Also by Ed Rasimus

FIGHTER PILOT
WHEN THUNDER ROLLED

PALACE COBRA

A Fighter Pilot in the Vietnam Air War

ED RASIMUS

St. Martin's Paperbacks

PALACE COBRA

Copyright © 2006 by Ed Rasimus.

Cover photo © George Hall / Corbis

All rights reserved.

For information address St. Martin's Press, 175 Fifth Avenue, New York, NY 10010.

Library of Congress Catalog Card Number: 2005040179

ISBN: 0-312-94876-X
EAN: 9780312-94876-4

Printed in the United States of America

St. Martin's Press hardcover edition / April 2006
St. Martin's Paperbacks edition / September 2007

St. Martin's Paperbacks are published by St. Martin's Press, 175 Fifth Avenue, New York, NY 10010.

10 9 8 7 6 5 4 3

To Bill Loyd and Bill Sparks,
who are two giants in a profession filled
with larger-than-life personalities.
They taught me what it means to be a fighter pilot.

CONTENTS

ACKNOWLEDGMENTS

The first indication that future historians will have that our Vietnam War was badly flawed will come from the static nature of the conflict. How we failed to notice that year after year we hadn't made any progress will confound them. They will look at the establishment of operating bases and the deployment of forces, and they will be impressed at our ability to create such massive infrastructure and conduct such intensive operations on the far side of the world. They will compare the force structure of the United States to that of its opposition and understand the reasonable degree of optimism we had at the start.

Then they will dig deeper, because that is what historians do. They will seek the rationale for our gradualism and caution in the buildup and targeting. They will nod their heads and sympathize with the caution we exercised as we tried to understand the complex relationship of client states to superpowers in a nuclear world. Yes, they will agree that we had to move slowly, and that it was reasonable to seek solutions with the minimum of military might. Certainly they will concede that the goal of democracy rather than Communism in a developing nation was a good one. They will have the benefit of more than thirty years of analysis as they acknowledge that George F. Kennan was right and that Communism, if contained, would fail. It will be apparent that the resistance to Communism anywhere in the world, espoused by the Truman Doctrine and then the Dulles domino theory, was fatally flawed in that it allied us with corrupt and often repressive regimes whose only redeeming quality was that they were anticommunist.

The political historian will link the politics of populism to the ebb and flow of the air campaigns. They will see seekers of the presidency counting the numbers and finding the resistance to a long-distance war as a more appealing constituency than the supporters. The cultural historian will view the failure of America to recognize the nuances of Asian culture as pivotal. Had we learned about the history of Southeast Asia and the traditions of the people, we might have understood what we were trying to do much better. The sociological historian will connect the Spock generation of self-centered baby boomers with the war's opposition and their desire for world peace at any cost with the failure. The organizational historian will examine the bureaucratic infighting of the American military and see the competition between Air Force and Navy as wasteful and inefficient. They will look at how the leadership fostered the McNamara era of body counts and analysis, square-filling and careerism. It may all come together.

I'm no historian. I was merely a participant in the games. I've been able to recount the stories and hopefully shed some light on the events. The stories are true, they all happened. Some are intense, others are mundane. They reflect the ethos of the time and shaped my attitudes on life. I've pulled few punches and have probably stepped on a few toes in these tales. I freely admit they are my recollections and impressions. The good guys were really good, and the bad guys were good as well, they just didn't measure up to the arbitrary standard in my mind. All put their lives on the line, following the orders of their lawful superiors and doing the best they could. War is a personal thing, and the recounting of a war is inevitably colored both by impressions at the time and by stewing in the juices of thirty years of memory.

I've been encouraged throughout the process by the support of my wife, Carol, who, despite nagging me incessantly about the technical details that bore her, always offers constructive criticism about the interpersonal descriptions. She's a great critic, and I take most of her advice. A fighter pilot, after all, can't take all of a woman's advice, or he would lose his credibility.

The impetus to get started on the tales came from my two significant writing mentors, John Sherwood, official historian USN, and author of *Fast Movers: America's Jet Pilots and the Vietnam Experience,* and Marshall Michel, author of *Clashes* and *Eleven Days of Christmas.* Each provided me with feedback on my efforts and direction. They opened doors and helped me to put a book in people's hands.

Memory is a fickle thing. I've drawn on friends and associates from the years in the fighter flying business to recapture names and understand perspectives on what was going on. Among the most dependable for background were Turk Turley, Tom Coady, Ed Cleaveland, Ed Rock, Bob Hipps, Swede Seagren, and Robin Olds. Occasionally the story exchanges run late into the night, and the potential for damage to either wallet or liver can be significant in those sessions.

No one who did not experience it can ever truly understand the POW experience, but the corner of the tent was raised for me just a bit by the ex-cons who were willing to talk a little about it. I owe a lot to Jack Van Loan, Paul Galanti, Ted Sienicki, and Dave Mott, who provided some glimpses.

Spell-checkers and grammar corrections from word processing software are fine, but they don't catch everything, and nothing is more informative than an old friend telling you when you are pontificating or sugar-coating. For their opinions, I need to thank Bill Stroud, George Marrett, "Bull" Kittle, and Joe Myers, who took a look at the manuscript in very rough form and offered input. Positive strokes are always good, but the occasional boot in the posterior is also necessary from time to time. My thanks to all.

Credo:

Because somewhere in me is still the little boy,
who wants to kick the can and write on walls,
and hitch rides on the tailgates of trucks,
and pull little girls' pants down.

And somewhere in me is still the go-to-hell pilot
in the go-to-hell hat flinging an aircraft
down boundless halls of space,
and talking with hands for airplanes,
and reliving the Po Delta and the Mekong Delta,
and reaching out to touch the face of God,
and profaning those who are tied to earth,
and pulling girls' pants down.

And somewhere in me is the Descartes and the Sartre
who philosophizes on the here and the hereafter,
and the deism of all that lives and not lives,
and the beauty of sky and water and cloven hoofs and man,
and girls with their pants down.

And deep inside me there is that uncompromising realist
who knows that this is all a terribly temporary gift;
that sometime, perhaps this next second,
he must run into that last hard object,
be it the side of a mountain, the slam of a bullet,
or the massive grasp of a giant's hand on a faltering heart.

When that time comes, if there is one thing to remember,
it will be that sweet memory that transcends them all,
the little boy, the go-to-heller, the philosopher, the realist;
it will be the ineffably beautiful picture of a girl . . .
with her pants down.

—Mel Porter, fighter pilot

INTRODUCTION

It is well that war is so terrible,
or we should grow too fond of it.

—Gen. Robert Edward Lee, CSA,
Fredericksburg, December 1862

IT'S EERILY FAMILIAR. THE SILVER-GRAY tanker flanked by the brown and green fighters laden with brown bombs and white missiles. The blue sky blending into the whitish-gray misty horizon, and then the dark green of the jungle below us form a static picture of war. Ahead for ten miles are four more sets like this one. Four thousand feet below us, another parade of chicks and hens stretches along the same course. Fifteen miles west and twenty miles east are similar assemblies of airpower, all preparing to head north yet again.

Nothing moves, yet everything is moving. The airplanes seem pinned by invisible wires to the wings of the tanker. The Phantom on the boom is engaged in a languid form of lovemaking in which the boom seems to slowly pump in and out of its metallic sheath, moving only a few feet back and forth as it injects its life-sustaining liquid into the receptacle of the fighter. It's positively Freudian.

Watch closely now, and you'll begin to see the movements. See the way his ailerons are cycling, up then down. It's not much. It's all so delicate. The airplane doesn't move, but still it is moving. Look down at the stick. It isn't apparently moving. Now, rest your hand lightly and follow along with me. Feel the little pressures? Ride the throttles. They weren't moving when you looked at them, but do you feel the life when you touch them? The tachometers don't show change in rpm, but look at fuel flow. See that jittering? That's the power that keeps us moving inches forward and back to maintain our position. There's life in everything. It's all moving continually. Look at the ground speed indicator. We're all moving forward at nearly 400 miles an hour. Thirty tankers, 120 fighters, more than 300 men, 2 miles up and loaded with several hundred tons of iron, all going to do the same damn thing we've been doing on and off for the last seven years.

I don't really understand why I'm here. I don't have to be doing this. I did my time at war five years ago. We aren't here to win. The American people don't seem to care about us. I'm not all that patriotic or courageous. But I love it. I love the challenge of air combat. I'm back in a fighter, challenging the best the enemy has to offer and knowing that I can win this contest, if not this war. I'm part of an incredible team. Men of courage and skill and the discipline to do the tough jobs that are demanded of them. Some fight for God and country. Some fight because they are ordered. Some believe in the cause. And some of us simply love it.

There is a fascination about war. It should not be entered lightly, and, once begun, should be waged to conclusion as quickly as possible. Once the threat to the nation, the challenge to world peace, the objectives of public policy have been met, the war should end. That would always be the ideal solution, but we recognize the loss of the ideal only long after the moment for effective action has passed. That was the problem with the air war over North Vietnam.

We had entered the war with resolution and patriotism. We overcame our fears and fought bravely for our nation, doing that which was asked of us and subjugating our questioning of policy, method, tactics, and strategy. We were the offspring of Tom Brokaw's "greatest generation," a combination of George Cohan's "Yankee Doodle Dandy" and John Wayne's oversize heroism that couldn't be beaten. We knew we were right and we knew we would prevail. But that was at the beginning.

When the air war started, no one thought it would last indefinitely. Certainly no one could have overlaid a series of starts and stops linking American political campaigns to the application of tactical air power. In 1965, '66, and '67, we went to North Vietnam delivering good capitalist iron on the evil communists and suffering incredible losses. It was bearable because we knew that our leadership sought victory and the American people supported us. But by 1968, it had become apparent that election victory for populist politicians on the home front was more important than victory in the war in Southeast Asia. That's when President Lyndon Johnson added one more stop to the sequence and announced an indefinite cessation of the air campaign against North Vietnam.

From 1968 until the spring of 1972, we entered a period that Robert E. Lee couldn't have begun to comprehend. We weren't there to win and we didn't seem to want to lose. Fighter pilots went because it was the thing to do. It had become a career move, absolutely required for promotion and conferring the authority to swagger and pontificate to others who either had not yet been to the war or had been earlier. A culture of combat grew that leaned much more toward the fondness for war than the need to aggressively pursue victory. We fought to fight, and with the most deadly targets suspended, it became simply a routine excursion expected of those who wore wings. While the ground troops facing the hell of jungle combat in the South still maintained a clear picture of the terrible nature of war, the fighter pilots in Thailand built a fantasized reality around the machismo of it.

Thailand became a place for those who hadn't made the cut as fighter pilots when they graduated from pilot training to get quickly credentialed. Bomber drivers and trash-haulers, training commandoes and desk jockeys went through the pipeline that turned them into instant heroes. The catch was that the war had become institutionalized. It simply droned on, and, with any real objectives gone, the daily pattern became finding a use for the sorties, with the rest of the day dedicated to designing new ways to demonstrate that somehow those assigned to fly fighters were special. Industries grew up to support the adrenaline addiction of near-combat as a third world nation tried to cope with the cultural overlay of tens of thousands of testosterone-pumped American men flooding their country. We brought our society with us, and, once removed from the constraints of home, family, parents, and civilization, we ran amok.

If there was sex in America, there would be sex in Southeast Asia, but without a senior generation to scold our excesses. If there were drugs in America, there would be drugs in the Far East, which was a lot closer to the source. If there was racial conflict in America, we could pack our racism and regionalism and redneck attitudes and live out the entire range of ethnic stereotypes without a need for solutions or consideration. Yes, we could package all that was breaking down in America in the late '60s and concentrate it for reconstitution in Thailand. And, of course, there was drinking. You've got to drink to relieve the stress of combat. It's been a tradition as long as there has been aerial warfare. Nearness to possible death provides a reason for excesses.

Then came April of 1972, and, with the Paris Peace Talks bogged down once again, a president who had been elected to correct the mistakes of the Johnson administration saw his Vietnamization policy coming apart. It was time to finish the job and force the recalcitrant communists back to the bargaining table. The Linebacker campaign resumed the bombing of the North, and, after three and a half years of relative security behind a political ceasefire, the targets of the enemy's heartland were again on the daily list. The defenses had the opportunity to concentrate and focus on the attackers, and our technology attempted to counter each technological advance. With the Linebacker campaign, we would again face a serious threat. Hopefully this time we would have the intent of winning.

I told of my first combat tour (1966) in *When Thunder Rolled: An F-105 Pilot Over North Vietnam* (Smithsonian Institution Press, 2003). This is the story of my return to combat in the summer of 1972, once again at Korat and once again flying to the same heavily defended targets in Route Pack VI, the valley of the Red River in and around the capital of Hanoi. The mind-numbing terror of first combat had long receded. Now it was a question of what we had become and whether I had grown "too fond of it."

This is as much a sociological view as a combat memoir; there was certainly more than enough combat to go around. But it is also the story of personalities and interactions, excesses and idiosyncrasies. It's a look at the microcosm of America's finest, taken out of the society that had forsaken the war. We were placed, for better or for worse, at the cutting edge of the nation's policy sword. Here's the Woodstock generation coming face-to-face with *Apocalypse Now*. But that is way too simplistic.

There are war lovers and war haters in this world. It is easy to rationalize hating war. Peace is so much more pleasant. But society has always had the subculture of the warrior. We are strange folks, living on the periphery of society, surrounding ourselves with the trappings of our trade and a mix of voodoo and superstitions, culture and custom that distinguishes us from the others. Outsiders look askance at our childish and immature pranks, our drinking and womanizing and bawdiness. We look back at them with disdain and disrespect, knowing that we walk closer to the edge and do, without fear, things that they cannot imagine.

SOUTHEAST ASIA

1. PALACE COBRA

Their element is to attack, to track, to hunt, and to
destroy the enemy. Only in this way can the eager and
skillful fighter pilot display his ability. Tie him to a narrow
and confined task, rob him of his initiative, and you take away
from him the best and most valuable qualities he possesses:
aggressive spirit, joy of action, and the passion of the hunter.

—General Adolf Galland, Luftwaffe

IT WAS TIME. THE CONFLUENCE of the moon and stars
could tolerate no other action. Besides that, I was not
going to go around for another year wearing a stupid
Recruiting Service badge on my uniform. It had started
simply enough. It was an opportunity for a conscientious junior officer. They had made me an offer I
couldn't refuse. I'd been slogging along at Willy Air
Patch,[1] teaching academic classes full of student pilots
the gritty details about navigation and flight planning,
then holding their hands through traffic patterns, acro,
spins, and instrument flight in the squealing terror of a
tiny T-37. It was a fairly innocuous existence for a
"smoldering boulder," combat-proven F-105 pilot, but

---

1. Williams Air Force base, located east of Chandler, Arizona, near Phoenix.

it was reasonably regular hours in a nice place to live, a fun job with a good bunch of guys. The joke was that flying a T-37 was like masturbating. It was fun while you were doing it, but afterward you were slightly ashamed.

The Air Force had determined that there would be no involuntary second tours to Southeast Asia for pilots. I'd been around once, and didn't have to go again until everyone else had his turn in the barrel. To ensure that no one slipped through the cracks, the personnel head-shed had created a program called Palace Cobra. Everyone was ranked by longevity on the base, and when you rose to the top of the list, the "big mutha snake" came down and bit you with an assignment to the war. If you'd already been, you got bypassed and were available for other opportunities. That's what they called your next uprooting from normalcy: an opportunity. Or you could volunteer to go back to the war.

There were a lot of factors that could compel you to volunteer for a second tour. The primary one was that it was the only route back into flying fighters. I'd been a fighter pilot once, having competed vigorously for the privilege. I'd found that I could do the job respectably well, and I knew that there was no other place I wanted to be in the Air Force. The problem was that to return to fighters from Training Command there was only one path, and that led through Southeast Asia. There simply wasn't any fighter qualification for pilots except those en route to combat.

I volunteered to go back when I'd had just over two years of stateside duty. I'd watched each month as the assignments came in and the Palace Cobra list slowly moved my name to the top ten. It had taken a while. For almost a year there was no movement at all, as there were way too many guys ahead of me with more than four years on station. Finally as I passed my third anniversary at Willy, things began to move. The real question was whether I was going to get tabbed for a fighter, or would I be funneled into some sort of forward air controller or support job. With a previous tour, it was a natural for me to be assigned to fast movers, but natural or sensible doesn't always determine what happens in the military. I was worried about having to choose between the F-4 and the F-105 Wild Weasel, with its SAM-suppression role that I'd supported during my first tour in 1966. Nothing else could happen. I was sure. Then the phone rang. Opportunity doesn't always knock. Sometimes it rings.

Would I like to go to Air Training Command headquarters to fill a major's slot in the personnel business? I would be running the undergraduate-rated officer assignment shop. This meant I would handle the assignment of newly commissioned officers to pilot and navigator training, then determine their assignments after they had received their wings. I would fly support aircraft, but primarily I'd be pushing a desk, working staff duties. It would be a chance to get major command-level experience and exposure to increased responsibilities. It might mean recognition by some general for quick advancement. It would mean moving to Randolph AFB outside of San Antonio. And it would mean dropping off of Palace Cobra.

They wanted an answer yesterday. I argued for some time. I must have been in demand, or else they'd been turned down several times already and couldn't fill the slot. They relented and gave me forty-eight hours to make up my mind. I thought about it for a day and a half, discussing it with my boss, coworkers, and my wife. Everyone thought it was a good deal. Eventually I managed to convince myself that it would be better than flying fighters again, in a war we didn't appear to be very concerned with winning anyway. I accepted the job.

Randolph was beautiful, and for the first year I found myself caught up in learning the ins and outs of staff work. I found out what talking papers and staff summary sheets looked like. I learned how valuable a senior NCO can be to a stumbling aviator wallowing in a paper mill. I wrote and read and briefed and explained. I traveled to the ten pilot training bases, and I even succeeded in getting a major change to the graduate assignment system for pilots just getting their wings, returning to the strict merit ranking for selection of their next aircraft. Graduate at the top of your class and you get your choice. Finish in the bottom and you take what's left. I felt that I'd accomplished a small something, correcting the errors of a personnel weenie who didn't know from which end of the jet the hot air came. Now the best students would get a shot at fighters. It wasn't bad duty; the only downside was the assignment to fly T-29s for my monthly four hours of flying time.

There were four aircraft types available for supporting pilots on the staff. There were the T-37s and T-38s used for pilot and instructor training on the base, and there were T-29s and T-39s for hauling generals and staff teams around the countryside. I arrived at Randolph as a qualified instructor pilot in the -37, and I had both student and pilot time in the -38. I even had thirty hours in the jet Sabreliner, the -39, which had been used as a radar and nuclear weapons trainer during my F-105 checkout. Of course, that made it natural to assign me to the twin Convair, a prop driven, forty passenger, mini-airliner, the only airplane I hadn't flown before and possibly the furthest stretch in the Air Force inventory for a Thud pilot on forced sabbatical from fighter aviation.

Checkout in the airplane was a disaster. It started with a local orientation flight. Half a dozen staff types loaded onto an airplane, and during a four-hour flight we sat in the airline-style seats reading magazines and waiting for a chance to take the controls for periods ranging from fifteen minutes to an hour. It was sort of an airborne Club Med experience, only without the fruity rum drinks. I was eventually called to the cockpit, where I was directed into the left seat. The view was pretty good, but the big steering wheel was clearly converting flying into an unnatural act. The throttle quadrant was between the seats, requiring power control with the wrong hand, and there were a profusion of knobs and levers on the quadrant that implied the airplane had a lot more than the two engines I knew were out there on the wing. Trim wasn't through an electrical thumb switch, but rather with a large wheel mounted vertically on the side of the throttle pedestal. My first attempt at a slight turn met with no result. It quickly became apparent that the fingertip flying of high performance jets wasn't the mode of operation for reciprocating-engine trash-haulers. It took considerable muscling to get the airplane to move out of straight and level. Control pressures weren't the solution, brute force manipulation of the wheel was.

After the instructor pilot's and the flight mechanic's chuckles over my control technique subsided, we entered the traffic pattern. "We're going to do a couple of visual touch-and-goes," the IP said. "Call for the before-landing checklist." It was Abbott and Costello time, checking out the infield lineup.

"Okay," I responded. Nothing happened.

"Call for the before-landing checklist," he repeated.

"Right. Give it to me," I tried again. Still nothing.

"You have to say the words," he scolded. "You have to say, 'before-landing checklist.' "

"You're kidding, aren't you? Okay, before-landing checklist," I intoned.

The flight mechanic opened his greasy yellow checklist and began reading. "Props?"

I looked quizzically at the IP. He pointed to two of the knobs at the top of the throttle quadrant, then held them down for about eight seconds until the rpm of the engines magically, without movement of the throttles, moved to 2,400. "That sets the props to proper pitch," the mech explained. "You're supposed to do that and then say, 'twenty-four hundred, set.' "

"Flaps," the flight mechanic continued, then looked expectantly at me again.

I looked out the window on my side of the cockpit and determined that I couldn't see any flaps. Without a clue about what was needed, I said, "Okay, set them."

"No," the mech warned, "You're supposed to say 'fifteen degrees'."

I'm nothing if not a quick study. "That sounds right. Okay, set the flaps." Nothing happened.

The IP gives me a Jack Palance, tight-jawed glare. He hisses impatiently, "You have to say 'fifteen degrees,' then the copilot will set them while you fly the airplane."

Determined to play the game, I say, "fifteen degrees." Now there's action from the IP, who fiddles with a little lever, and Jack Palance momentarily becomes Mr. Magoo. He leans myopically forward to stare at the flap position indicator, setting it to exactly fifteen—not fourteen, not sixteen, but precisely fifteen. He's gotten where he is today by being precise.

The flight mech continues down the list. "Mixture?"

I ask what the proper response is. The IP says to set the red levers to full forward or rich. I ask who is authorized to do that, and the IP motions to the flight mechanic sitting between us and hovering over the throttles. I tell him to go ahead.

"Sir, I can't do it unless you say 'full rich,' then I move the levers." The enlisted mechanic is frustrated by my manifest incompetence.

I'm in an airplane that barely responds to control inputs, that requires some sort of Gilbert and Sullivan duet to get something done, and that apparently is dependent upon an exaggerated Simon Says game before anything happens. Frustrated, I ask the IP, "Why, if everyone here but me knows the answer, do we have to ask the questions? If I ask for the before-landing checklist, and now you know that's what I want, why don't you just do it?"

He shakes his head at the ignorance of this former single-seat, single-engine fighter pilot who is now adrift on his many-motored, trash-hauling turf. It begins to dawn on me that I'm dead meat in this game of aeronautical one-upmanship. I'm learning about something called crew coordination.

Had someone told me that flying wouldn't always be fun, I'd have called him a fool. Now I found myself using staff work as an excuse to avoid flying the T-29. We could bank flying time up to four months in advance, and then, if we missed our requirements, we could pick up two months' back pay by flying more hours. I planned flights to take a trip every four to six months, then made myself unavailable in between, whenever the schedulers called, by claiming an important briefing for the general or a short suspense on a major staff project. That sort of rustiness could kill me in a fighter, but in this school bus I would always have a competent, experienced bus driver and mechanic to take care of me.

I thoroughly detested the T-29 and actively sought to minimize my exposure to the beast. Worst of all, six years after receiving my wings, I now had some copilot time in my logbook. Pushing the gray, government-issue, six-drawer steel desk in my office was preferable to driving the unmaneuverable, air-thrashing, slow-moving, fifties-era people-mover. Worrying about flight lunches and baggage and passenger manifests and billeting arrangements for the sandbags in the back was not my idea of a good time. My secretary knew that if the flight schedulers called, I was always out.

By the spring of 1972, the war was well along the path to being Vietnamized. President Nixon's program of turning the fighting for their country over to the residents of Vietnam and bringing Americans home was increasingly popular. The pipeline was still pumping pilots into the war, but the numbers were decreasing, and the long-range planning for both undergraduate and operational flying training showed a definite reduction. Senior people in the headquarters were beginning to look for new missions and responsibilities to keep their empires in business. The folks at the Military Personnel Center, which was also at Randolph, began to covet my responsibilities at Air Training Command. They prepared a briefing for the generals of ATC and the Air Force suggesting the efficiencies of assuming assignment handling for pilot training graduates along with their existing job of managing the training of senior pilots. It made sense, and the function moved across the base. I, however, remained in ATC personnel. The headquarters Air Force folks over at the center wanted the positions in the bureaucracy; they didn't want the people that occupied them.

With the job moved, I stayed in the personnel branch for less than a month, then an examination of the remaining functions of the student personnel branch led to the conclusion that it would be better handled under the leadership of the general who ran Recruiting Service. Now the needs of the Air Force could be handled by a single manager, from finding the body on the street of Anytown USA, through basic training to tech school, all the way to the end unit. Basic training at Lackland, for both officers and enlisted, would be getting their raw material from the Recruiting Service. My office staff, my boss, and my boss's boss all packed our files and pencil sharpeners and moved out of our third floor offices to a converted World War II barracks building a block away. Each of us was issued a shiny recruiter badge, with instructions to wear it on our left shirt pocket proudly. I chucked it into the desk drawer. Each morning when I came to work, I pinned it on to wear in the building. When I went out the door, the badge went back in the drawer.

It was definitely time. I'd been in the staff job long enough to get an effectiveness report, two of them actually. I'd briefed the generals and gotten noticed. I'd filled the square, and now, if I was ever to get back into fighters, I had to stop diddling around. I went down the hall to see the first pilot upstream of me in my chain of command. Politely I mentioned to my boss, Colonel Bob Baldwin, a professional personnel staff whiz, that I was going to get out of this business while the getting was good. He nodded, probably somewhat relieved that there might be a solution for what to do with this head-strong pilot who wasn't totally comfortable with the glories of the personnel business and really didn't have a job any longer anyway. He blessed my visit to Colonel Denton.

Jack Denton had flown F-84s in Korea. He was a crusty old guy, loaded with experience and common sense, dedicated to the Air Force and doing the best he could in a job for which he had never volunteered. He'd been grounded several years earlier for an ulcer, and would never fly again, yet he exemplified all that the term *fighter pilot* means. He was in his office, wading through a stack of briefing slides, when I asked his secretary if Colonel Denton had a minute or two. He yelled through the open door to come in. Before I could salute or report, he motioned me to one of the two leather armchairs in front of his desk. I hadn't said a word when he looked at me and said, "So you want out, huh?"

I wasn't surprised. He knew where I'd been, and he knew the way fighter pilots think. He knew I wasn't a career personnel officer, and he knew that the recent reorganizations had made it a hell of a lot more difficult to really demonstrate much in my job, which now held a mere shadow of its former glory. I acknowledged his query about the purpose of my visit. "Yes, sir. I've got to get back into fighters and with the war winding down, if I don't move soon, I'll never be able to. I'd like you to release me for assignment, and, if it isn't too much to ask, put in a good word for me with the permanent-party assignment people to get one of the training slots next month."

He nodded. "I know how you feel," he said. "I'd do

the same thing if I were you. It's what, February? I think we can still get your name against one of the April slots. F-4s alright? I think the command's got four holes to fill. Let me check." He turned and picked up the phone to the ATC assignment section. In seconds he was talking to my close friend in the assignments shop, George Teas. George had also flown F-105s as a first lieutenant, then had an instructor tour in Training Command and after that to the headquarters. He still had a job, and a pair of cute kids at home, so he wasn't quite as ready as I to return to high threat flying. Colonel Denton simply asked if the month's F-4 levy had been filled. When George said the names hadn't yet been firmed up, Denton told him to put me on the list. Surprised, George could only answer, "Yes, sir."

Colonel Denton looked up at me and grinned. "That was easy. Now, jump in your car and head over to MPC. You know the guys in Air Force assignments, don't you?"

I worked almost daily with several of the action officers at the center, more closely in recent weeks as they orchestrated the takeover of my office's functions. Yes, I knew them well.

"I'll give them a call while you're driving over to tell them it's all greased. See what they've got available for training and where the end units are. You've got my blessing to do whatever looks good to you."

It was the fastest I'd ever seen an assignment made. I wasn't sure what the record was, but short of the chief of staff of the AF demanding someone to fill a position immediately, I doubt that it could have happened more quickly. I saluted smartly and left the building so fast I found myself walking into the personnel center with my Recruiting Service badge still prominently displayed. It didn't matter anymore. I was on my way out and back into fighters.

I walked the long basement hallway at MPC from the parking lot to the front of the building, then up the two flights of stairs to the rated assignment offices. I found Cliff Tatum hunched over one of the front desks. We'd flown the abominable T-29 together on a weekend trip. As two fighter pilots flogging a load of shoe clerks on an inspection tour to one of the training bases, we'd commiserated about the good old days in fighters. He'd flown Phantoms and I'd driven Thuds, so we naturally kidded each other with a whole series of jokes and jibes about the aircraft. Cliff was just hanging the phone up as I approached.

"Denton?" I asked.

Tatum nodded and grinned. "So you've finally seen the light and decided to fly a real fighter."

"No, it's all that's left now that the single seat Thuds are all used up. Now we single seat guys are going to show the Phantom community how it really ought to be done. You've had it screwed up for way too long. I've come to set it right." He laughed and reached behind his desk for a loose-leaf binder.

"Okay, Raz, here's what we've got next month. Where do you want to train? You'll be getting the Cat IV checkout, that's sixty days and about thirty hours of flying time. You can go to Homestead, George, MacDill, or Luke. What's your druthers?" Homestead was outside of Miami. MacDill was on Tampa Bay. George was in the high desert a couple of hours out of Los Angeles. I was more familiar with the Phoenix area from my time at Willy, so I said I'd take Luke. Cliff warned me that Luke was still using the old F-4C model, while the other three bases were training in the E. I stuck with Luke.

"You want to name your follow-on poison while you're at it? I can send you to any of the Thailand bases. If you go to Ubon, you'll probably have to go through LGB[2] or Igloo White[3] training first, but that shouldn't be a problem. Korat will take input from any of the training sites. Udorn prefers E-model training 'cause they're doing mostly air-to-air. Oh, and you can go to Danang still, but there's a chance that the 366th will pull out in a couple of months."

It didn't take more than a second to choose Korat. I'd been through my first tour there and thought it was the best of the bunch.

"Alright, brudder, you got it. I'll send a message over to the training commandoes in the basement and have your name on it. They'll cut the orders and you'll probably be officially alerted for assignment in two weeks. Act surprised when they call you."

It was 4:30 in the afternoon, so I headed for the club rather than back to the office. The Recruiting badge went in the glove compartment, and I headed upstairs to the bar. I was about twenty minutes ahead of the after-work crowd, so I got a good seat, able to look straight into the steely blue eyes of the dashing young fighter pilot, formerly a personnel puke and Recruiting Service staffer, who appeared in the mirror behind the

2. LGB or laser-guided bomb training for the first generation Paveway weapons system, sometimes called "zot," in which an aircraft illuminated targets for other bomb droppers using a laser pod on the left wing.
3. Igloo White was a system of sensors, air-dropped along the Ho Chi Minh Trail to detect vehicle movement and then help target key interdiction strikes.

bar. Damn, I felt good. I couldn't tell the guys that I worked with about my good fortune yet, that would have to wait until the official paperwork flowed. But I knew, and that was more than enough.

Not all was smooth, of course. I'd have to tell my wife about this quick change in our lives. It shouldn't be a problem. We had a nice home near the base in Universal City. She was active in the wives' club and had several close friends with whom we regularly socialized. She would understand.

"You bastard!" was her first reaction. I'd expected something a bit surprised, possibly slightly upset, but the vehemence of the response shocked me. "Can't you be satisfied? What the hell is the matter with you?" She obviously wasn't as happy about the assignment as I was.

"It's what I do," I explained. "I'm a fighter pilot. I dealt with the first tour and now, if I ever want to get back into the business, I've got to do this." I tried to generate an understanding of my lifelong ambitions and what it meant to me. I should have known that if she didn't understand it after six years of living with me, she wouldn't experience any sort of epiphany tonight.

Dinner was over. There was a definite chill in the air that didn't relate to the February weather. She ended the discussion with an ultimatum that must have been simmering, undisclosed for a long time prior. "If you do this, don't expect me to be waiting for you."

And a year later, she wasn't.

2. A NEW WAR

You love a lot of things if you live around them,
but there isn't any woman and there isn't any horse,
nor any before nor any after, that is as lovely
as a great airplane, and men who love them are
faithful to them even though they leave them
for others. A man has only one virginity to lose in
fighters, and if it is a lovely plane he loses it to,
there his heart will ever be.

—Ernest Hemingway, August 1944

PAPA WAS RIGHT ON. I'D lost my cherry to the Thunderchief long before I got my Phantom assignment. I'd wanted to fly the Thud from the first day I'd seen one and had been lucky enough to meet the girl of my dreams, woo her, and take her to bed in the vicious days of Rolling Thunder. I'd lost my heart, my soul, my virginity to an airplane with one seat, one engine, and a gun. I'd been alone in Bad Guy Land in what was absolutely the best airplane in the world, and she'd brought me home safely more than a hundred times. How could one not love her?

Now I was headed to F-4 school. I'd spent the last five years sparring with Phantom drivers, sometimes seriously, sometimes jokingly, about the deficiencies of their airplane and the superiority of mine. There were some deep-rooted issues regarding the views of the airplanes. On the one hand, there was the simple issue of assignment out of pilot training. I'd been fortunate enough to have the skills, the desire, and, most important, the healthy dose of luck required to gain an assignment to a single-seat fighter. The numbers told the story. There were eight undergraduate pilot training bases pumping out US Air Force pilots in a class every six weeks, all year-round. That meant about 325 new second lieutenants joining the force every month and a half, 9 of which would get to fly the F-105. The Phantom community was restricted, at that time, to experienced pilots in the front seat and new graduate pilots in the rear cockpit. In my graduating class there had been 140 guys sent to backseat pilot duties in the F-4. It wasn't difficult to feel a bit superior. Nine guys got laid by a queen of the prom, and 140 got sloppy seconds with a fat, smoky, double-breasted ex-Navy airplane that didn't even have a gun.

There was more in the background, too. When I went to the war in the Thud, the heavy lifting was all done by the F-105 forces at Korat and Takhli. It was easy to be influenced by the experienced fighter pilots who led me through my first tour and, arguably, were responsible for molding me as a tactical aviator and helping me survive the losses. They didn't like the idea of flying with a helper, and they were eager to point out that the Phantom community was populated by lesser pilots than themselves. It wasn't always true, of course, but it was natural to believe that it was. I'd seen situations in which F-4s didn't get to the target areas while Thuds did, and I'd seen situations in which Phantom crews were capped and rescued by -105 pilots after being abandoned by their flight. It was purely anecdotal, but it laid an almost subliminal attitude regarding which of the two aircraft was superior.

All those experiences had been little more than snapshots in time. What I'd encountered had been true for only a short period, and there were considerably different policies with significantly different results during different phases of the war. By the time my hundred-mission tour was finished, the Air Force was no longer assigning brand-new pilots to the F-105. The program was being filled with senior pilots who had lots of flying time and, regardless of whether they had any tactical background, could be qualified in half the time of a new lieutenant. For some it was an opportunity to achieve greatness in combat, but for most it was a task fraught with peril and often leading to death or long-term imprisonment in North Vietnam.

For the Phantom community, the clear transition point between bumbling escorts and respectable war fighters was the leadership of Robin Olds in the 8th Tactical Fighter Wing at Ubon. Robin had been a leading ace in World War II and was sent to Thailand in late 1966, to put some fangs in the F-4 program. He led by example and became a virtual legend among SEA fighter pilots. With four MiG kills over the North, he showed that the Phantom could be as good as anything the bad guys could put up against us. There was never again going to be the slightest insinuation that a two-place F-4 might be any less capable than a single-seat fighter when it came to combat effectiveness.

I had seen yet another change very directly in my role at Air Training Command headquarters. The USAF had finally seen the error of putting a pilot in the rear cockpit of the F-4 and changed to weapons system operators, navigators rather than pilots. No longer did a new graduate of UPT have to be placed in a subordinate and frustrating position as backup pilot and radar operator while a more experienced pilot flew the airplane. A WSO was a specialist, rated as a navigator and trained to operate the aircraft's systems in support of the pilot. Rather than compete for control of the plane and lobby for an upgrade to the front seat, the WSO formed a team with the pilot, supporting rather than challenging. You got synergy rather than erosion. Two heads, two sets of eyes, and two pairs of hands could increase the effectiveness of the total weapons system. It was a good solution. Not perfect, but much better than before.

With navs in the rear, and the AF policy of no involuntary second tours, there were a lot of F-4 front seats to fill, so the job was opened up to new pilot training grads. The circle was now complete. Just as the Thud had been the hottest ride on the block when I'd graduated, the Phantom was now the assignment to which the best young pilots would aspire. For a prior F-105 driver, however, there still was a deep-seated love for the first airplane and a nagging antagonism toward this ugly pug-nosed bird that was trying to replace her.

I clipped the F-105 hundred-mission patch off the shoulder of my flying suits and vowed to stay away from aircraft-versus-aircraft discussions when I got to Luke. My job would be to learn about this aircraft and how to work with a partner while trying to avoid the inevitable comparisons between my new weapon and my old love. It wouldn't be easy, but I would have to try.

I arrived at Luke in late April and started academics almost immediately. There were nine guys in the Cat IV checkout, some with tours in other aircraft and some with no prior fighter time but lots of hours in training aircraft or interceptors. The Category IV requirement was supposed to be prior fighter qualification, but there was apparently considerable latitude in who could fill the slots. At the same time, a new class of recent UPT graduates were starting a long six-month, 120–flying hour course in the airplane. They were matched up with new navigators for the program, while we in the Cat IV would fly our twenty or so training missions with instructors in our backseats.

Classes lasted all day long for the first week, describing the various systems of the Phantom, ranging from engines to hydraulics, fuel, and electrics. We got lessons in radar and weapons, some of it new and some of it modifications of the information we already knew about our old weapons. The new lieutenants were scrambling to absorb it all, while the guys with prior fighter time were inevitably comparing the F-4 with their previous aircraft despite our resolutions to the contrary. In some places the differences were major, while in other areas the similarities made it easy to understand how the bird functioned.

We got a couple of simulator rides to learn our way around the cockpit, and we were told to go out on the flight line to get some cockpit time, sitting in a parked airplane familiarizing ourselves with the location of switches, knobs, and controls. The lieutenants eagerly roared onto the ramp, seeking an unscheduled airplane where they could sit in the cockpit of their first fighter for an hour or more. The older students, experienced captains and majors like me, recognizing that in Phoenix, the temperature on the flight line was well over 100 degrees even in April, remained in the air-conditioned squadron building and got our cockpit time by sipping a cold Coke and flipping through flight-manual pictures.

The Phantom had been designed first for the Navy as a fleet air defense interceptor. The USAF had made some modifications to outfit the airplane for the other tactical missions of which it was capable, but the blue water influence was apparent in several areas. The wings folded at the outboard sections, and there was a huge tail hook that could be used to snag the arresting gear and bring the airplane to a quick halt on landing. All the Century Series of fighters had tail hooks,[1] but they were small, lightweight affairs that were used for relatively low speeds at the departure end of the runway. The Phantom's hook was industrial-strength, designed for carrier operations and capable of being routinely raised and lowered from the cockpit. Approach-end barrier engagement was part of the bag of tricks available to the Phantom crew. Lots of emergency procedures and bad weather techniques required that even in the Air Force, we could be expected to use the approach-end arrestment procedures.

The radar was the whole reason for the aircraft to exist, yet it was in many ways inferior to what I had been familiar with in the -105. As an interceptor, the Phantom was designed primarily to find other aircraft in flight; the rudimentary capability to use the radar for ground mapping was an afterthought. The radar scope itself was square, with a vertical cursor that scanned left and right across the screen rather than sweeping like a windshield wiper from the vertex of a pie-shaped wedge. The con-

---

1. The Century Series were those AF tactical fighters numbered in the 100s, starting with the F-100 and going through -101, -102, and so on, to F-106. The Phantom, called the F-4C in its first AF iteration, had originally been numbered F-110. The last Century Series bird was the F-111, after which the AF revised the numbering system, bringing us the "teen" fighters.

cept, called a B-sweep, was that as you got closer to a
target you needed more detailed information; therefore
the whole bottom of the radar screen represented close
range. Rather than disappearing into the apex of the
wedge, the target stayed clearly visible, with azimuth
and range data shown in a broader view. The catch was
that it didn't look anything like the real world. Mile
markers on the radar were horizontal lines representing
distance, rather than the more familiar arcs found on a
ground mapping radar. For mapping, the square picture
the radar created required more than a little bit of interpretation. It would take quite a bit of getting used to.

We spent a lot of classroom and simulator time
learning about intercept geometry as well as the capability of the aircraft's two air-to-air missiles, the
Sidewinder and the Sparrow. I had carried the heat-
seeking Sidewinder on the Thud so was reasonably familiar with employment of that weapon. The capability
had increased markedly since the earlier versions I'd
used, but the principles remained the same—put a heat
source like an enemy aircraft tailpipe under the pipper
and the missile seeker head would see it and confirm ac-
quisition with a buzz or growl. Growl, shoot. No growl,
don't shoot. Even a fighter pilot can understand that.

The Sparrow, however, was an entirely different story.
This was a radar missile. It had considerably longer
range than the Sidewinder and could, under optimum
conditions, reach well beyond visual range to engage
and kill other aircraft. The radar, the airplane, and the
missile were a tightly integrated package that functioned
under the management of the backseater. The aircraft
had room for four of the missiles, semi-embedded in the
underside of the fuselage. The radar detected targets, the
WSO designated which target to attack, and the system

fed information to the missile. When the missile was fired, it headed off to the target designated by the aircraft's radar, homing on reflected energy transmitted by the aircraft and received by the missile's own antenna. Keep radar energy bouncing off the bad guy and the missile drove right down the beam to kill him. The Sparrow had a much longer range than the Sidewinder, but it couldn't be used at close range where the complex system might not have time to function.

While the pilot performed engine-start and preflight checks, the backseater went through a series of BITs, built-in-tests, that checked the radar and the missile's ability to perform. Maybe the WSO knew what it was all supposed to mean, but for the nose-gunner it was too much like some sort of video game. Circles expanded and contracted, gaps in arcs rotated around the scope, and tiny dots chased each other in a track between two electronic rings. If the dots did one thing, all was well. If they did something else, something was wrong. The checklist spoke in an esoteric terminology of things, like V-sub-c, min range, break-X, and English bias. It might as well have been Greek or Latin for as much as it meant to me. Those of us in the short course were going to have to learn the details on the job rather than in the schoolhouse. Dependence upon a WSO was becoming a necessity.

The instructor force was composed mostly of guys who had been backseat pilots, then upgraded to the front cockpit after a combat tour. Many had multiple combat tours during the long years of the war, but surprisingly few had North Vietnam combat experience. The 1968 bombing halt announced by Lyndon Johnson during the presidential campaign had held for four long years, and, with only a few minor incursions into the

North, the war had become almost routine; we had greatly reduced losses in a lower-threat environment. Combat was always going to be dangerous, but removal of radar-guided SAMs and MiG interceptors from the equation made the risk appreciably lower. All that remained were the flak, small arms, and basic risks of operating high performance aircraft under heavy loads and in all kinds of weather, day or night. Piece of cake, as they say. No sweat, no threat, loads of glory, flying in a relatively benign war. The reduced threat was one of the major factors that had made it easy for me to choose to return to combat.

There were instructor-WSOs in the squadron as well. They handled a lot of the academic load relating to radar operation, intercept techniques, air-to-air weapons, and even nuclear deliveries. They flew with student aircraft commanders once the new guys had qualified as pilots in the airplanes, and they taught student WSOs on the ground how to be part of the team that ran this complex aircraft. For former single-seat types like me, they were essential to understanding how the partner concept would make the two-place airplane into a more effective weapons system. I wasn't sure whether the second guy was going to be a good thing or bad when I got to the war, but I knew that having someone to share the load in training was definitely going to be appreciated.

Two days before my first scheduled ride in the F-4, headlines broke in the morning edition of the *Arizona Republic*. The gradual escalation of the war against the North was apparently over. On May 10, 1972, President Nixon finally decided that four years of negotiation without measurable result wouldn't do in an election year. It was clearly time to make the price for continued recalcitrance at the Paris peace table too high for the North Vietnamese.

Major air strikes were launched against targets throughout North Vietnam. Hanoi and Haiphong were heavily hit by forces launched from carriers in the Gulf of Tonkin as well as USAF tactical aircraft stationed in Thailand and South Vietnam. Several aircraft were lost, defensive reaction was intense, and there was every indication that this was not an isolated action. Duke Cunningham, a Navy F-4 pilot, got three MiG kills in a single mission and became the first fighter ace of the war. Operation Linebacker commenced. If it lasted more than sixty days, when I got to Korat I'd be going to North Vietnam again.

FLYING THE PHANTOM WAS SURPRISINGLY easy. Takeoff and landing speeds were considerably slower than those of the F-105, thanks to something called BLC or boundary layer control. A system of ducts and slots routed high pressure air from the turbine section of the engines to the leading and trailing edges of the wings when the flaps were down. This airflow energized the air over the wings, making them much more effective in producing lift at low speeds. Where the Thud would take off at 190 knots or more after six or seven thousand feet of ground roll, the F-4 lifted off at 40 knots less, in just under four thousand feet. Landing showed a similar 40- to 50-knot lower speed.

Handling of the F-4 in every region of flight, from traffic patterns to high performance dogfighting, was based on angle of attack. Rather than use indicated airspeed and calculations of weight of fuel or stores remaining, the optimum speed was simply an angle of attack of the wing. Regardless of weight, temperature, density altitude, or anything else, the wing's best angle of attack was always the same. A simple gauge calibrated in "units" told you what the AOA was. The units were arbitrary, not denoting any particular measurement standard, simply "units." There was no need to look in the cockpit for the AOA gauge: there was a head-up display of three tiny lights mounted on each side of the gun-sight combining glass. Lighted yellow arrowheads showed whether your AOA was above or below the optimum, which was denoted by a tiny green donut. Go too fast and the upper light pointed the arrow down, indicating a need to lower the nose slightly or ease off the back-stick pressure. Strictly a Goldilocks arrangement: you could be too hot, too cold, or just right. The whole mess was supplemented by a tone that buzzed in your helmet earphones. As you slowed the airplane and increased the AOA, a tone started a slow, low beeping. Slow to optimum AOA and the tone went steady. Slow too much or get the nose too high and in danger of a stall, and the beeping increased in pitch and rate until the frantic gibbering couldn't be ignored.

Landings were Navy style, by design. The recommended technique was to fly the AOA to an "on speed" indication, steady tone and donut light lit, around the final turn and onto final approach. Control the nose position with the stick and use the throttles to determine the landing point. There was no flare involved. Simply drive the airplane onto the runway as if you weren't even aware that it existed. The huge landing gear struts absorbed the shock, and even though it looked extremely firm, the ride was smooth and the impact hardly noticeable. From outside it looked like a controlled crash. From the cockpit, every landing was a grease job.

The only downside to the aircraft's handling was something called adverse yaw. I'd heard lots of old F-100 pilots talk about adverse yaw. The Hun was notorious for it. Aerodynamically, it was the issue of the down aileron creating more drag than the up aileron when the stick was moved to the side rolling into a turn. The drag made the nose yaw away from the intended direction of flight. No big deal, you're probably thinking. Well, part of what goes on in the process of the nose moving the wrong way is that part of the upper wing blanks in the turn and the lower wing moves into a more advantageous position to generate lift—a lot of lift. The result of a ham-fisted airplane driver throwing major aileron into an aggressive roll is that the aircraft suddenly and dramatically flips in the opposite direction. Many F-100 people died as a result of not learning to deal with adverse yaw, and virtually everyone who flew the airplane had great respect for it. The recommended technique was to fly with the stick controlling pitch and the rudder controlling roll. Ailerons were generally ignored. The F-4 had adverse yaw issues.

Most of the first flight in the aircraft was spent orienting a new Phantom driver to the advanced handling characteristics. At altitude in the training area, the instructor demonstrated the proper control techniques, showing how rudder effectiveness increased as back pressure was introduced. Aileron deflection was an emphatic no-no. The AOA indications were demoed, meaning you slowed the airplane down and listened to the tone transitions and watched the lights and AOA gauge as you went through the optimum on-speed conditions, first a light burble or tickle on the controls and then a more substantial buffeting indicating an impeding stall, and finally the chattering warning tones. At high AOA the stick lightened noticeably, causing a slight nose rise if you didn't ease off the back pressure. The next event after that was a rapid yawing, or nose slice, which was pretty much the last controllable event before departing from controlled flight. Departure was something to be avoided, as it took lots of altitude to recover and often required inflight deployment of the drag chute. Coming home without your drag chute was looked down upon as poor form.

After the demonstrations the new pilot trainee was talked through the exercises, flying the airplane to the same condition of nose rise, and trying to recognize the hints that nose slice and departure were imminent. The real danger was that experienced pilots would use techniques that had worked well in previous aircraft but would be dangerous in the F-4. The frustrating part was that the younger instructor pilots were seriously apprehensive about letting the upgrading pilots go too far in their demos. After several maneuvers in which I could feel definite restrictions to stick movement as the IP guarded and then guided my control inputs, I simply eased off the stick grip entirely. I turned my head left and right, held the throttles, and let my right hand rest on my knee. Without missing a beat, the airplane flew through the maneuver exactly as the instructor was directing and coaching me. He remarked at my smoothness and how quickly I had benefited from his instruction, abandoning all of my old and ingrained bad habits. I thanked him for the compliments and reassumed my grip on the stick.

The "quickie" checkout was brutally brief. The assumption was that student pilots were experienced tactically and knew the basics of formation, weapons, navigation, and combat applications. A fast half-dozen sorties and a pilot qualification check assured that we could take off, land, fly instrument approaches, and

safely avoid going out of control while airborne. I had
nearly fifteen hundred hours of flying time, but I hadn't
been in a fighter in more than five years. I was safe
enough to fly the airplane around the local area, but
wasn't quite sure whether I was competent to go to war.
Each morning the newspaper reported on the progress
of the reinvigorated air war over North Vietnam. The
daily updates seemed to parallel our training, showing
us what we would need to do when we arrived in theater and mocking the very obvious superficiality of the
short training syllabus.

The *Arizona Republic* reported that MiGs were encountered during a bombing raid and two Phantoms
were lost, running out of fuel after chasing the enemy
without results. At Luke we were flying three air-to-air
sorties, all single ship 1-v-1 maneuvering and all without consideration for mutual support, radar employment, or the fighting characteristics of the enemy's
aircraft. Two-airplane flights would head to the training
area, practice some tactical formation turns, then conduct a brief sequence of tail-chase engagements in
which the object apparently was to see who could pull
the most G the longest. The young instructors had little
detailed air-combat training, and the experienced students in the short course generally knew more about
three-dimensional maneuvering than the faculty. The
prevailing policy seemed to be that flying fighters was
very dangerous and, while it would be easy to write off
a combat loss, an accident in training would be inex-
cusable. Our maneuvering was tightly controlled,
strictly choreographed, and, with the inevitable stick
guarding by the instructors, left a distinct impression
that the F-4 was not a very agile airplane.

I spent quite a bit of time in the squadron weapons

office, digging through the classified manuals held in the big green safe. There was a serious effort going on in the Fighter Weapons School at Nellis AFB to develop new ways to fight air-to-air. The concepts of the Korean War that I had been taught during my F-105 training weren't doing the job in this war. The basic idea that the flight lead was the shooter and the wingman was supposed to support him from a "fighting wing" position in a 30 degree maneuvering cone fifteen hundred feet off his tail was inherently flawed. Fighting wing didn't offer support in any way. It merely meant that the wingman was going to be filling the space that an attacker would need to shoot the lead aircraft. Wingmen during Rolling Thunder had paid a heavy toll for the elitist concept of fighting wing.

The new tactics had been developed years earlier, but the bureaucracy of the Air Force had been reluctant to change. Change meant training, and training inevitably meant risk, and risk led to accidents, and when accidents happened, wing commanders lost their jobs. Don't change your tactics and the boss stays in the running to make general.

The Weapons School had explored the geometry of aerial combat. Pulling on the stick harder and longer than your opponent might only work for a short period, and even then only if your adversary was flying a similar aircraft. We knew for certain that the MiGs were lighter and generally more maneuverable. Our aircraft were multimission capable and superior technologically. We had better radar, navigation equipment, air refueling, and load-carrying capability. We could deliver the iron at a long distance. What we didn't have was turn rate and turn radius. If we tried to out-turn the MiG, it didn't matter whether it was a -17, a -19, or a -21, we would lose.

The answer wasn't obvious until you thought about it, and the Fighter Weapons School was paid to think about it. Don't chase the bad guy. If he can out-turn you, it's foolish to try to deny it. The solution is to get out of the enemy's plane of maneuver. If the bad guy turns horizontally, your choice is to maneuver in the vertical. If you are faster than he is, you pull up and out of his turn circle, slowing down in the process to reduce your turn radius, avoid overshooting him, and retain the ability to pirouette and reposition in a lead predicting descent. If you are slower than the enemy, descend inside his turn and cut across the circle to close on him and kill him. Whatever you do, you don't want to track along the same flight path, trying to squeeze an extra degree or two of turn out of the maneuver.

The real advantage of the out-of-plane maneuvering was something we referred to as God's G. When an aircraft turns, it fights the tendency to go in a straight line. By rolling and pulling into a turn, the G force squeezes you into your seat, and it isn't simply a shove, it's downright serious pressure. The more G you can pull, the tighter you are turning at a given airspeed. More G is better until you reach the structural limits of the aircraft. It's not considered good technique to pull the wings off. The F-4 had enough thrust and enough wing to pull and maintain more than seven Gs. If you could keep your airspeed above roughly 450 knots, you could pull seven Gs. That defined a turn radius.

If you made your turn in the vertical, however, something interesting happened. The force of gravity, that one G that we all experience all of the time, added to the effective G of the turn. If you pulled up and over the top of a loop, as you were pulling down inverted, the turn radius was smaller. It was as if you had one additional G on the aircraft. If you pulled seven Gs across the top of a loop, you effectively got an eight G turn. Conversely, if you flew across the bottom of a loop while pulling seven Gs, the impact of God's G was to decrease your effective radius and make a larger turn. A loop, it turned out, wasn't really a circle but actually an egg, with the narrow part on top.

This could be used to advantage in air combat. It was no problem to read about the egg and visualize it, but few of the instructors understood it. Anyone who tried to get more than a few degrees out of the horizontal was cautioned that he was too aggressive, and that huge pitch excursions weren't needed. Simply chase the other guy around the sky and roll your socks down around your ankles at six Gs for a minute or so.

At the same time that the Weapons School was rewriting the concepts of single aircraft maneuver, they were also benefiting from the lessons that the Israeli air force had learned in their wars. When outnumbered, as they usually were, it wasn't a good idea to stay engaged with an opponent for very long. Unlike the combats of World War II or Korea, in which fighters paired off and battled to the death, the IAF learned that it was smarter to "shoot and scoot." Don't stay engaged with an enemy for more than 30 to 45 degrees of turn. Shoot your missiles or gun when in range, then break away while your energy is still high and the bad guy is busy defending against your weapon. Use your wingman not as a cushion for your six o'clock, but as a fighting partner. Either aircraft in an element can be the shooter, without regard to whether he is lead or wing. If the shooting aircraft is turning in one direction, the wingman should be maneuvering in a different plane of motion. Tail chasing is a mistake.

All this was in the books, but it wasn't in the Cat IV

syllabus of instruction. We didn't get any mutual support element tactics. We didn't get any max range missile shooting. We didn't get any dissimilar fighting against aircraft that looked or flew like our expected enemy. We got fighting wing and close-in horizontal turning. We got scolded when we broke out of plane too much, and we only got three sorties to learn how to get maximum performance out of our airplane. The instructors, many of whom had flown their combat as backseat pilots, weren't comfortable or trained in the new concepts of air-to-air, so they weren't going to let us take them into areas with which they were unfamiliar.

As the daily news reported attacks on airfields, transportation facilities, fuel storage dumps, and other targets, we were going to the gunnery range, dropping 25-pound blue practice bombs in 10-, 20-, and 30-degree dive-bomb attacks. The important issue for qualification to go to war was that bombs released from the aircraft would hit somewhere on the face of the earth. Refresher training for those of us who previously had some skill at weapons delivery took a fast half-dozen missions. The details of how best to cope with crosswinds, adjust for nonstandard release conditions, or even deliver from a tactical popup were left for individual study or learning by experience when we got to our war assignment.

There was a day refueling sortie and one at night. The refueling receptacle for the Phantom was on the spine of the airplane, just behind the canopy of the backseater. Unlike the F-105, in which the door opened in front of you, the F-4 required considerable dependence on the capability of the tanker's boom operator. The procedure simply required you to fly a stable formation position under and slightly behind the tanker, following terse corrections issued by the boomer or responding to directional signal lights on the bottom fuselage of the KC-135. A good boom operator could aggressively reach out and poke you with the boom, while a timid one spent agonizing minutes giving short, "up one foot, back one, left two" instructions. Faced with a weak boomer in the Thud, you simply told him to hold it steady, and you flew the receptacle onto the nozzle. With the receptacle behind you in the F-4, there was a definite feeling of vulnerability to an inexperienced boomer.

Night refueling was combined with a night range mission. We had never done night attack in the single-seat -105, but there was a distinct possibility that we might be assigned to a Phantom unit that had round-the-clock responsibilities. To designate the aim point we used air-dropped flares, or "ground logs," that burned as target identification signals. The darkness of the range on a moonless night with nearly the same number of lights on the ground as stars in the sky led to almost continual vertigo. Here was a good example of the value of the backseater in a two-place airplane. I knew the importance of believing my instruments and not trusting the whirling fluids of the inner ear that give us our sense of balance. The turning, banking and G forces of the bombing pattern were a nightmare of dizziness, and the calm voice of the WSO describing altitudes, attitudes, airspeeds, and position in the gunnery sequence removed the monsters and helped quiet the mind.

The total training added up to twenty-eight hours in twenty-three flights. It took barely six weeks and wasn't designed to make you fully capable in the aircraft. The gaps in the training were huge. We didn't get any training in intercept options, we didn't fire any of the air-to-air missiles, there was no information about missile defense using the electronic countermeasure pods, we never got to carry full-scale heavyweight ordnance, and there wasn't any training in nuclear weapons delivery. I was fairly confident I'd figure out the nuke business someday in the distant future if the need arose, but the rest of it was an acknowledgment that we were big boys, and we would have to draw upon our past experience and trust our leaders in the immediate war. I wondered if this was similar to the Japanese kamikaze philosophy of fighter checkout.

Operation Linebacker was rolling at full speed, and I was now technically a fully, albeit marginally, qualified Phantom pilot. I was headed for Korat, back to the scene of my first combat tour a bit more than five years earlier. I had a lot more flying experience than the first time, and I knew about leadership, formations, tactics, and surviving in the high-threat environment. I was familiar with Korat, and strangely, the fact that we were going against North Vietnam again gave me a feeling of confidence. I knew the area well. It was going to be interesting to see how much had changed and what had remained the same.

3. SWEET HOME KORAT

We sleep safe in our beds because rough men stand ready in the night to visit violence on those who would do us harm.

—Attributed wrongly to George Orwell

AS THE DOOR OF THE C-130 swung open, it was pure sensory overload. The assault was incredible. The brilliant sunshine after the gloomy interior of the transport made your eyes squint and water. The blast of heat from the humid jungle air was made even hotter by the hours of cold soaking your body in the air-conditioned cargo compartment during the four-hour flight from the Philippines. The noise was an instant headache. There was no abatement from the drone and whistle of the turboprops, to which we'd become acclimated over the duration of the flight. Now the noise came from beyond the airplane. It was a cacophony of jet engines, propellers, afterburner blasts, trucks racing across the ramp, sirens on fire engines. Everywhere you looked there was intense activity. Aircraft taxied, maintenance trucks darted between fuel tankers and dodged refueling hoses stretched across the tarmac, and trains of bomb trailers snaked their way to an assigned tail number for upload. Takeoffs and landings added steadily to the din.

But the sense that took the most severe hit was olfactory. The American nose is not conditioned for the odors of Asia. Jet fuel and exhaust were the almost pleasant foundation for a soupy perfume that seemed to define Thailand. Blindfold me and drop me into the country with no other clues and I'll immediately recognize Thailand. The diesel generators that provided electricity ran day and night, putting charged electrons into the wire grid to light the lights, then dumping unconsumed hydrocarbons and soot into the atmosphere. Cooking fires of the entire nation added a nice layer of carbon monoxide, the inevitable byproduct of incomplete combustion of charcoal, tempered slightly by the marginally pleasant aroma of garlic, soy sauce, and somewhat rancid cooking oil. The heat meant that everyone was perpetually sweating, and the sweat was of an intensity for which no Ban, Secret, or Right Guard had been designed. Lurking, and not timidly, in the background of this mélange was the unmistakable smell of decomposing sewage. The klongs, those open ponds and canals that seem to cover half the landscape of Thailand, added the final distinctive odor of shit to the package. Yes, the smell was noteworthy.

The twenty or so other passengers each went through their own unwinding and stretching exercises, shaking loose the stiffness of the flight, then gathering their briefcases or tattered brown envelopes containing orders and critical military paperwork. We shuffled out the door of the Herk and stood somewhat dizzily on the cement ramp. Korat was still the Korat I remembered from '66, but it was also much more. What had once been a bustling fighter base hosting two, then three, then four squadrons of single-seat F-105s would be deemed a ghost town in comparison to the crush of the base now. The revetments could be seen off to the east along the parallel taxiway, but there was so much more. There were fighters parked on the main ramp, overflowing from the neat row of corrugated steel revetment slots. Beyond, there was more ramp space with C-130s bristling with antennae, then beyond that were camouflaged EC-121 radar picket planes, and still farther off was a ramp extension containing EB-66 radar jammers. In front of our newly arrived C-130 sat at least half a dozen other cargo planes in various stages of loading, unloading, or refueling. To the west of where I stood were several KC-135 tankers. Throw in a helicopter or two, some for flight-line fire protection and some for apparent liaison transport, plus a few light planes that might have been forward air controllers or maybe engaged in some sort of shadowy CIA/Air America operation, and the whole scene was overwhelming. It seemed as though every square foot of concrete had an airplane on it, and almost all of them were making noise.

There was no personal greeting by pilots from a shorthanded squadron, as there had been for my arrival in the F-105 days. This time it was a tech sergeant from personnel in olive drab jungle fatigues who shepherded us onto the Bluebird school bus. We rolled away from the airplane and slowly wended our way between parked aircraft for the two hundred yards to the terminal building. The sergeant stood at the front of the bus, checking off names on his clipboard and advising us that we could collect our baggage in a few minutes, as soon as the pallet was offloaded, and we would then be going to billeting, where we would be assigned quarters and given an instruction and welcome packet to

Korat. It seemed that eight years of combat operations at Korat had allowed for development of a smooth and impersonal processing system. A few first-tour folks at the front of the bus peppered the tour guide with questions, while I simply looked out the window trying to absorb the changes that had taken place over the intervening five and a half years since my first tour.

With B-4 bags, the military-issue soft-sided version of a two-suiter, and fiberglass Samsonite suitcases blocking the aisle, the bus moved out from the terminal area and headed down the main road of the base. I recognized the fighter operations quadrangle from my first tour. The squadron buildings looked virtually unchanged, but the command post now had a seven- or eight-foot-high barricade of sandbags inside the chain link fence. Korat had never been under attack during the entire war, but some past commander must have decided that building a better wall would make him more promotable.

New cement, stucco-clad buildings lined the road, and signs identified these as maintenance, supply, munitions, avionics, and other support offices. A right turn away from the flight line on a road that hadn't been there in '66 took us past the old hootch area and disclosed almost triple the number of aircrew housing units on the west side of the street. Ahead a sprawling teak building displayed a large sign over the entranceway, declaring it the Korat Officer's Open Mess. The club was new and clearly a much more sophisticated facility than the old one. A quick left onto a side street and we pulled up in front of a building labeled Billeting Office. The tech sergeant announced that officers would dismount here with their bags, while enlisted personnel would continue aboard the bus. I got off.

The billeting clerk was ready. She had a list of inbound personnel and a file drawer filled with briefing packets, all organized alphabetically. There were seven officers in our group, some aviators and some support. Each of us completed a housing registration form and got our appropriate packet. Mine indicated that I was going to be assigned to the 469th Tactical Fighter Squadron. The clerk assigned me a room and a building number, then told me I could get a ride from a base taxi that would pick us all up in about twenty minutes. I asked her if the 469th hootches were in the same area they had always been. Although she wasn't sure, she pointed to an area of the base map on the wall behind her, and it was clear that nothing had changed. It was only about two hundred yards away. I told her I'd walk.

It was probably a poor choice. The heat and humidity had me huffing and distinctly pitted out by the time I got to my room. The hootch was just around the corner from the building I'd stayed in six years earlier. A green F-4 silhouette rather than an F-105 on the door signaled the most apparent change. A television was on in the central screened porch area. The room to which I'd been assigned seemed unusual in that the picture window was boarded up with a large plywood sheet on the inside, spray-painted with the large warning, "Quiet! Night crew sleeping!" I tried the door handle gingerly, hoping not to disturb whoever might be inside. It opened to a refreshing blast of air conditioning and the glow from a single small light bulb on the desk lamp. A slender, dark-haired young guy in shorts and rubber sandals sat at the desk, feet up, reading a magazine. "Hi," he said. "You Raz?"

"Yeah. I just got in and I guess this is gonna be my room. You were expecting me?" Apparently the new arrival process had been automated down to the notification of squadrons, billeting clerks, and even roommates. "I'm Ed Rasimus, how you doing?" I dropped my helmet, bag, and briefcase and extended my hand.

"Bob Slockbower. Backseater, Spectre escort, night owl. They call me Socks or Sockblower." He shook my hand, then pointed at the bed across the room from his desk. "That'll be yours. Don Logan had it, but he got shot down about three days ago. I'm waiting for the word to inventory and pack up his stuff. I moved it all to one side of the closet. I'll have it out of your way in a day or two." I nodded slowly, remembering the losses of friends and squadron mates during my first tour. It was the first of what would be many instances of déjà vu.

"You need a hand with anything?" he offered. I shook my head and slung my B-4 onto the bed. Then I retrieved my helmet bag and briefcase from the doorway, flicking on the ceiling light so I could scope out the full glory of the room. It wasn't much different from the one in which I'd spent that intense six months of my life as a lieutenant F-105 pilot. My section of the closet held a half-dozen hangers with pants and shirts or flight suits, all pushed to the far left. The shelf contained an array of yellow boxes of Canon photography equipment. Lenses, cases, flash, motor drive, filters, tripod, and more were stacked up. Logan had been into picture taking in a big way. I wondered if he'd been taking pictures when he was hacked.

"What happened to Logan?"

"He was backseater on an escort for a Pack VI mission. We lost two airplanes that day. Everybody seems to think the MiGs came slashing through on a high-speed pass and got them both. It was just north of Kep."

"How's it been going?" I asked. "Have you had many

losses?" I'd been to Kep before and knew that the flak and SAM threat could be intense. I wondered if the change from Laos and South Vietnam missions to the higher threat North Vietnam targets was having an impact on the squadron. "You been getting a lot of Pack VI flights?"

"Not me. Not yet at least. I've been on nights for the last couple of months. We do some night stuff with FACs near the DMZ, and a lot of escort for the AC-130s. I like flying at night. It's cooler. The air is a lot smoother. You can see where they're shooting from. Hey, did you know Bill Elander? He was in Logan's front seat."

Elander had done a -105 tour in '65, one of the first to get a hundred missions completed. He'd been before my time in the airplane, and I'd never encountered him. "Nope. He did his hundred before I got here," I said. It wasn't a very auspicious beginning. In fact, it recalled my arrival at Korat the first time. Too many squadron losses, a bed that had belonged to someone lost only a day or two before, and an indication that things might be getting worse before they got much better. The last time, they did. We lost nearly one hundred F-105s during that six months.

While we talked, I unzipped my bag and hung up flight suits. Getting unpacked in a tropical combat zone doesn't take a whole lot of time. I got out of my uniform, grabbed the clean, folded white towel off the end of the bed and started out the door in my Jockey shorts. The showers were in the center of the bungalow. "How's the new club?" I asked Bob on my way out.

"It's okay," he shouted at my back. "Booze is cheap and the food's tolerable. Hey, watch out for Mama-san, she's probably still in command of the latrine."

The warning wasn't necessary. Mama-san, a stocky,

self-assured Thai woman, was the hootch housekeeper. She was just gathering up her working clothes, stowing the ironing board, and taking a last check of the refrigerator contents before heading off to catch the bus to Korat city. She looked about thirty-five, but it was virtually impossible to tell. To an untrained *farang* observer,[1] all Thais other than children and the elderly possessed the smooth, unwrinkled skin, jet black hair, and twinkling eyes of young adults. She looked me up and down, probably judging instantly whether I was a threat to her domain and whether I would be a neat guy or a slob causing her extra work. "Sawadee, kah," she greeted me.

"Sawadee, kup," I responded, surprising her that a new arrival knew the greeting and the proper gender for response. She smiled. I'd gained approval.

"You come Korat before?"

"Chi, kup." I immediately exhausted the rest of my Thai vocabulary with a positive reply. "I was here in 1966. You know Dang? She was my hootch maid. She took good care of me."

"Ahhh, Dang. She still work here. She over there." Mama-san pointed at my old hootch building from the -105 days. It appeared that little had changed over the intervening years as far as domestic issues. "I tell her you come back." She didn't need to ask my name, she would see it daily on my flight suit nametags. She continued to bustle around the screen porch, gathering her belongings and not allowing the social niceties to interfere with meeting her bus for the ride home. She headed out the door as I headed into the shower area.

The flash heater on the wall responded appropriately

---

1. Farang: a "foreigner," or non-Thai. Much like the Japanese gaijin, but without quite as much negative connotation.

to my demand for hot water. The erratic nature of the small water system made it critical to get your showering done in a hurry, before the hot water ran out and the heater couldn't keep up with the flow. It didn't take long to get the travel dust off. Five minutes and I was showered, shaved, and ready for a drink. Bermuda shorts and polo shirt was still the off-duty uniform of choice, and I was properly supplied. Before leaving the hootch I took a minute at the desk in my room to open the brown manila envelope I'd been given at billeting, to see what was going to happen tomorrow.

I was welcomed to the 469th "Fighting Bulls," humbly described as "the World's Finest." I'd report to personnel tomorrow morning for in-processing and collection of my various records, forms, and paperwork. Then I'd visit my squadron, the flight surgeon's office for flying clearance, the command post for security access, and finally the personal equipment section to be outfitted with parachute harness, survival gear, and flight equipment. Finally, I would report the day after tomorrow to "new-guy school," a three-day training course on local procedures, rules of engagement, weapons, and tactics. The war had apparently been going on long enough that bureaucracy had built substantial empires. Absent the intense pressure of small units suffering heavy losses, we now had the time and the volume of fresh input to the squadrons to allow for square-filling, lesson-planning, briefing, testing, recording, and detailing. Maybe it was a different war.

Slockbower watched me read the packet, then offered, "You're just gonna love new-guy school. They've loaded two hours of information into a three-day course."

"Well, with my twenty-eight hours in the airplane, I've probably got a bit to learn here. I've never even flown an E-model." I figured it couldn't hurt too much to be up-front about my basic inexperience in the F-4. "I'm gonna head over to the club and check it out. You hungry?"

Socks demurred with the excuse that he was on the schedule later that night, so would be heading down to the squadron shortly. I waved, then turned and headed back the way I'd come an hour earlier, past the billeting office to the club.

THE OFFICER'S CLUB WAS HUGE, a giant teak complex surrounding a swimming pool and garden area, with two sprawling wings flanking an open breezeway capped by a second-story banquet and party floor. One approached down a white gravel driveway and a welcoming sign identifying the building as KABOOM— the Korat Air Base Officer's Open Mess. A bit of sick war zone humor there. On the right of the breezeway leading to the pool was the bar, and to the left was the dining room. Straight ahead, an array of chaises longues and pool chairs surrounded gleaming blue water. Several men in swimsuits, obviously aircrew members, splashed in the pool, lounged in chairs reading paperback books, or conversed with a surprising number of clearly American women. Some things had changed considerably since my first tour.

The bar seemed like the better starting point. It was much like bars in the States: dark and a bit garish, with neon signs touting several brands of beer; a huge jukebox, and a slightly sour smell of cigarettes, stale beer, and sweaty bodies. The bar itself filled the entire wall down the left side of the room. A brass plaque above the huge bell mounted over its center proclaimed that this was "the longest bar in Southeast Asia," as well as restating the standard rules of every officer's club in the US Air Force: "He who enters covered here, shall buy for all a round of cheer. He who rings this bell in jest, shall buy a round for all the rest." Translation: If you wear your hat into the bar, someone rings the bell to alert the crowd and the offender buys drinks for the house. Ring the bell as a joke, and the ringer picks up the tab. Whenever the bell rings, someone will be buying drinks.

The bar was teak. The floor was teak. The walls were teak. The dark reddish wood was everywhere. To the left of the entrance, arrayed on the wall were three large teak shields. Each was roughly three feet tall and nearly as wide. Across the top on a large brass banner, each displayed the same words: "100 Missions—North Vietnam." Two of the three were filled with neat rows and columns of smaller brass tags, 120 per shield. The third was less than two-thirds full. Midway down the first one, I found my name and that of my 1966 squadron mates from the F-105 days. I looked around at the dozen or so guys in flight suits sipping drinks. Their names weren't on the plaques yet, but with the resumption of bombing of North Vietnam, they might someday make it.

It was inevitable that I would flash back on that previous life at Korat, thinking of all the names that weren't on the plaques, the lieutenants and captains and majors that had gone into the grinder and wound up dead or, worse yet, prisoners of war for these intervening years. I wondered what their thoughts were as the time rolled on, seemingly endlessly with the parade of pacifist visitors coming to the prisons around Hanoi to pose on an antiaircraft gun, wave at the cameras, and inevitably to demoralize the American fighting men who were suffering at the hands of our enemy. I hoped they had survived those quiet years from the end of 1968 until the spring of '72. I wondered what had become of their buddies and friends, the guys who should have been flying overhead to punish the enemy and bring their release closer. We were going back now, and maybe this time we'd get the job done right.

At the far end of the bar, a small sign over a hallway entrance announced the club office. I headed that way and noticed the smiling, familiar face of Jimmy the bartender, still at his post six years later. I doubted he'd ever anticipated that a job at the Korat officer's club would lead to long-term employment. Down the hall I found a large room with two pool tables, and to the left a cashier's cage and small manager's office. Behind the cashier's window bars was another familiar face, one of the prettier waitresses from the club dining room back in '66. It was Nit, now chief cashier of the club. Like Jimmy, she had made the war into a career. She didn't recognize me, but looked puzzled when I slipped a blue laminated card through the bars and said I wanted to renew my membership. I had card number 207. Nit studied it, then looked at me and smiled. No, I wouldn't be able to use that card. I needed a new, plastic, credit card. And, no, I couldn't keep that number either. My new one would be in the four thousand range. So much for seniority. I kept the old card anyway. Bureaucracy is blindly obedient to regulations at the expense of memorabilia.

With the business of membership taken care of, I returned to the bar and ordered a Heineken. I found a place at the end farthest from the door, giving me a vantage point from which to get a general feeling for the pecking order of the place. Traffic was picking up

as the end of the regular duty day came. Strangely, I
didn't see many F-4 crews coming in. Neither the green
Fighting Bull of the 469th nor the black Fighting Ram
of the 34th were apparent in any numbers. There were
mostly C-130 and EB-66 crews and a smattering of
transients, folks spending the night on business from
some other SEA location. Strange.

IN-PROCESSING WENT SMOOTHLY AS AT a stateside base.
Records were collected, forms were completed, orientation lectures were conducted, and a string of installation high rollers came through the classroom to
welcome us all to Korat and wish us good luck in the
war. There was none of the frantic dashing between
temporary offices to fill the processing squares that had
characterized my first tour. Clearly the efficiencies of
permanence were demonstrated. Manpower was being
pumped into the operation at a much higher rate, meaning shortages were fairly rare in crews, maintainers,
bomb handlers, and support personnel.

A day later, I checked in with the squadron. The
building was the same; it had always been the 469th
TFS. It was the first structure on the right as you entered the quadrangle of squadron operations buildings.
On the left, the old 421st squadron where I had flown
my -105 tour was now the home of the 17th Wild
Weasel Squadron, flying F-105Gs. Farther ahead on the
right was the 401st Tac Fighter Wing deputy commander for operations. To the left past the 17th was the
other remaining F-4 squadron, the 34th. On the opposite side of the quad, what had once been the home of
the 13th TFS was now a centralized personal equip-

ment center, with helmets, parachutes and harnesses, survival equipment, and G suits for all the fighter crews in a single site. At the far west end of the quad was Fort Apache, the operations and intelligence center. As grim recognition of the inability of most Americans' digestive systems to cope with Asia, the center focus of the quad remained a four-holer latrine. Except for a few signage changes, it was much as I remembered.

The 469th was considerably different than it had been in the F-105 days. A single-seat fighter squadron typically had eighteen or at most twenty pilots. As an F-4 squadron, the unit now had twenty-four aircraft assigned, and more than thirty two-man crews. The commander, Ed McHale, had been a T-38 instructor when I'd gone through pilot training. The operations officer, Fred Smith, was a West Point graduate and son of a general officer. The rest of the squadron was a mix of new and old, experienced and beginners in the tactical aviation business. There were some second- and even third-tour fighter pilots on the roster, but most of the captains and majors had only recently been qualified in the F-4. There were some ex-bomber types, ex-airlifters, and former training command instructors. A few of the senior guys had been around the F-4 for a few years but had been successful in dodging the war until now. The lieutenants were almost all on their first assignment out of nav school or pilot training. The number of guys to meet and remember was overwhelming, and it raised a warning flag in my mind about the importance of knowing the capabilities of the guys on your wing and the ones leading you. It could make the difference between survival and disaster.

Slockbower was right about new-guy school. It was

an empire built to indoctrinate the new arrivals. What I'd learned independently in '66 after a couple of hours' study now took almost three full days of classes. Parts of the new-guy course were filled with descriptions of the base along with the local flight patterns. Other lesson blocks covered the rules of engagement, those convoluted regulations under which we operated that seemed specifically designed to protect our enemy from danger. There were bits of history, geography, and math, and a lot of butt-covering. If it was briefed in "new guy" it meant someone couldn't be blamed later when the inevitable rules violations occurred.

There was some valuable info, however, for those like me who had only a handful of flight hours in the F-4 and absolutely no experience in the E-model of the aircraft. I learned about the improved radar, the weapons release computer system or WRCS, the electronic countermeasure pods, and the newer radar warning receiver. The cliché goes, "you can tell a fighter pilot, but you can't tell him much." This was very operative when I was told that the bombing computer system could drop more accurate bombs than an experienced pilot using manual dive bombing. The cliché held true when they told me about the ECM pods and how they would "increase miss distance" for SAMs and flak. It even lasted through their explanation about the effectiveness of the EB-66 jamming aircraft and the SAM-suppression tactics of the F-105G Wild Weasels. I'd dropped a lot of bombs, seen a lot of SAMs, and flown with a lot of Weasels. You couldn't tell me much about any of that.

4. SHARK-MOUTHED PHANTOMS

> So it was that the war in the air began. Men rode upon
> the whirlwind that night and slew and fell like archangels.
> The sky rained heroes upon the astonished earth. Surely the
> last fights of mankind were the best. What was the heavy
> pounding of your Homeric swordsman, what was the
> creaking charge of chariots, besides this swift rush, this
> crash, this giddy triumph, this headlong sweep to death?
>
> —H. G. Wells, *The World Set Free*, 1914

THE SQUADRON WAS WAY TOO big to learn everyone's
names, particularly when I was spending most of my
duty days at new-guy school. Throw in the concept of
round-the-clock operations and it was virtually impossible to even encounter most of the folks. The club
wasn't the answer either, I soon discovered. Other than
meals, most of the guys avoided it and chose instead to
gather at a squadron bar in the small green building in
the center of the hootch quadrangle. Originally con-
structed as a central shower facility, with the only hot-
water heater in the area, the building's original purpose
had long been rendered obsolete. Showers were now in
the hootches themselves, and the vacant shack had

been commandeered at some time between 1966, when I'd left Korat, and '72, when I returned.

It was only the second evening when one of the guys asked me if I'd found the "CTF." I had no idea what that was or where it was. He quickly explained and told me it was right around the corner from my room. The initials stood for crew training facility. It wasn't necessary to ask why. The growth of the base explained it clearly. With tanker crews, airborne command post operators, various trash-haulers, and the proliferation of nonflying bureaucrats on the base, it was too restrictive for fighter pilots to spend their after-hours time at the officer's club. Besides, with the apparently significant population of officers' wives that somehow, despite the prohibition of accompanying husbands to remote tours in combat zones, seemed to be everywhere, it was inevitable that there would be conflict with the fighter pilots. To accommodate our colorful vocabulary and rather bizarre concepts of nightly entertainment, the CTF made a lot of sense.

Fighter pilot bars always have rules and hazards. In the isolated environment of the CTF, the rules had grown in complexity. There were the basics, recognized around the tactical world, but there were a couple of local twists about which no one was going to tell the new guy. The CTF door opened into a small, smoky room filled with guys in sweaty flying suits. It wasn't more than twenty feet wide and forty feet long. Straight ahead on the back wall was a small bar, manned by a petite, smiling Thai girl who boasted considerable— probably not natural—breast development. The bar had six rickety stools and the requisite brass bell hanging overhead to signal whenever someone was buying a round. On each side of the door stood a round table, the one on the left with a nonstop poker game for six or seven players, and the one on the right with a conversational group or occasionally a dice game such as craps or four-five-six. On the floor immediately on entry was a large tile mosaic of the squadron patch, depicting the 469th Fighting Bull in all of his fire-snorting glory. It didn't take a genius to figure out that one didn't step on the unit symbol. Accidentally step on the bull when you come in, and you'll buy a round. Hung in the doorway, at forehead level, were the six barrels of a 20mm Vulcan cannon. Watch the bull to avoid transgression, and you got hit on the top of the head with sixty pounds of chrome steel gun barrels. Watch the barrels to save your skull, and you ran a good chance of offending the bull. It took some agility and situational awareness to get in and out of the CTF without cranial injury or an exploding bar bill.

Booze was cheap, and a profit margin wasn't part of the CTF equation. One of the younger lieutenants got the additional duty of running the bar, keeping the supplies stocked, hiring the busty Thai barmaid, slipping a few bucks a month to a hootch girl to swab the place out each morning, and making sure the books got balanced at the end of the month. No money changed hands; it was an honor system among honorable men. Take a drink and enter a hash mark on a clipboard. The total was paid off at the end of the month or when you departed. Combat losses of folks with large bar tabs were an accepted cost of doing business. The name of the CTF gave the place a quasi-official status, so that the young officer responsible for the operation could be recognized on his periodic performance reports for the great job he did in maintaining unit morale.

Within the space of a few beers, I met all the folks in the squadron that I would want to know. In an organization that contained a mix of multi-tour fighter pilots, reluctant warriors whose number had come up on the Palace Cobra list, and young aggressive new crewmembers, it was a given that those who spent the most time in the CTF were the hard core, the warriors and squires hoping to learn the fighter business and survive. There were a couple of old friends, lieutenants who had passed through my classes in training at Williams. These were the kids to whom I'd repeatedly said I wouldn't let them graduate until I was ready to fly their wing in combat. It had been flamboyant rhetoric at the time, but now it was likely to become reality.

There was also a friendly golden-haired dog with a scar across his snout and a tail wag for every aviator that entered the CTF. It was Roscoe, the squadron mascot that Ray Lewis had brought to Korat in 1966, before he was shot down in his F-105. Roscoe had survived the long years and was clearly the senior dog on all of Korat. More than anything I'd yet seen, Roscoe's big brown eyes and wagging tail made me feel welcomed back. He walked slowly up to me and raised his head by my knee. He looked as though he remembered me as well as I remembered him, but maybe he simply wondered if I might be a good source of an occasional Milk-Bone from the cookie jar behind the bar. I rubbed his ears and got him a treat. A flood of memories hung like an aura around the dog. Good times, bad times, friends who'd died and others who'd survived, it all came pouring back. Bartenders, hootch maids, waitresses, old students, and now Roscoe. Did Roscoe remember? I'm sure that he did.

◆ ◆ ◆

GETTING BACK INTO THE AIR was a battle. There were too many people doing too many things, and too many bureaucratic squares to fill to generate much urgency. I hoped I could get a local sortie to figure out what the E-model did differently than the primitive C that I'd flown at Luke. At the very least, maybe I could get one or two permissive environment sorties before having to face the defenses of North Vietnam again. Certainly the two-place aircraft made it easier to transition, but I didn't want to endanger a WSO, a flight, or folks on the ground if I could help it.

Major Dee Lewis, the senior WSO in the squadron, grabbed me from in front of the ops counter and became my guide and mentor for the week. Whenever I showed up at the squadron, if Dee was around he put me to work getting my gear organized, reading some local tactics manuals, or watching a mission brief or debrief. He dragged me down the hall to a small cubicle and dug out the dash-1 flight manual and helped me isolate the important differences between the C and the E. We talked about the radar, the gun, and the dive toss system for weapons delivery. We talked about formation and refueling and target area tactics. He told me what we were doing in Linebacker, and I told him how it had evolved from the days of Rolling Thunder. He told me to get to the Thai tailor on base and get a party suit.

"A what?" I couldn't help but ask.

"A party suit," he explained. "When we have squadron parties, we wear party suits. They're sort of like a tailored flight suit, but in the squadron color. Didn't you have party suits the last time you were here?"

Feeling a bit out of step, I sheepishly pointed out that we didn't have a lot of parties, except for some small get-togethers when guys were fortunate enough to finish a hundred missions. The idea of some sort of special festive uniform for partying didn't jibe with my concept of a war, and it certainly didn't track with my F-105 tour when the losses were so high that a celebration of a tour completion was almost a solemn occasion. "Do I have to have one of those, or can I get away with civvies?" It seemed like a reasonable question.

Dee gave me a funny look, not sure whether he'd offended me, or was I someone of an unusual religious persuasion that didn't allow for drinking or parties? "Everyone's got one. They cost about twenty bucks for the basic model and whatever patches you want on it. Some guys do flared legs or shoulder gussets in a different color, but most stick with the basic flight suit pattern. Ya' really need to have one. C'mon, let's grab a truck and I'll take you down by the BX and get you measured up." It seemed that resistance was futile.

THE FOLLOWING DAY I GOT a spot on the schedule. New-guy school had loaded my brain with some good stuff and some old stuff, complicated with some legal stuff like the rules of engagement. Operations from Korat hadn't changed a whole lot. The radar agencies were the same, the approaches and departures were the same, the tanker tracks were the same, and, when it came to Linebacker and the North Vietnamese, the targets, defenses, and losses were nearly the same.

The different stuff was the size of the attacking packages, the integration of the various missions into a much more complex scenario than we'd used in '66. Now we had not only MiGCAP flights to keep the enemy aircraft away, but escorts armed with air-to-air missiles accompanying the bombing flights to the targets. We had a newer version of the two-seat F-105 Wild Weasel, the G-model, to attack SAM sites. There was a new radar warning receiver, the APR-36/37, to tell us about what defenses were looking at us, and there were electronic countermeasure pods to befuddle the defenders trying to target our aircraft. We had chaff flights dropping corridors of radar-blinding Mylar strips to shield the attackers. And we had precision guided munitions, laser guided bombs to make it easier to hit pinpoint targets. It seemed that we had out-technologied the enemy, and victory should be ours momentarily.

My reintroduction to combat was not involved with such a production. It was a good, old-fashioned, two-ship loaded with Mk-82, 500-pound dumb bombs, assigned to attack a "suspected truck park" about five miles from the long-destroyed runway at Dong Hoi in the southern panhandle of North Vietnam. Six years and two months earlier, I flew my first combat mission to virtually the same place. Maybe technology wasn't winning the war all that fast.

I was crewed with Dee Lewis. The pairing demonstrated a whole range of factors taken into scheduling consideration. I was second tour, so I didn't go to South Vietnam or Laos. I was an "experienced" pilot, so I got an instructor WSO rather than an instructor pilot to ride with me. I was very low time in the aircraft and zero time in the E-model Phantom, so I got the most experienced IWSO in the squadron. He could take off, land, refuel, fly formation, and keep my bumbling butt out of serious trouble if needed. I got a two-ship flight so I wouldn't jeopardize a larger formation with poor positioning or bungled radio calls. And the target was unimportant, so the sortie wasn't going to be missed if I screwed things up.

The flight briefing was short and to the point. We'd take off, fly route formation to the tanker, take some gas, drop off, and go to tactical spread into the target area. We'd drop pairs of bombs in multiple passes, killing as many trees as we could, then come home for a tactical TACAN approach, visual pattern and landing. Weather was good, defenses were minimal, and we weren't dependent upon anyone else for support.

Dee spent more time one-on-one with me in the crew briefing. His job was to teach me the way combat flights went at Korat, to ensure that I was safe to fly with the other WSOs in the squadron, and to orient me to the things that the F-4E did differently than the C-model I'd flown at Luke. Most of the discussion centered on the weapons release computer system, usually referred to as dive toss. Lewis had already briefed me on the Korat dive toss emphasis. Our wing, more than any in the world flying the F-4E, had worked hard to optimize the dive toss system. Every aircraft had every drop plotted to determine trends, and then every parameter tweaked and refined to improve accuracy. The reputation was that dive toss could drop better bombs than the best manual dive bomber. "Put your pipper on the target, punch the pickle button, and fly your ass over the target," Dee repeated the mantra. "You'll hit whatever you designated."

With typical fighter pilot reticence, I replied, "bullshit!"

Dive bombing was a complex exercise of preflight calculations, precision aeronautical parameters, incredible aviator skill, detailed weather and wind information, and a soupçon of magic. I'd dropped lots of iron over North Vietnam and knew positively that dive toss was not the match of my weapons delivery skills. It might work for some of these new punks in the squadron and some of these minimal-skills retreads from bombers and airlift, but it wasn't necessary for me and I wouldn't bother with it.

"Will you at least give it a chance? Try it out on your first pass. The target's not important and we're going to make multiple passes, so try it out. Then, if you aren't convinced, we'll do what you want and you can drop the rest manually." Lewis was adamant about the superiority of the system. I was adamant that he'd never seen my skills. I conceded a trial.

The mission was another one of those déjà vu moments when you're positive this has all happened before, but there are just enough differences to tell you that this isn't the dream you had last week. Suiting up for the sortie was the first example. The personal equipment shop was still that locker room sort of place, with smells of sweat and fear punctuated by sophomoric humor, nervous jokes, and scatological references that don't get a laugh anywhere else. There were the helmets and parachutes, G suits and survival vests on rows of steel pipe racks.

But for the F-4 drivers it was harness, not parachute—the chutes belonged to the F-105 Wild Weasel crews. Our parachutes were integrated in the airplane's ejection seat, and we simply connected our harnesses to the chute canisters when strapping in. The helmets were the same, but they were no longer white—common sense had prevailed, and they were now spray-painted in dull camo colors or covered with plastic camo patterned tape. The guns were a macho mix of standard issue Smith and Wesson .38s, along with personal favorites like Browning Hi-Powers, Colt 1911 autos, Dirty Harry .44 magnums, and even one cowboy-style Single Action Army. A standup freezer in front of the entrance was loaded with plastic pint flasks, olive drab in color and filled with ice. On the way out, each crewmember picked up a pair and stuffed them in the lower leg pockets of the G suit. They would melt for a cool drink on the way home, or else when you hit the ground after bailout. It was a tacit assumption that you'd live at least another two hours while the ice melted.

The ride to the airplanes in the blue step-van was the same, except when I arrived at the revetment that held my airplane, two of us dismounted rather than one. The airplane was a menacing, brutish linebacker of a bird rather than the sleek, slender, wasp-waisted running back of my F-105 days. Rather than poising itself for flight, this one lurked in the revetment waiting for the unsuspecting victim to pass. It didn't have the pug-nosed ugliness of the F-4C that I'd flown at Luke, however. This one was sharp-nosed with a longer snout, and an underslung jaw thrusting the six shrouded barrels of the M-61A-1 Vulcan cannon out below the radome. The low wing seemed lower still, with virtually all the ground clearance filled with twelve Mk-82, 500-pound bombs and two 370-gallon fuel tanks. Under the belly, from their semi-submerged carriage stations sprouted the fins of three AIM-7E-2 Sparrow missiles. The left front missile well held an ALQ-87 electronic countermeasures pod.

The aircraft's nose, behind the black of the radome and extending back from the gun muzzle shroud, was painted with the shark's mouth made famous by Claire

Chennault and his American Volunteer Group in World War II, the Flying Tigers. It was a bit of flamboyance that showed Chennault's enemy that while camouflage might be prudent, it was less important to hide than to threaten. The teeth looked damn good on the P-40s of the AVG, and they seemed perfectly appropriate on the F-4s of the 388th Tac Fighter Wing at Korat. I didn't know if the bad guys on the ground up north would be able to see the teeth, but if so I'd be glad that their last thought might be that they'd been killed by Korat. Of course the teeth were also a responsibility, since wherever we went, whatever we did, we'd be visibly identifiable, distinct from the other wings in theater. I liked it.

The cockpit of the E pounded home my sense of déjà vu. It felt like my limited experience in the F-4: the stick was too short, the parachute canister hovered over my shoulders, the throttles required too long a stroke to get max power, and you couldn't quite get the rudder pedals cranked far enough out. Yeah, all of the discomforts were still there. It was the instruments that weren't quite right. The weapons release switches were all different than the C-model. The flight instruments were familiar, but the radar controls were labeled differently, the radar warning receiver was different, and the big combining glass of the lead-computing gun sight was totally unfamiliar. I instantaneously got over any reservations about going into combat with a WSO. Dee Lewis was going to be my salvation, at least for this first flight in the F-4E.

The radio check-in snapped me back to familiarity. Lead called us over to ground control frequency and directed engine start. I acknowledged the channel change, and Dee switched the radio. I leaned over the left canopy rail and twirled my upraised left index finger in a "fire it up" motion, then pressed the right engine start button when the RPM came up. The next ten minutes were filled with the business of starting two engines, checking systems, exercising flight controls, cycling flaps and speed brakes, then watching out of the corner of my eye as Dee worked the radar through the BIT checks. I hadn't yet quite figured out what the tests were supposed to show, but each one had a list of expected scope presentations and a checklist page devoted to "what was wrong if" explanations. Circles appeared and disappeared, dots flashed, and cursor bars moved magically up and down the scope. Occasionally Dee requested a verification from me, or a switch input to make sure the front cockpit systems were properly integrated with his radar.

"Oak check," came from the lead aircraft four revetments down the line.

"Oak two," I responded, then asked Dee if he was ready to roll.

"Cleared primary and sync," was the expected call from the back, indicating that the inertial navigation system was aligned and we could safely taxi. I flipped the toggle from gyro to INS and rotated the knob momentarily into the sync position, watching the attitude indicator for the characteristic twitch as it shifted from one reference to another.

"Korat ground, Oak, taxi two of the finest," was the call. The tiny ads for your squadron appended to local radio calls were a new feature. Now that we were on ground channel, I would hear calls for "the finest," from 469th crews referencing the squadron motto across the bottom of the green fighting bull patch,

"World's Finest." The 34th used "men in black" when Will Smith was just a gleam in his daddy's eye; and the F-105G squadron simply used "Weasels" to tell the tower who was calling.

"Roger, Oak, taxi runway two four, altimeter three zero point one one. Call when ready for departure."

We rolled out of the same revetments, down the same parking row, out to the same parallel taxiway past the same control tower and fire station, to the same arming area we'd used in '66. The heavily loaded Phantoms rumbled along the tar strips and wanted to coast increasingly fast on the downhill undulations. I picked up about four hundred feet of spacing, and maintained position on the right side as lead taxied on the left half. As we passed the lines of airplanes, I noticed that every Korat plane, regardless of type, showed the shark's teeth. The Weasels had teeth. The EB-66 electronic countermeasures airplanes had teeth. The RC-121 radar surveillance aircraft, a military version of the four-engine Super Constellation airliner, had teeth. Even a pair of the C-130 Airborne Command Post transports showed gaping, tooth-filled mouths stretching down the nose just aft of the radome.

Arming was a familiar exercise. Safety pins were pulled from bombs, suspension racks, missiles and fuel tanks. The gun was charged and electrical plug connected. The airplane was checked for loose panels, leaks, and security of all components. The tires were checked for cuts, then rolled forward and checked again. The lead of the inspection crew snapped a crisp salute at the leader and then flashed a thumbs-up. We were ready to go.

Tower cleared us onto the runway and we rolled into

position. Canopies came down on both aircraft, front and back canopies together on lead's signal. A run-up signal and we started the procedure of checking the engines one at a time at full power, configuring the flaps and handling the last-minute checks before flight.

CLEARED FOR TAKEOFF, WE RUN the engines up to 85 percent power and hold the brakes. Lead waves and rolls. I watch as the two tailpipes light off with the yellow glow of the afterburners. I punch the clock and watch the sweep second hand start moving. When twenty seconds elapse after lead, I roll down the runway and back to the war.

Dee says, "watch this." I'm checking the airspeed, steering down the runway, and watching my leader lift off ahead. I've got line speed, the check that acceleration is normal at one thousand feet of roll. We'll get nose wheel liftoff at about 145 knots, and should get airborne at about 170 after a little more than four thousand feet of roll. I see, out of the corner of my eye, the radar on five-mile scope suddenly shift to a lock-on presentation. He's grabbed the lead aircraft, just as we would if we were departing into weather rather than the clear blue morning sunshine.

We're airborne now, and I reach for the gear handle, then the flaps. I let the airplane's nose down slightly, and we accelerate to 400 knots and roll into a right turn to cut off lead, who is now about two miles ahead and 30 degrees right of the nose. "Check the VI meter," says Lewis, and I look at the clocklike gauge in the upper left corner of the panel. It shows our closure rate on lead, a combination of overtake in speed and angular

convergence. It's just one of the many tweaks that the
E-model adds. Rejoins are always a function of practice and judgment: now, with the VI or visual identification meter, we can actually see how fast we are
approaching another aircraft. As I increase my cutoff
angle on lead, I watch the closure go from 100 to nearly
300 knots, then as I merge and finish the rejoin, the
radar displays a breakaway "X" and the speed drops to
50, then 30, then 0. I am on the wing in close formation. I look over my leader, checking his bombs and
aircraft for anything abnormal. I see his backseater
checking me. We exchange "okay" hand signals, and
lead kicks the rudder quickly back and forth in a signal
to move to route formation for cruise to the tanker.

The radar warning receiver lights up, and the flashing and beeping tell me that Lewis is busy checking out
the presentations. I adjust the volume of the warning
tones, making sure it's loud enough to hear but won't
drown out critical radio calls. The bearing pointer
swings from the lock onto the Korat TACAN around
the instrument to point at the direction we're heading,
the contact point for Red Anchor refueling track. The
radar display shows me the airspace a hundred miles
ahead, and I can already see Dee working the antenna
sweep high and low, searching for a beacon from our
tanker. This is my first experience with a "real" WSO
doing his thing in the rear seat, and I'm frankly daz-
zled. All of the mundane housekeeping and navigation
that I would have had to handle by myself in a single-
seater are taken care of, almost before I can think of it.

We go through the radio channels from Korat departure control to Invert, the controlling agency for northeast Thailand, then, following radar vectors to our
tanker, to the refueling primary. Join-up is routine, and

we're watching the lead aircraft take fuel barely twenty-five minutes after takeoff. Unlike the stateside routine, here there are few rituals to enact. The purpose is to get gas and go to war in minimum time. The resumption of bombing of North Vietnam and the associated large, coordinated strike packages have had an impact on air refueling efficiency.

Lead takes about six thousand pounds of fuel in just over three minutes on the boom. Now it's my turn, and, with the help of a good boomer, I'm hooked up and taking gas in seconds. Lewis is giving me position corrections and discussing the pros and cons of looking over or under the front cockpit canopy bow when refueling. It's too much of a good thing, so I ask him not to be offended, but please shut up for a few minutes. He takes a break.

Fully fueled, we drop off the tanker and head east toward the panhandle of North Vietnam. We cruise at just over 20,000 feet and 450 knots. Lead kicks the rudder to signal a move to route formation, then kicks again, and I break away from him to tactical spread. I pick up a position on his right side, about 3,000 feet away and 1,500 feet higher up sun. I'm line abreast, never forgetting the lessons we learned in the F-105 days about always remaining where your leader can easily see you. Lagging gets you killed, and when you fall behind you can easily gobble up the flak that shoots behind your leader. Oak lead calls a channel change and we switch to Cricket, the airborne command post, to confirm our mission number and target.

We've just passed the muddy Mekong, crossing from Thailand into southern Laos. I know from the map at this morning's briefing that Cricket is orbiting high and to our right. I watch the radar scope out of the corner of my eye and see Lewis searching the area, then locking on to the C-130, 30 degrees right at forty miles. He doesn't say anything, waiting for me to acknowledge the lock. I take the opportunity to tease him, "That's outside the formation, you should be calling it, or lead. I'm looking left forward, high and low. At least that's what the book says. Seriously, Dee, I'm still not convinced there's anybody qualified to check my six o'clock but me." As I say it, I raise the nose slightly, roll up on the right wing and kick top rudder to move the tail out of the way. We're both looking outside the formation and below us for threats. It's an exercise that I'll do every couple of minutes until we're out of hostile territory. Left, right, high, low, always looking, hopefully seeing before it's too late.

Dee said, "You'd be surprised how many guys haven't figured that out. I was just showing you where Cricket orbits. I like your formation position. I can never get the young guys to move far enough forward." He breaks the lock, and the radar resumes sweeping ahead of us. The INS is set to the target coordinates, and I see that we're still eighty-five miles away from Dong Hoi.

"That's Ban Karai pass down on the right about ten miles ahead. See all the bomb craters?" Dee points out a familiar landmark along the Laos–North Vietnam border. The area covers several square miles and is a virtual moonscape.

"We used to call it De Gaulle's nose back in '66. I dropped a lot of bombs there during my first tour. You can't see the primary road anymore so you can't see the nose outline, but it was a pretty good likeness." Despite the bombing, it's obvious that supplies still flow through here. It's a veritable spider's web of tracks and detours around bomb craters and washouts.

In a matter of minutes we're within sight of the coast. The deep blue water of the gulf, the white sand of the beaches, and the vibrant green of the jungle paint a beautiful picture of an Asian tropical paradise disrupted by the bomb craters that pockmark the coastal plains. The runway at Dong Hoi is clearly visible, a mile of decrepit asphalt that's been bombed and repaired repeatedly since the French occupation. There won't be any airplanes using it in the near future. Dee begins walking me through the switch setup to drop our first pair of bombs. He reminds me that I've agreed to try dive toss, and he explains once more that all I have to do is let him lock the radar onto the ground return when we roll in, then put the pipper on the target and hold the pickle button down as I make a wings-level pulloff. The bombs will come off when the computer decides that the time is right.

Oak lead repeats the briefing we went through at Korat: "Okay, Oak, the target area is about two miles inland from the north end of the runway. Take spacing for left hand roll-ins and we'll make multiple passes. I'll be rolling in from the north in about twenty seconds." I ease up on the left turn we've been in and allow the lead aircraft to drift away from me. If I've got to do this dive toss business, I'm going to give the system a challenge. It won't be easy to make me a believer. I see the lead aircraft overbank and roll into his bombing pass. I ease my airplane a bit higher and watch the altimeter lazily rotate through twenty thousand feet. Lead's aircraft is flying over the indicated target area, and I can tell that he's released his first pair of bombs.

We've orbited the target area, and now it's my turn to deliver. "Oak two's in from the south," I call to let lead know what I'm doing. I'm planning on using the south edge of the smoke from his bombs as an aiming point.

I pull up still a bit more and then roll over into a 30-degree dive. I put the pipper below the smoke, and it only takes a second or two before Lewis tells me he's got a system lock. The gun-sight reticle is tied to the radar boresight line and shows a slight offset to the west to correct for wind drift. I ease the pipper up to the target, shallowing out my dive, and then punch the pickle button and start a pulloff. I've pickled and pulled without ever going below fifteen thousand feet. If this thing works, it won't be because I've given it the slightest bit of help. I'm ridiculously high, decidedly shallow, and really didn't let the airspeed build very much. As a dive-bomb pass, this one is lousy. The airplane shudders slightly as the bombs come off. I jink once to the right for about 30 degrees of turn, then come back left into the circle to follow Oak lead. "Two's off hot," is my call.

I look back at the smoke from lead's bombs and then watch as my pair impacts precisely on the southern edge of the smoke. It's exactly where I had the pipper. The bombs aren't short, they aren't blown by the wind, they're on target. It's like magic! I hear a chuckle from the backseat, where Lewis has been biting his tongue trying not to say, "I told you so."

We make five more passes from an orbit over the target area. Each time I try to screw up the dive toss, and each time the bombs hit exactly where the pipper was at the time I hit the pickle button. It doesn't matter what the dive angle is, what the airspeed is, or what the altitude is. As long as I fly a wings-level pulloff, the bombs come off the airplane at the point necessary to reach the target. We don't see any defensive reaction, and the RWR never emits a single beep. As far as we can tell, there's not a soul on the ground anywhere near our target. I know that's wrong, and I know that this deceptively peaceful area has claimed a lot of airplanes during the last six years. It lures you into a false sense of security and then kills you in an instant. It's important to never become complacent.

Oak lead calls that we're done and heading home. I cut across the circle of our bombing pattern and close the distance between us. He waggles his wings, indicating he wants me to close up for a visual check. His WSO looks at us as we close to fingertip formation and raises a thumb and extended forefinger in the shape of a checkmark. I drop low on the wing, looking at the underside of his aircraft, then reduce my power slightly and drift back to nose-tail clearance. I cross to his opposite wing and move forward and up into position. His bomb racks are empty and his aircraft looks intact. I give an okay sign and watch as lead signals me forward. He returns the inspection favor, looking at my aircraft and then returning to the lead of the formation. We cruise home in route formation, front-seaters with arms draped on the canopy rails, showing each other that the WSOs are flying the jets.

That night, before I head to the CTF for a cold beer and after Socks has left for his nightly excursion over the Ho Chi Minh Trail, I reach in the back of the closet for my crumpled A-3 parachute bag. It held most of my flying equipment on the trip over—flight suits and boots, a light flying jacket, two G suits, and one more item. Crushed nearly flat in the bottom of the now almost empty bag is my first-tour jungle hat. The olive drab hat has a single small patch attached to the right side of the turned-up brim, with the embroidered word,

"Thailand." I look at the dusty, sweat-stained hat and think for a minute about what it meant back in 1966. Here is the record of my first hundred missions over North Vietnam. In black felt-tip ink, there are a series of hash marks, each recounting a trip in an F-105, each representing a "counter" that eventually added up to 100. Some of the marks are in red, darkened now so that only I notice them among the row of black lines. From the right front, the hash marks march in orderly sequence halfway around the hat's band. On the back, a much shorter group of marks indicates the few missions I flew that didn't count toward completion of that tour. There are 110 total marks. I reach into the desk drawer and pull out a black marker, then slowly mark the first hash of the second tour, precisely above the starting point of the existing row. One hundred and one missions over North Vietnam are now recorded on the hat. It is impossible not to wonder how many marks will eventually adorn the hat, and whether there isn't some penalty for challenging fate too many times.

IT WAS LITTLE MORE THAN bluster when I started saying it in briefings and classroom presentations as a pilot training instructor. As the hot-rock junior warrior with a hundred missions over the North, I told my students that the criteria for their passage included my willingness to fly their wing in combat or have them fly mine. It was simple to say and it made sense. The job was to train military pilots, and it was all too easy to compartmentalize the possibility of combat in the near future. I wanted my students to be aware that part of the price of those silver wings they coveted was the requirement to go to war. I never thought it would actually happen.

It was now my third mission. I'd shown sufficient presence with Dee Lewis that I was cleared to fly with a regular, but experienced, WSO. Since the twenty-four-hour operation made it a problem for roommates to work opposite sides of the schedule, it was a natural event to crew me with Bob Slockbower. He wasn't too crazy about leaving his night job, but acknowledged that flying with a second tour guy was probably conducive to his longevity. Since he was three-quarters of the way through his year tour, it wouldn't be possible to avoid going on the big Linebacker raids, and if that was inevitable, then make the best of it with a demonstrated survivor. I had no objection. Socks had a good reputation, and we got along well.

The weather was atrocious at briefing time. A stationary front had parked itself over the Southeast Asia peninsula, and low ceilings and soaking rain were the order of the day. The mission was a four-ship into South Vietnam to work with an O-2 Skymaster forward air controller. We carried twelve Mk-82, 500-pound bombs apiece, six on the centerline rack and three on each inboard wing station. We'd hit a tanker over Laos and then proceed to contact the FAC. The flight lead was George "Nordie" Norwood, one of the first students with whom I'd flown during my years at Williams.

Nordie was one of those confident, aggressive types who wants to get into the battle and has both the skills and tenacity to make it happen. He'd worked hard in pilot training, but hadn't been fortunate enough to get one of the very few single-seat jet slots. He'd taken an A-1 Skyraider assignment knowing it was a quick ticket to the war, then he'd gotten into the F-4 as an "experienced" pilot. Now he was a junior captain, with his sec-

ond combat tour almost completed. He knew me and I
knew him. Not a word was said about the cliché of the
student with his old instructor on his wing.

WE PREFLIGHT IN THE POURING rain and can only be
thankful that the day is warm. With the canopies down
as we taxi, the cold air from the air-conditioning vents
seems to ferret out all the places where wet Nomex
touches bare skin. Water runs down from under my helmet, and the condensation threatens to fog over the
flight instruments. Rubbing clear spots to peek out of
the canopy soon leaves our gloves soaked. It is going to
be a miserable couple of hours.

On the active runway cleared for takeoff, after
Nordie rolls I have just twenty seconds to tweak the
temperature with the engines at full throttle, trying to
hit a balance between freezing wet and steaming overheat. Socks reaches out and locks the radar onto the
lead aircraft just about the time I release brakes and
light the ABs. As Nordie rotates, the burner plumes
blow clouds of water and steam off the runway. He extends straight ahead about two miles from the departure
end, then enters a right turn for our rejoin, staying below the thousand-foot ceiling. I raise the gear and flaps,
then hold the burners until we hit just over 400 knots. I
start the cutoff to rejoin, trying to stay far enough forward on the rejoin path to help out the number three
and four aircraft, which will be following. Socks calls
out distances and closure speeds from the VI meter, so
that I can stay focused visually on my leader.

I slide onto the inside wing in the turn and whistle
softly in appreciation, as three and four come into view

from behind and ease into their position on the left wing. It is an almost perfect rejoin for all the players. Nordie checks both sides and gives a quick push-up move forward with his throttle hand, signaling that he is going to continue climbing into the clouds. It will be the last time we'll see the ground or horizon for the next hour.

Formation flying requires lining up a reference on the lead aircraft. In the case of the F-4, it means positioning so as to place the trailing edge wingtip light in line with the blue star on the aft fuselage decal, then doing whatever is necessary to keep the reference in place. Rather than depending upon instruments for orientation or flying with reference to the ground, you abandon everything but those alignment points. If lead rolls and turns, climbs or dives, it makes no difference. Keep the points aligned by small corrections with the stick and the throttles, and you'll always be in position. You might be topside up or upside down, but you'll be next to the leader. The purpose isn't for a Thunderbird demonstration, but to allow multiple aircraft to efficiently transit the airspace. If the weather is bad it shouldn't make a difference—but it does.

Clouds aren't solid, and they aren't even consistent. Sometimes they are little more than a foggy haze, allowing you to see the entire formation and fly comfortably with room for error and correction. Other times, such as during the rain in Southeast Asia, clouds can be dense, dark, and turbulent. They can become so thick that you lose sight of the other aircraft on the leader's opposite wing. They can become so dark that you have difficulty making out lead's entire airplane. They can, at the extreme, blank out even the wing of your lead, leaving little in view but a steady dim green or red light and a flow of mist, almost like a wind tunnel demonstration over a wingtip. They can do that for an hour as you curse and swear, sweat and struggle to keep in position. They can force you to fight the airplane and wrestle with conflicting sensations as your inner ear tries to tell you you're turning or climbing, when you know nothing but that you are momentarily out of position on the wing. It's that kind of a day today, and Slockbower is earning his keep. He's working the radar, updating the navigation, changing the TACAN stations, and moving us through the radio channel changes as Nordie maintains head down on his instruments, flying as smoothly as I taught him all those years ago in Arizona.

We get to the tanker track, still in the clouds. Invert control has us on ground radar and provides vectors to the refueling aircraft. We are in the clouds, but the tanker radios that he's in some thin stuff that will probably allow us a mile or so of visibility. We follow the vectors from the ground radar controller, and out of the corner of my eye I try to find the blip on the radar scope that is the KC-135. The distance rolls down from ten miles to five, then three, but we still don't see the tanker. The sky is a bit lighter now, but only the difference between skim milk and heavy cream. There is no horizon, no up or down—just a wing and a nav light. The controller tells us we're down to two miles, and I watch as Nordie starts to split his cross-check between the instruments and a visual search for the tanker. I ping Socks to keep a close watch on the altimeter, because I know the tendency to ease up into the tanker's altitude in the hope of catching a glimpse. Then I find myself easing forward on my leader and see the speed brakes fan out on his airplane. A shadow catches my eye, and suddenly we are on the wing of the tanker.

Norwood drives right onto the extended boom and almost immediately starts taking gas. With a brief radio call, he clears us off his wing and onto the wing of the tanker. I move up onto the right side, while three and four ease forward onto the refueler's left wing. It is fast, smooth, and a serious demonstration of pro flying by all the players: tanker, fighters, and radar controller. We cycle through like a well-rehearsed ballet. Lead, then three, me, then four. No horizon, no blue sky, no green jungle below. Just four bomb-laden Phantoms and a converted airliner, touching each other and passing the lifeblood of fighter aviation at 3,500 pounds per minute. The whole operation takes less than twenty minutes, and we are ready to drop away, back into the murk on our way to a still-unknown target somewhere in South Vietnam.

We change radio channels and call the airborne command post, Cricket. We tell him our call sign, mission number, ordnance load, and fuel state, along with a position off a nearby TACAN station. The frag order that morning told us we would be working with a forward air controller, call sign Covey, in the area west of Danang. Cricket has the option of letting us continue to a rendezvous with the O-2 Cessna, or if he hasn't found a suitable target for us, reassigning us to someone who has a better use for our bombs. Today, Covey 41 is going to get us.

"Covey 41, Covey 41, this is Redwood," Norwood starts the contact with the FAC.

"Redwood, Covey 41, how copy?" The FAC awaits us.

"Loud and clear, Covey. Are you ready for a

lineup?" The bureaucratic details need to be taken care of before anything like combat can happen. The FAC acknowledges his readiness and Nordie begins relaying the confirmation of details that Cricket probably already passed to the pilot in the slow-moving control aircraft. "Redwood's got four Phantoms, mission number alpha foxtrot seven two four three. We've got twelve Mk-82 slicks each and 20 mike-mike with twenty minutes of playtime. We'll be at your position in about five minutes. How's the weather look? Over."

"Roger, Redwood, copy all. The weather's workable. I've got an open area about ten miles across with some mid- to high-level clouds overhead at about fourteen thousand feet. Visibility is good, so we should be able to do business. Are you ready for a target brief?" Covey appreciates that with bad weather all around, we'll probably want to get our bombs off and get on our way home with plenty of fuel, in case we need to divert to another base. Fuel is always a concern, and the heavy rain or low visibility can move a flight into an emergency situation in minutes.

Getting the details for a target brief is a challenge for single-seat fighters flying close formation in the clouds, but in the F-4 the WSOs play stenographer while the front-seaters do the flying. Nordie acknowledges that we are ready to copy.

"Okay, Redwood. The target is a suspected truck park in the trees," code words meaning the FAC doesn't have anything substantial and is simply flying a sortie and using up some available fighters. "When you get here I'll mark with a smoke, then you'll be cleared flight lead discretion on the number of passes. Random run-ins approved, your choice on pulloff," he continues to affirm there's not much here, and we won't be winning the war today. "Haven't seen any enemy reaction today, but in the past there has been reported small arms fire from this location. The FAC will be holding to the southeast of the target area at 4,500 feet while you work," he tells us, conveying that the enemy probably isn't home and hasn't been very concerned about protecting anything that might be here. The danger here is from our own airplanes running into the FAC, each other, or the jungle while trying to maneuver and deliver ordnance within the hole in the clouds that lets us establish contact with the ground.

It's only a minute or two before the clouds lighten, then break into wisps that intermittently shroud our formation, then give us hope of some time in the clear. Socks has the coordinates we've been given for the FAC displayed on my HSI, a bearing to the location, and a decreasing distance in miles to the rendezvous. We're less than ten miles away and now in the clear, although walls of cloud remain on both sides and we're covered by a solid ceiling of murk above us. Nordie kicks the rudder back and forth rapidly, signaling us to loosen our formation so that we can relax, set our weapons switches, and look for the FAC's tiny airplane. We're in a loose fingertip formation, four bomb-laden Phantoms arrayed like the four fingers of your left hand—I'm the index finger as number two, Nordie's in the lead as the middle finger, and the three and four aircraft are on the left as ring and pinkie digits. We're in the target area in a relatively tight formation, in miserable weather, and about to be directed by the equivalent of a civilian light plane. This is surely a different war than the hundred missions over North Vietnam that I previously experienced.

"Redwood, this is Covey 41, I've got you in sight. Check your low left eleven about five miles. I'm in a left-hand orbit at 4,500 feet. Call visual." It's a whole lot easier for the FAC, unencumbered by trying to fly formation, to spot the lumbering herd of bombers, belching smoky exhaust and silhouetted against the light gray clouds overhead.

"Roger, Covey, Redwood lead has you in sight. Redwoods, echelon right for a left-hand wheel, take spacing and call the FAC in sight." Norwood isn't going to waste a lot of time on this.

I spot the FAC below my leader's radome and call, "Two's got the FAC." The backseaters of the three and four aircraft call their visual contact. We're ready to go. Socks has the radar in five-mile boresight, my scope switching from the regular sweep back and forth to a solid line down the middle of the display, as the radar ranges down the line designated by the gun sight's pipper. The flight is now aligned in order on Nordie's right wing, in an easy left turn around the FAC aircraft. I start to set weapons switches, calling them out so Socks can be sure that I've got them all. Bombs selected, salvo, dive toss, center and inboard stations, fuse nose/tail, master arm coming on. I'm ready to go with a one-pass, haul-ass strategy. If lead directs something different, I'll change the bomb quantity. Socks tells me he's ready to go.

"Covey 41's in to mark." We watch the tiny gray airplane pull up into a momentary climb, then roll inverted and drop the nose into what appears to be an almost vertical dive. A split-second later, two puffs of smoke behind the FAC indicate that he's fired his pair of rockets. Almost immediately a pair of flashes among the dark green trees of the jungle show the hits from white phosphorus charges. Bright white smoke begins to billow into a pair of columns, indicating a spot for the fighters to reference their bomb runs. "Okay, Redwood, if you've got the smokes consider the distance between them to be 100 meters and the line formed by the two points is north-south. Lead's cleared in, hit the south smoke." Despite the lack of a meaningful target, the FAC is showing a lot of experience and efficiency. He knows how to get us on and off the target, and everything he does is direct and to the point.

Nordie calls in, and I watch his airplane overbank into a 30-degree dive-bomb pass. The FAC immediately gives him clearance to drop. I maintain altitude in an easy left turn around the white markers. The lead F-4 begins a pullout from the dive, and the high humidity of the jungle condenses across the upper surface of the wings in a flickering cloud of moisture. As he turns, the bombs detonate below and behind him, obliterating the white smoke and covering the jungle with an ugly black, gray, and red storm of fire, metal, and shrapnel. "Nice bombs, Redwood. Two, if you're ready, come 200 meters north of lead's bombs. Cleared hot," Covey keeps the pace up.

With the first "if you're ready" from the FAC, I'm already rolling into the bomb pass. It doesn't take a lot of correction to align the pipper where the FAC has indicated he wants the bombs. Socks calls, "Locked," as he scrolls the range gate down onto the ground return in the radar scope. I give the system a second or two to settle, then push and hold the pickle button and start my pullout. The airplane shudders through the release of the twelve bombs, and as the nose comes above the horizon, I check turn quickly to the right, then reverse to the left turn to keep our formation wheel around the target. I look back over my left shoulder to see the bombs hit exactly where the pipper was. The dive toss works as advertised once again.

I'm into a cutoff to close on lead as the remaining two aircraft of Redwood follow the FAC's instructions to dump their loads. Four minutes later, the number-four aircraft cuts across the circle to close up into a route formation, just like coming off the gunnery range in training back in the States. Covey thanks us for our time and work, expresses a bit of regret that he couldn't offer us a better target, and clears us off his frequency. Nordie acknowledges and gives a quick wing rock to move us into close formation as we had back into the cloud bank west of the target. In forty minutes we're back at Korat.

Maintenance debrief, intel processing, and the flight debrief go quickly. Not much has happened, and the whole procedure is little more than bureaucratic paperwork. We've added sorties to the daily count, tons of bombs to the totals for the war, and another debit to the taxpayer's wallet.

DEE LEWIS HUDDLES WITH THE schedulers working on the next day's frag as we walk out of our flight debrief. He calls to the group, "Hey, you guys know there's a party tonight for a couple of guys who finished up this morning? Dinner at Veena's at seven. We'll have a couple of buses to take ya'all from the hootches at 6:30. Party suits. Meet at the CTF when you're ready to go."

The rest of the flight mumbles an awareness of the invitation and continues out the door to head back to the hootch area for a shower and maybe a nap before the party. I stop for a few minutes to talk to Dee. "Did I

hear you say Veena?" I ask. "We used to have parties at
Veena's Hideaway when I was here in '66. Is that the
same Veena? Had a neat little place on a dark side street
downtown. Pretty good food, but I think the 'beef' was
really water buffalo."

"Probably the same woman. There's still the place
downtown, but she built another joint out here by the
base, just off the departure end of the runway. Calls it
Veena's Farm. She handles a lot of parties for the base
when guys finish their tour. Did you get your party suit
yet?"

Clearly the party suit thing is a priority for Dee.
He's probably in charge of making sure all the
squadron guys comply with the custom.

"Nah, I got measured up and ordered one last week,
but the guy at the tailor shop said it won't be ready for
a couple more days. I guess I'll have to blend in with
civvies."

Reassured that I've at least got one on order, Lewis
lets me leave the squadron. I spot a truck leaving the
quadrangle and get a ride back to my room. By 5:30 the
banging doors and shouting from the CTF indicates that
folks are starting to gather for the party. I emerge from
the cool of my room to find a group that looks like a
cross between Robin Hood's Sherwood Forest gang and
an audition for a Jolly Green Giant commercial. Thirty
or more guys lounge on lawn furniture spread around the
grass in front of the squadron's bar, sipping beer from
cans or various forms of iced booze from plastic cups.
Each is dressed in a bright green facsimile of a flying
suit, short-sleeved and festooned with patches indicating
squadron membership, aerial achievement, or ribald
comment on the war, the enemy, or life in general.

Socks is on the grass near the CTF doorway, holding

a can of Bud. Since we flew this morning, we can't be excused from the party. Another group in Nomex flight suits stops to exchange a few words with their squadron mates, then they head to the club for a quick meal before reporting down to the squadron for the night sorties. They'll miss the party, fight the war tonight, and be having a Scotch and soda while the majority of us are having breakfast. The twenty-four-hour-a-day schedule makes for some odd patterns.

Socks is resplendent in his party suit. The green coverall isn't adequate to really display his flamboyance. He's added a heavy silver chain around his neck, with a three-inch-diameter chrome disk that even at a distance is recognizable as a peace symbol. Around his waist he's got a belt of chromed 7.62 mini-gun bullets. It's heavy, but it somehow seems to be appropriate. On one shoulder is an F-4 patch, on the other a patch designates his "Spectre escort" role—flying night escort duty for the heavily armed AC-130 gunships that patrol the Ho Chi Minh trail. Above his embroidered wings on the left breast pocket is a 469th Fighting Bull. On the right to balance the decoration is another patch declaring him "SAM-qualified." He'd get a lot of strange looks in the States, but here he's just one of about thirty similarly attired young men.

A pair of Air Force Bluebird buses arrive on the street in front of the hootches, signaling that it's time to head for Veena's. We form a line, each with a drink in hand, to go off to the party. As a new guy in the squadron, I wait my turn to board. I find myself sitting near the back of the second bus, sharing a seat with Dee Lewis. "What's the occasion for the party?"

"We've got a couple of guys finished their tour. They flew their EOT missions yesterday and they'll be leaving

tomorrow. We'll give 'em a plaque from the squadron
and probably get stupid." Dee confirms that some things
remain the same as in years prior. Finishing a combat
tour is an important occasion. It's a moment for rejoicing
that you've survived, and for recognizing that the associ-
ations made through the experience are special. I'm recalling the almost solemn dinners we had in the F-105
squadron. Some were tinged with bittersweet recollec-
tion of losses suffered at nearly the same time as the successes of tour completion. Some were almost mournful
occasions, while others reflected an incredible intensity
of joy, as a close friend was going home and had survived to return to his family and a more normal life.

"Some of these guys would never leave the base if
we didn't have parties at Veena's or somewhere else
downtown," Dee continues. "If it isn't on base, they
don't care much about it. Some'll head for Bangkok
when they get some R and R, but a lot of them never
see Korat city, and a few don't want to go anywhere for
R and R but back to Hawaii."

"I know how that works," I interject. "When I was
here last time, I think I got to Bangkok twice and didn't
get into Korat city but about twice more. We were
pretty busy, and it didn't seem like there was much opportunity. Maybe there's more to do now."

"There are a few guys who spend a lot of time downtown. A lot of the maintenance troops are shacking up
with Thai girls in places downtown, and a lot of them
just head to town every night. There's the bars, the tailor and jewelry shops, and then the massage joints. The
'rub-n-scrubs' get some serious GI traffic." I don't realize then—how could I? —that Dee's comments will be
a map to my own future.

It only takes about fifteen minutes, passing down the

flight line road and out the west gate, around the perimeter that skirts the end of the runway. At the intersection of the base access road and the Bangkok-Korat highway is a sprawling, one-story teak roadhouse. A hand-painted tin sign identifies the building as "Veena's Farm" in English and again, apparently, in Thai. The buses pull into the large gravel parking lot, and we file into a large concrete-floored hall. Long tables are covered with paper and set for dinner; folding chairs await us. Immediately to the left of the door is a bar, manned by three Thai bartenders. Already they are falling behind in serving the green-clad partiers.

The buses head back to the CTF to pick up stragglers, so we have a half-hour of drinking, storytelling, and talking with our hands about flying escapades. The pert Thai waitresses scurry in the background to line up the salads and wine bottles at the tables in preparation for seating. Parties for Americans are what Veena's Farm is all about, and they are obviously experienced in the ritual. The whole process unfolds like a well-designed and properly oiled machine.

When the time comes to be seated, we go through the standard ceremony of rising for a Pledge of Allegiance—a somewhat superfluous exercise for a group of men twelve thousand miles from the States, risking their lives daily in high-performance aircraft operated as instruments of a national policy that is being seriously questioned at home. Then there are the ritual toasts to the president, the chief of staff of the Air Force, and finally a few humorous and lighthearted glass-raisings to locals, friends, traditions and idiosyncrasies of the fighter pilot community. By serving time the group is well lubricated and definitely not combat capable.

Dinner is an eclectic mix of American meat-potatoes simplicity and Thai local specialties, designed to showcase neither cuisine but simultaneously to offend not a single palate. There is a green lettuce and tomato salad, left largely untouched by many who have gleaned their medical advice from Mexican border town visits and timid flight surgeons: don't eat the greens, drink the water, or use the local ice. Then a roast beef plate with fried potatoes, supplemented with a traditional Thai fried rice on the side garnished with cucumber slices and scallions. Rolls, of course, with chilled butter. Dessert is vanilla ice cream and locally baked cookies, clearly not using a local recipe. Red wine bottles are distributed between every three seats. It is a menu for abuse.

Almost before the dinner is complete, Ed McHale, the squadron commander, rises to conduct the ceremonies. He acknowledges the wing commander, the deputy for operations, and the other wing officials in attendance. Then, one by one, he calls forward the four captains who have completed a one-year tour, flying the F-4 from Korat. He shakes their hands, hands them a plaque acknowledging their achievement, and gives each an opportunity to say a few words. They don't say it, but they seem grateful to be making their escape from a situation that has escalated in intensity recently, with the resumption of North Vietnam missions. As expected, each receives a bit of respect and a ration of derision. An initial brief applause as they acknowledge their peers, and then increasing snickers and hoots as they inevitably veer off into the maudlin. One is nicked in the shoulder by a carefully buttered and then wine-soaked dinner roll. Another ducks just in time to avoid a well-aimed cucumber slice.

With formalities concluded, the party deteriorates

rapidly. The wing senior officers and the squadron
commander leave almost immediately, with most of the
revelers still at our tables finishing the wine and plot-
ting tactics for the next engagement. Rolls are collected
from serving plates, wine bottles are emptied, cucumber slices and tomato wedges are lined up. Soon the air
is filled with grocery-based missiles. Barrages cross the
room at random angles, sometimes in response to an attack and often in a preemptive strike against a potential
adversary. The waitresses scurry for cover to one side
of the room, and the clatter of a corrugated tin shutter
announces the closure of the bar. It's a long way from
the solemn and respectful dinners we had in the -105
days. It explains a bit about the party suits that have
clearly evolved to save wear and tear on the civilian
wardrobe. It definitely seems disrespectful to the Thais
who, as I well know, often subsist on a very meager
diet. And it doesn't seem like the mature actions of a
group of military professionals. I am disappointed in
the spectacle. I walk, well, maybe scramble, out of the
room and wait outside for the buses. Several others are
lined up, some nondrinkers and some prior tour veter-
ans, all somehow appalled by the conduct of the group.

5. LINEBACKER DRAFT CHOICE

> If you're planning on this being an easy job . . .
> you've got another think coming. You can end up
> dead in this line of work. War is dangerous!
> If you have any thought of chickening out . . .
> now's the time to do it.
> Being any kind of pilot in enemy territory means
> having your life threatened on every mission.

—Joe Foss, Medal of Honor recipient, Marine fighter pilot

IT DIDN'T TAKE LONG TO get the call. The squadron had sorties to Pack VI on the schedule every day, and I was someone with a load of prior experience, so I couldn't miss being tabbed to head downtown. Pack VI was still the essence of intensity. It was high-value targets and high-threat defenses. It had the most concentrated flak in history, seasoned with an array of surface-to-air missiles and topped with a meringue of MiGs. It was the flatlands of the Red River Delta, peppered with MiG bases, surrounded by radars, and quarantined by the now-familiar restrictions of the politically driven rules of engagement, the ROE. It was a place where people died and prisoners were taken; where heroes were made and the challenge to each day's survival was very real.

I was on the schedule by mission 5, flying number two on an escort of a bombing flight, headed to a military storage area next to Phuc Yen airfield. It was the real deal, and I didn't need to wait for the briefing to know what was coming. There would be the whole gauntlet of defenses, the probability of marginal weather, and an array of threats that could include the weapons of your friends and the possibility of midair collisions as a hundred or more aircraft tried to find a target, do the job, and survive.

I'd done a bit of independent research in the command post, and a lot of background had been supplied in new-guy school. The pattern had become one of specialization at the Thai bases. It was a good concept. Each base would have one or two specialties for which they were primarily responsible. Udorn was the home of the reconnaissance squadron as well as the 555th "Triple Nickel" squadron, which specialized in MiG hunting. They held a select group of Fighter Weapons School graduates and instructor pilots who were trained in air-to-air tactics and weapons employment. We all should have been fully qualified to fight MiGs, but that wasn't the way the Air Force thought. The Udorn wing did the MiGCAP (combat air patrol) and sweep missions that looked for and engaged enemy airplanes. It was a job that every fighter pilot wanted but of which few were really capable.

Ubon, home of the 8th Tac Fighter Wing, which had been made famous by the leadership of Robin Olds, did the precision-guided bombing mission. They had the handful of laser pods to illuminate targets for laser-guided bombs. It took concentration and a wheelbarrow full of cojones to find the high-value target, place the laser spot on it, and then orbit amid flak and SAMs while another airplane maneuvered to release an LGB in a position from which it could fly to target. Ubon also did the sensor planting along the Ho Chi Minh trail, and carried a lot of dumb, unguided iron bombs as well, both day and night.

Takhli, to the west of Korat, dropped conventional bombs and handled most of the chaff laying. Chaff had become a big component of the Linebacker packages. Confounding the enemy radars to minimize the effect of SAMs, radar-directed antiaircraft artillery (AAA), and intercept controlling radars for the MiG had become big business. Formations of three or four flights of four aircraft would lay huge corridors of chaff, flying at twenty thousand feet or higher and releasing chaff bombs that airburst and spread miles' wide trails of radar-reflecting Mylar foil for the follow-on forces to fly in, shielded from the tracking of the enemy radars. In combination with the self-protection ECM pods that each aircraft carried and the standoff electronic jamming of the EB-66 aircraft, the chaff seriously degraded the ability of North Vietnamese radar to target individual airplanes.

Korat's specialties were escort of the strike and chaff flights to provide protection from MiGs that escaped the Udorn cappers, and SAM suppression using hunter-killer teams of F-105G Wild Weasels and F-4Es armed with CBUs. We often carried plain ol' iron bombs when needed to fill the packages. Korat also hosted the EB-66 electronic jammers, the EC-121 airborne early warning radar planes, and the C-130 Airborne Command Post squadron.

The main briefing room in Fort Apache was standing

room only. Every seat was packed, and guys were lined up along the side aisles and back walls. The briefing sequence hadn't changed since '66, but the size of the package certainly had. Now, instead of four or five single-seat flights of four, we had twelve or more flights, all two-seater F-105 Weasels or F-4s. Today we were going to provide two escort flights for the chaff layers, two more for the bomber stream, three hunter-killer teams and four flights of bomb droppers. Every four-ship would have their own pre-strike tanker, and there would be another tanker to give a drink to eight airplanes on the way home if they should need it. At Korat, Takhli, Ubon, Udorn, and Don Muang, outside of Bangkok, there were similar gatherings of aircrews. All to bring continuing pressure upon the North Vietnamese, by moving the rubble around at what was only a suspected storage area that had been bombed regularly since the summer of 1966, and that was right next door to an active MiG base.

Yeah, we should have this thing wrapped up any day now.

The operations briefer gave a time hack, then flashed a slide on the screen showing the entire Southeast Asian region, with tanker tracks, extension routes for the tankers to deliver us to 20 degrees north latitude, then arrow-tipped lines from the drop-off points to the familiar turn point just downriver along the Red from Yen Bai, and finally east toward the southern tip of Thud Ridge and the target, marked with a small red triangle. Orbits for the EB-66 jammers were shown near the western edge of Route Pack VI, while the EC-121 circled in northern Laos. Each of the orbits had a nearby supporting orbit for its personal MiGCAP in case the enemy decided that a big slow mover would be a more attractive target than a swarm of angry fighters.

Anyone who was leading a flight or had been there before knew the drill without the graphics. The briefer flipped an overlay onto the map with a broad shaded area covering the ingress route. This was the chaff corridor that would be released by the first wave. Alongside the dusky smear were the call signs of the four flights of chaffers. Tiny airplane silhouettes on each side of the smear were labeled with the call sign of one of our escort flights. On the right side of the corridor was an elongated racetrack labeled "Parrot" flight, which would be the hunter-killer flight aligned on the high threat side of the force to defend against SAM attacks.

After a few seconds for the crews to absorb the alignment, the briefer pulled the first overlay and replaced it with a second sheet illustrating a lighter, more dissipated chaff corridor, now with the bomber stream and their escorts and SAM-defenders. This time the Weasel flight was "Crow" and the MiG escort would be "Dallas." I was Dallas two, with Socks in my pit. I cross-checked my lineup card to make sure I had the right sequence of bomb-dropping flights. The time-on-target was correct, and the various CAPs and support flights were all as shown on the briefing slide. I had what I needed.

The ops briefer finished up with a list of tankers and assigned fighters, noting the refueling tracks, tanker cell frequencies, and a sequenced time for drop-off at the northernmost extension. With everyone on their proper tanker and all the tankers stacked in sequence on each of the three refueling tracks, if we all went by the clock, we'd be neatly lined up for the big show.

Operations turned the stage over to intel. His first chart showed a larger scale map of North Vietnam, with colored circles showing the array of air defenses. From the foothills of the mountains across the Red River basin, the entire spectrum was covered by the large red outline of SAM circles. Small missile silhouettes were scattered across the landscape like so many grains of rice. Black circles formed an almost overlapping array of radar-guided 85mm heavy guns, while a bumpy blue outline depicted the nearly identical area covered with radar and visually sighted 37- and 57mm batteries. The 23mm rapid fire cannons were not even shown on the map. It could be assumed that they were everywhere.

The next slide showed the air order of battle, the listing of intelligence estimates of how many MiG interceptors of each type the North Vietnamese air force had. It hadn't changed much in seven years of war. They always had about 120 aircraft; the only difference was that over time, the ratio had shifted from older MiG-17s to more of the newer, faster, and more threatening MiG-21s. Yep, we had the full array of threats. It was just like the good old days. Simply amazing. Here we were six years later and still doing the same thing to very little effect.

Next was the weather brief. It was always a challenge in Southeast Asia. The seasonal monsoon pattern meant that when weather was good in the target area, it was marginal at the Thailand bases. If it was good in Thailand, it was probably going to be crap at endgame. Either end could kill you, but it was far worse with bad weather in Pack VI. Clouds and rain meant you would be funneled into a smaller area for the bad guys to concentrate their firepower at you. Low visibility meant more difficulty navigating and finding the target. SAMs and radar could see through the clouds, but we were mere mortals and we needed some clear air to see the ground. The good news today was that the weather was decent at home, visibility was unrestricted in the refueling tracks, and the target area had only scattered puffies.

With the mass briefing over and our maps, lineup cards, target photos, and code-word lists stowed in our flight suit pockets, we headed back to the squadron for our individual flight briefings. Our flight of escorts would fly as two discrete pairs, stationed as outriggers on each side of the inbound bomber stream. Two Phantoms to the left and two to the right, paralleling the course of the four flights of bomb droppers. Should MiGs threaten the package, we would veer off and engage them. We'd have a bit of help from the EC-121, Disco, who supposedly would provide warning of the approaching interceptors. That, at least, was the theory. It seldom worked that way in practice. Anyone who'd been up north knew that most of the warnings from Disco came about two minutes after the action had taken place, usually as a result of Disco monitoring a fighter's radio calls. Someone sees MiGs or calls a SAM; shortly thereafter Disco tells us there's a MiG or missile airborne. A minute or two in aerial combat is a lifetime, or maybe even longer than the remainder of a lifetime, for an airplane that's been targeted.

We spent about a half hour talking about the "standards" for engine start, taxi, takeoff, en route to the tanker, and refueling. Most of the discussion dealt with noncritical garbage that the majority of competent folks could do adequately without any briefing at all. The "meat" of the mission, what we would actually do if engaged by enemy aircraft, took less than five minutes. It was an accurate reflection of the level of air-to-air training. You didn't spend a lot of time discussing "magic" that you didn't understand and probably couldn't execute anyway. We would turn into the threat. We would let the element lead shoot. Wingmen would cover the element leaders' six o'clock. We would comply with the rules of engagement to visually identify the target. We would return to our escort positions as soon after the engagement as possible. Yeah, right. The briefing ended with a detailed discussion of the route back to Korat, a plebiscite on whether everyone thought we might need the post-strike tanker (we agreed that our fuel state at the middle of northern Laos would be the deciding vote), and a debate on whether we should fly a visual approach or practice instrument procedures when we returned.

Surprisingly, the mission went far more smoothly than the briefing had indicated. The sequencing at Korat was exactly as briefed, so flights got to the active runway in the proper order. The rendezvous with the tanker, co-ordinated by Lion, the ground radar station near Udorn, was flawless. Flights from the four bases approaching three different refueling tracks, each pair of cells of three or four tankers stacked at various altitudes was handled with remarkable precision. Twenty tankers, twenty flights of four aircraft from three or four bases, all trying to occupy a remarkably small chunk of airspace at the same time, most of the little airplanes concentrating on staying on the wing of their leader while trying for a desperate peek around every once in a while; a gaggle of high-powered, bomb-laden, heavy-metal thunderers all

coming together precisely. Flights turned onto their assigned tankers, no one came close to a midair, and everyone was taking gas in short order.

IT'S A FAMILIAR DANCE. FOUR fighters per tanker, each
airplane taking six to eight thousand pounds of fuel,
then sliding to the opposite wing of the tanker. Sequencing through the flight with little radio chatter.
Then the tanker streams turning northward out of Thailand, across the dirty brown Mekong River and heading
to the drop-off points in central Laos. We cycle one
more time through the boom, one after another taking
the last possible drops of fuel, barely a thousand
pounds at a time, trying to reach the 20 degree north
latitude drop point with all four airplanes in each flight
as close to fully fueled as possible. You're working
hard on the boom. You're sweating a bit and concentrating on the task, the formation, your position over the
ground, and the mission ahead. There's no time for
fear, no time for chitchat with your WSO, no time to be
outside the moment. You've got your game face on.

The escort flight is as heavily laden as the bombers.
We've got three fuel tanks, four AIM-9 Sidewinder
heat-seeking missiles on the inboard pylons, three
radar-guided AIM-7E Sparrows in the fuselage missile
wells, an ECM pod in the left front missile well, and a
full load of 20mm ammunition for the Vulcan in the
nose. As soon as the tanker drops us and turns back
south, we start checking our weapons. We take turns
dropping slightly back of our element partner and
checking the alignment of the heat-seekers with the red
bull's-eye of the gun sight. With the pipper on the
tailpipe of an F-4, the missile should "growl," indicat-

ing with an audio tone that it sees a heat source. We step through the four missiles, checking each one's alignment and finishing with the best aligned missile or strongest growler in the start position. The inanimate missiles don't care which goes first, but if we get a shot at an enemy, we humans want it to be our best shot.

We follow a similar sequence stepping through the radar missiles. We don't lock onto each other, but we select each missile in turn and wait for it to light up on the instrument panel, telling us that it is properly tuned to the guidance signal that our aircraft will emit when we fire. Socks is busy in the backseat, updating the inertial nav system to our next turn point and then the coordinates of the target beyond. He's cycling the various modes and lights of the APR-36/37 radar warning receiver. He hasn't seen many SAMs during his Spectre escort duties over the Trail, but he's well aware that today we're going to be in serious SAM country. He's flipping the ECM pod through its modes and watching the active lights and checking for faults. Through it all, he's keeping an eye on the radar scope, scanning forty miles ahead of us for whatever might be lurking.

Our flight has now taken up stations on either side of the bomber stream. We've got the bombers' line of flights bracketed. Each bomber flight of four is in tactical spread, three thousand feet apart, the element stacked high or low depending upon which side of the leader they are flying and what the position of the sun is. The flights hold spacing between themselves to give three to five minutes between their times on target. We watch the radar to see the first flight, now nearly forty miles ahead of us. We're abeam the third flight in the stream; I'm with lead on the right side of the bombers, while Dallas three and four are nearly five miles away on our left. Both elements are stacked high, to let us look down at our charges and scan the area below, the most likely place for MiGs to come from. We'll eat up the forty miles by the time we get to the steel mill and be nearly with the first flight, then we'll fly past the target area and reverse our sides, Dallas lead and I crossing from south to north of the bombers while three and four do their reversal to come from north to the south side of the formation. When we recross the target area, we'll almost be even with the last flight on target. Assuming, of course, that we haven't been engaged.

The weather is as promised. No refunds from the weather-guessers today. It's severe clear, with just a few scattered alto-cumulus to break up the monotony of bright blue and emerald green. I've seen it before, but the beauty of the countryside belies the violence of the war. The limestone karst breaks through the jungle canopies in ragged fingers, thrusting toward the sky. The mountain ridges promise great hunting, fishing, peaceful camping, and respite from the world. But that would be in a different time. Today there's a war, and the mountains mean refuge if we wind up damaged and bailing out. The mountains could be the key to survival. The flat areas of lighter green, pastures and glens, are the spots to be avoided. That's where the people will be, and the odds are a whole lot better than even that the people who meet a descending parachute won't be a fan club.

We're almost to the North Vietnam border now. The RWR is beeping regularly with the sweeps of some sort of air defense radar. There's a weak intermittent buzz and the flash of a tiny, short strobe on the warning receiver's scope, indicating a spurious signal from a distant Firecan gun radar. Otherwise, silence. Radio discipline is surprisingly good. No chatter, no missed frequency changes, no managing of the flights by weak leaders over the radio. I can see heads swiveling in front and backseat cockpits. A glance at my radar scope confirms that Socks is slowly sweeping the antenna high and low. My canopy bow rearview mirrors show his helmet regularly looking up, out, back, then down to the scope. He's busy and so am I.

"Dallas has bogies. A pair, low right, two o'clock, opposite direction." Lead doesn't use a position number. He's Dallas. I look right, away from the leader and our bomb-laden charges. There they are. Two white or light gray airplanes, easily ten thousand feet below us. It's Banana Valley, a jungle pocket among the steep mountain ridges, just inside the border in the northwest corner of Route Pack IV. It's a known lurking place for MiGs. My heartbeat surges momentarily as I anticipate an early baptism of fire. Then, "Disregard, Dallas, they're smokers."

It's the Marine F-4s we'd been briefed on. They're a BARCAP, a barrier patrol to stop any MiGs that might think it a good idea to take a high-speed, low-level run at our unprotected tanker fleet, extended to 20 degrees north latitude over Laos. It's a possibility that scares the tanker drivers, and I don't blame them. I'll soon learn that the conspicuous smoke trail laid by the F-4s' dirty engines will be a mixed blessing. It gives us away from a distance, but it's also a great protection from misidentification by some trigger-happy and poorly trained wingman in our own flights.

We cruise along. The centerline tank is thumping, signaling that it's empty and demanding that it be released before we get into any high-G maneuvering.

The huge white 600-gallon gasbag isn't stressed for anywhere near the aircraft's limits. When full it barely handles two G, and even when empty is only certified for four. There's no way to fight another airplane or even to evade a SAM with the tank still aboard. It will only be a few minutes until we'll be jettisoning.

It doesn't take long. "Dallas, tank jettison on my call . . ." I glance down at the switch by my left thigh. I've already broken the safety wire after dropping off the tanker. Now I lift the red plastic guard and find the toggle. "Dallas, ready, now!" Lead's nose rises and I match his four G pull, then flip the switch. A mild jolt tells me that the ejector cart has fired and the tank is blown away from the belly. I pull for a couple of seconds longer to match my lead, then roll inverted and search for the tank beneath me. We're back level with the bombers in seconds, and I can see the tanks from the element falling away, trailing a white exhaust of remaining fuel and vapor.

It's only psychological, but the airplane feels lighter, more responsive, ready for a fight. "Dallas, fence check," is the next call. It's the signal that we're approaching the time that things might get serious. Socks asks if I want the checklist read. We're still a relatively new crew, and he's not sure how much help I want or need. It's a prudent act on his part, ensuring that I've got all the help I need and he's got the protection of a competent front-seater to keep him alive. I simply summarize my preparations for battle. I've got the stab-aug roll channel turned off—the aileron/rudder interconnects make rolling at high G jerky. I've got all my loose maps, gear, and whatever tied down; I don't fly with a lot of extraneous junk. I've turned the TACAN to receive-only to stop one of many transmitters on the airplane; I've got the weapons switches set, a radar missile selected, the sight on. And I've taken a refresher look at the toggle that will quickly switch to AIM-9 heat-seekers and the gun if needed. He's satisfied that I'm ready.

The valley of the Red River is about ten miles ahead. To our right, the delta spreads into the broad flatland that becomes Hanoi, then onward to the Gulf of Tonkin. To the left the valley rapidly narrows, and the built-up area around Yen Bai stands out against the dark green vegetation. The black circles on the map strapped to my left thigh tell me that we're now in range of the first SAM sites, and the red arcs mean we've got 85mm threats as well. After years of bombing, the folks at Yen Bai are notoriously aggressive. If you get in their range or even if you don't, they'll put something in the air. The RWR has several lights flashing now, and the center of the small vector scope shows a bright green octopus with several tentacles reaching outward, indicating a number of radars looking at our formation. Several arms of the creature point to Yen Bai, and several more to our right to the small heavily armed towns between us and the capital. It's going to get interesting in just a few minutes.

"Dallas, you've got Crow passing on your right, low at four o'clock," is the alert from the Wild Weasel flight. We're doing about 450 indicated now, and the SAM suppression flight is clearly at least 100 knots faster. The F-105G element leading the hunter-killers is between us and the most likely SAM threat. His job is to detect SAM signals, warn us of launches, and kill anyone with the audacity to threaten the strike package.

If they emit radar, he'll stuff a Shrike down their antenna. If they shoot, he'll follow the missile smoke trail back to the source and attack them. If they aren't well camouflaged, he'll seek them out visually and dump CBU on them. He'll be first to the target area and the last to leave. His supporting element is a pair of F-4Es that will protect him from MiGs and attack the SAM sites that he discovers. They will be lower than the rest of us, faster than the rest of us, and in the arena longer than the rest of us. I don't envy them.

The chaff strike has already done its work, and we can make out a light smear on the radar scope where they've been. The strips of chaff, called dipoles, are cut to length according to the frequency of the radar to be jammed. Unless we're really looking for the corridor we usually won't notice it very much, but it's supposed to be a significant degradation to the air defense radar. I'm wondering if it comes with a money-back guarantee. The chaff flights have been on their own discrete frequency, so we haven't heard any chatter from them. If they had experienced much defensive reaction, we didn't know for sure. Disco would have been yelling if there had been SAMs or MiGs airborne. At least I hope so.

"Crow's got activity just south of Phuc Yen. Heads-up, guys," is the first indication that the enemy is awake today. There were plenty of SAM sites on the maps at the briefing; the catch is, those were only the known sites. On any given day, they might or might not harbor a SAM battery. The SAMs move regularly from site to site and often spring up at brand-new locations. The shell game of finding them is what keeps the Weasels fascinated. New photos, new electronic intelligence and, of course, real-time detection of SAM site radars are all input to the game. The most likely reaction area is near the target, and while the chaff partially blinds the SAMs, it also creates a huge pointer to identify the direction of the strike flight. It routinely ends at about the final destination of the bombers. Somewhere in the big cloud are attacking jets, so the focus of the enemy's attention becomes quite clear.

It's mere seconds later that we see the first orange trail arcing upward from the area near the MiG base. A second SAM from the same site begins to rise in trail. We're still not in range, so they may be firing at the hunter-killer flight or possibly someone in the chaff package. A long strobe on the RWR scope points straight ahead, and the yellow "activity" light is flashing. As the rising plumes draw my attention, I see the flashing white popcorn puffs of 37 and 57mm bursting well below our altitude. "Crow's got a launch. Crow's got a launch." The RWR audio is a nearly deafening buzz now, as flights that hadn't yet turned on their ECM pods react almost in unison. I grab for the volume knob without looking at it and turn it down to a more manageable level.

We're almost to the target, and I can see the first flight of bombers pulling up in pairs, bracketing the target area and rising only slightly to roll into a dive-bomb pass and reverse course outbound. The SAM launches and the flak mean it's unlikely we'll see MiGs here, but they can always be lurking up the Red waiting to pounce on an outbound straggler. My left arm has involuntarily straightened, pushing the throttles forward until they are right against the resistance that needs to be overcome to go to afterburner. I'm line-abreast of Dallas lead, and I'm not about to lag behind. I'm

rolling right and left, now; fast enough to thwart anyone sneaking up behind me, slow enough to take a
good look high, low, and behind on each side. The maneuvers keep a bit of G load on the bird, and that bleeds
off enough speed to keep me from overrunning lead. I
hear Socks straining against the G as he turns with each
reversal to check for threats. He's good, and I appreciate it.

Dallas is past the target now, as the second flight is
calling their roll-in. We should be cross-turning shortly,
but at this point every second is a year and every passing mile goes too quickly. It seems as though we'll be
halfway to Kep before we get turned around. One MiG
base is bad, but being between two is a lot worse. The
countryside ahead is flat and clearly developed. There
are roads and villages, rice paddies and rivers, and, of
course guns and SAMs out here. Mountains are our
friends and flatlands our enemies. Rough terrain means
the bad guys can't easily get their defenses moved; flats
mean easy access and high mobility. I'd sure like to get
reversed and start heading outbound. I'm still on the far
right side of the right-hand element on the right side of
the strike package, and the only thing farther right is
the city of Hanoi and a whole bunch of SAMs, guns,
and guys who don't like me very much.

"Dallas, cross-turn," finally comes. Lead banks hard
away from me in a descending left turn. We start hard,
then ease off a bit to cross nose-to-nose with our element, then tighten up again to establish our outbound
course parallel to the egress heading of the bombers.
Now I'm headed southwest and watching the last flight
of F-4s dropping on the target area, which is bathed in
grayish smoke, flecked with flashes from the antiaircraft batteries. Directly below is the wide cement run-

way of Phuc Yen airfield. Nothing appears to be moving, and there are no visible airplanes on the ground.
Little is clearly discernible beyond the pavement. Taxiways disappear quickly into trees and bushes. Buildings
can barely be made out against the olive drab foliage.
The North Vietnamese have become masters at camouflage, and it is only the runway that marks the air base.

I float my turn high and almost directly above my
leader. I learned long ago that the worst place to ever be
is directly behind another aircraft. Protection for each
other involves always being seen, and once behind it
becomes all too easy to lag farther and farther back.
Trailing another airplane means you stand a good
chance of sucking up the flak that's aimed at him but
doesn't lead enough. I'm always forward and always
trying to look through my partner at the areas of greatest threat. It's purely a survival reflex. I reestablish my
spread, now on the right side of the right element, again
to the right of the bomber stream as they head outbound. I can watch Hanoi and the flat delta of the Red
River, twenty miles to the south. We've got maybe forty
miles to go before we're clear of the SAM rings and
back into the relative safety of the mountains. Clear of
the SAMs will mean that once again the MiG threat
will go up. It's too early to relax.

Back across the Red River, we spread wider in our
formation and ease higher. We'll save fuel and cruise a
bit faster. We're low on gas now and in relative safety
over the mountains. Laos is just ahead and then the post-
strike tanker. No one has been lost today and there are
no emergency beepers. No MiGs, just a few SAMs and
light flak. It's gone pretty much as briefed. I turn control
over to Socks, who always wants more stick time. He
likes to fly the jet, and it's a good insurance policy to

have the second crewmember able to maintain formation, handle a refueling if necessary, and maybe even get you lined up for an emergency landing. The water bottle in my lower G suit pocket is melted now, but still cold and refreshing. It's good to be alive. Another hash mark will be logged on the jungle hat tonight.

"RAZ, LIEUTENANT COLONEL MCHALE WANTS to see you." The lieutenant on the duty desk greets me with the sort of message that no one ever really wants to hear. Exchanging a few words with the boss in the hall is fine. Having a brief conversation over a cup of coffee in the lounge is good too. Shooting the breeze over a beer in the club or at the CTF will do, but getting called to the boss's office is way too official for most fighter pilots. Nothing good can come of these encounters.

I head down the hall to the squadron commander's office. I've known McHale since I was a student pilot at Williams and he was an instructor. The years have passed, but I knew him then and he knew me. The first sergeant looks up from his desk and tells me that the boss is at his desk. "Go right on in, sir."

I knock on the doorjamb, then walk in and salute. "You wanted to see me, sir?"

"Yeah, Raz. Have a seat." Ed McHale is tall, athletic, blond, with a thick crew cut and a ruddy complexion. He's been the squadron commander for several months now and has almost completed his one year tour. I've only been here for a couple of weeks. We haven't talked much since I arrived, so maybe this will just be a welcome aboard interview. "I'm hearing good things about you," he starts out. This isn't going to be good, I can tell already. It was the first principle they taught us at instructor pilot school. Always start the bad debriefing with some good comments. I sit quietly without responding and wait for the other shoe to drop.

"The guys I've talked to that have flown with you say they like the way you work. You're doing a good job in formation, you appear to handle the airplane well, and they say they can depend on you to be where you're supposed to be." It's nice to hear positives, but I've been doing what I know to stay alive. The skills that I learned flying into North Vietnam in the F-105 are the same ones that I intend to use to get the job done this tour. I wait for him to continue. I know this isn't a pat-on-the-back session. Something's up.

"We had a visit a couple days ago from the Seventh Air Force deputy commander for operations. The DO is touring all the bases and checking out the Linebacker folks. Apparently there's quite a bit of emphasis on the Pack VI missions."

"Yes, sir," I respond. "There's always been a lot of emphasis on Pack VI. That's where we lose most of the airplanes."

"Well," the boss continues, "the DO says that we need to select 'designated Linebacker crews' so that we're sending the best folks on these missions." Flashing lights. I can already see it coming. Somehow, I know that with barely fifty hours in the F-4, I am about to become one of these best available.

"The Pack VI mission was always pretty tough," I offer. "But, we were always darned careful back the last time I was here to make sure that the threat got shared equally. Nothing tears a squadron apart quicker than some guys carrying all the load while others aren't facing the same threat." It's true, but I already know that things are different this time, and my rationale isn't equal to the pronouncement of the two-star from Saigon. McHale is about to "designate" me.

"You've got that right, but it doesn't sound as though we've got a choice, Raz. You already know that the various bases have some specialties. The guys up at Udorn who are going to become primary Linebacker crews for CAP are mostly Fighter Weapons School graduates who have a lot of air-to-air experience. It makes sense to fight the MiGs with the best at that business. Here at Korat we do two things: escort of the strike flights, and hunter-killer against the SAM sites with the Weasels. The designated crews will be doing the same mission every day. They'll be first on the schedule for the missions going north. We'll fill the rest of the schedule with the other guys, so they'll get to go as well, just not every day." It's hard to argue with the principle of sending your best for the most difficult missions. It simply wouldn't appeal to the average life insurance underwriter. Going to Hanoi everyday is not conducive to a long career.

"Here's the deal," he leans forward, "Which would you rather do? We need you as a designated Linebacker crew. Would you rather fly escort in the air-to-air role, or would you rather fly with the Weasels and kill SAM sites?"

It doesn't take me long to respond. The choice is clear. There's the high-altitude profile, cruising along with the strike above most of the flak, waiting for the glory of a chance at a MiG. Or, there's the alternative of rooting around at low-level, down nose-to-nose with the guns every day. Being first in to the target area and last out, all the while not avoiding the SAM sites but actively seeking them in the midst of the heaviest defenses they can assemble. It isn't attractive in the slightest. "I'd rather kill MiGs, sir. I'll fly escort." This is the logical and safer alternative.

"What's your second choice?" The standard AF response. You always get one of your first two choices. It's a done deal. It was sealed before I walked in the door.

"It makes sense," McHale goes on, actually trying to sell me on it. "You've got previous F-105 experience. You're familiar with the mission and the Weasel. It's a great opportunity for you." Here's that damned opportunity thing again. I nod. I have a bit of insight into how a convicted felon must feel when given the choice between a life sentence and capital punishment. I got my second choice. I flash back on the patch that many of the Wild Weasel crews wore: a cartoon weasel curled around a bull's-eye and holding a missile aloft to hurl at the target. Across the bottom of the patch were the letters YGBSM, the response of one of the first of the Weasel "bears" when he reported to training and found that the mission was to hunt for SAM sites and then kill them. He verified what the briefer had just described as the new job, and then exclaimed, "You've gotta be shittin' me!" It became a motto for all Weasels.

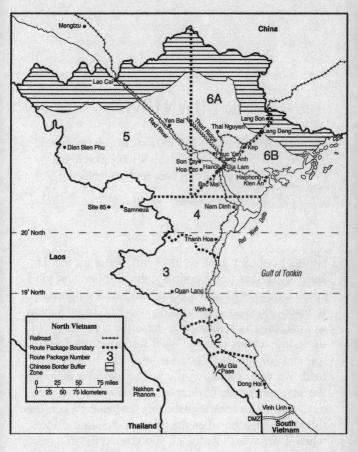

China

Mengtzu

Lao Cai

6A

Yen Bai
Red River
Thud Ridge
Thai Nguyen
Lang Son
Lang Dang

5

Dien Bien Phu

Phuc Yen
Dong Anh
Kep
6B

Son Tay
Hoa Lac
Hanoi
Gia Lam

Bac Mai
Haiphong
Kien An

4

Site 85
Samneua
Nam Dinh

20° North
Red River Delta

Laos
Thanh Hoa
Gulf of Tonkin

19° North

3
Quan Lang

Vinh

2

Mu Gia
Pass
Dong Hoi

1

North Vietnam

Railroad	+—+—+
Route Package Boundary	• • • •
Route Package Number	3
Chinese Border Buffer Zone	▤

0   25   50   75 miles

0   25   50   75 kilometers

Nakhon
Phanom

Vinh Linh
DMZ

Thailand
South Vietnam

NORTH VIETNAM

6. DOWNTOWN

The aircraft G-limits are only there in case there is another
flight by that particular airplane. If subsequent flights
do not appear likely, there are no G-limits.

—Frank Chubba, fighter pilot

THINGS COULDN'T HAVE WORKED OUT better for me. Despite my wishes to the contrary, the absolute best job I could have was to be a specialist in SAM suppression. It made sense to do what the two-star from Saigon wanted, even if it seemed to raise the threat level for those individuals chosen. We'd lost so many folks in '66 and '67 precisely because we were spreading the load. We were spreading it among guys who included the inexperienced, frightened, occasionally incompetent, and sometimes unjustifiably arrogant. When the threat was highest, when the mission was most critical, when it was fourth and goal, you wanted the first team in place. If we had to have primary, designated, go-downtown-everyday crews, then I was a natural choice, and I was going to be better able to survive and do the job if I was surrounded by guys who were the best. Yeah, it made sense on a lot of different levels.

I didn't get my first choice, but the second wasn't

going to be that bad. Flying escort wasn't the best place
to get a MiG: escorts seldom engaged enemy aircraft.
More often they were used as a blocking force by the
radar controllers who provided detailed information on
a discrete frequency to the hotshots from Udorn. They
were "cat-herders," tasked to funnel the day's designated target to the preordained hero of the moment.
When MiGs got airborne during Linebacker, we knew
it immediately through a combination of radar surveillance, embedded human observers who reported, and
electronic monitoring of enemy aircraft transmissions.
The poor guys, defending their homeland as best they
could, didn't have much of a chance. But the F-4s flying escorts for the bomb and chaff packages were mere
pawns in the game. Not many MiGs for them.

SAMs, on the other hand, still raised the heartbeat,
made the palms sweaty, and forced even the staunchest
of tactical aviators to react. Killing SAMs (and avoiding
being killed yourself) was a challenge, but it was a mission with immediate rewards. Getting the strike package
in and out without losses was a measurable outcome
every time we went. Finding and destroying a SAM site
in the process was even better. And, since the enemy
hadn't grown up with Steve Canyon, Terry and the Pirates, or Sky King in their comic books, they didn't
much care about daring dogfights with escorts or CAP
flights. The MiGs' objective was to attack the guys who
were attacking them. Hunter-killer flights were more
likely to encounter MiGs than the escorts, by a long shot.

A fringe benefit to becoming a full-time hunter-
killer team member was that I knew quite a few of the
F-105G Weasel pilots. They had been single-seat Thud
drivers during my first tour, or among the first contingent of Weasels. The best of the bunch had been in the

Weasel business for five or six years. That was an incredible level of experience, one that was seldom encountered at any time in any other specialty during the war. The ones that had less experience weren't going to be on the primary Linebacker roster. They would build experience flying support for other strikes in the panhandle of North Vietnam or along the Ho Chi Minh Trail, where the SAM threat was less intense. Almost all of them knew through the grapevine that I had a hundred-mission tour in my background. I knew them or they knew me. The comfort level established by that exchange made it a lot easier to work together. I was a little bit more than one of those "Phantom drivers," and a lot more than a former UPT instructor.

The 17th Wild Weasel Squadron occupied the old squadron building in which I'd spent my first tour. The Linebacker effort had them augmented by a detachment of aircraft and crews from the Weasel squadron back in the States, the 561st WWS. The commander of the 17th, Lt. Col. Ed Rock, had been an instructor in the F-105 when I'd trained, and then among the first F-105F Weasel pilots. His operations officer, George Bowling, had been around the -105 for nearly as long. Other Weasel front-seaters were almost legendary in the SAM-killing business. There was Lucky Ekman, a lieutenant just finishing his first 100 missions and then the first to extend beyond a hundred North Vietnam counters, now a major wearing a patch that said, "200 Missions N. Vietnam—F-105G." Tom Coady, another 100 mission survivor in single-seat Thuds, kept coming back or extending tours until he would eventually become the record holder for F-105 combat hours. Jim O'Neil, Tom Edge, Ed Cleaveland, and others made the "hunter" side of the roster pretty impressive.

On the F-4E "killer" side of the team we had more to draw from, with two Phantom squadrons available. There would be roughly eight crews from the two squadrons to be the primaries, with occasional help from other pilots and WSOs when there were more hunter-killer flights scheduled. We would always fly the element of the four-ship, the number three and four positions, and, based on the point in the mission, we might be flying wing off the Weasel, leading the Weasel pair, or even operating autonomously as an armed reconnaissance two-ship. By flying together constantly, we would all know the mission, aid in the development of tactics, and, hopefully, generate the almost mystical teamwork that occurs with people who fly together so regularly that they know without apparent communication what the partner is going to do next. It worked for air-to-air units, and it would work for defense suppression teams too.

IN THE RED CORNER, NEARLY 35 feet tall, weighing in at just over 5,000 pounds, the defending champion of North Vietnam, the SA-2 Guideline. This feisty little battler has a reach of nearly 30 miles and punches at an amazing 3,000 miles per hour. He's quick, he's sneaky, and he comes with some partners who aren't afraid to jump into the ring with him. Always in his corner are the Fan Song radar and his little brother the Firecan. They'll spot the opponent a long way off and help Guideline deliver his knockout blow of more than 440 pounds of high explosive. Usually he's accompanied by his gunner buddies, ranging from tiny 23mm, who may be small but unleashes his punches in a blinding flurry, all the way up to Guideline's oldest, biggest, and loudest partner, a heavyweight champion in his own right, the 100mm antiaircraft artillery gun. They're a vicious team, and they've chalked up an impressive series of wins. With several hundred victories and an undisclosed number of losses, Guideline remains the world's airspace defense champion ever since gaining the title in an upset victory May 1, 1960, over the U-2 spy plane flown by Gary Powers.

In the blue corner the aging and slightly overweight challenger, the F-105G Wild Weasel. At 67 feet and a bit bloated 54,000 pounds, he greatly outweighs the champion but he's nowhere near as fast, only occasionally displaying a quarter of the champ's flashing speed. He comes to the fight with a one-two punch of Shrike and Standard ARM, a pair of missiles that won't touch the champ but will strike and befuddle the champ's associates, Fan Song and Firecan. The challenger has taken a few hits over time but has won a lot more than he's lost. He's been known to jab and feint, then sneak in a Shrike when the champ is looking the other way.

The two arms of the challenger are quite literally ARMs, or antiradiation missiles. They detect the transmissions of the ground radar and home on the signal to deliver a small payload with great accuracy. The Shrike has been around since the first Wild Weasels and has been updated to provide better frequency discrimination, a rudimentary memory to keep guiding to approximately the last signal location if the radar shuts down, and improved cockpit displays to better inform the Weasel "bear," or backseater, about the radars it is detecting. It's a smart little missile.

The Standard is a newer missile, sort of a big brother to the Shrike. It's nearly three times the size with a bigger rocket motor, bigger warhead, and more capable electronics. The bear can program the Standard with in-

formation collected by the Weasel aircraft, preloading
it with data about a selected target radar. When
launched, the Standard can supposedly turn around and
attack a radar site behind the aircraft. That might be
what the manufacturer's catalog tells the customer, but
no one is quite sure that it really can do that. The best
data gathered so far is that based on the projected time
of flight of the missile; there is occasionally a correla-
tion with the chosen target going off the air. In practice,
it doesn't make much difference. The goal is to put the
enemy's eyes out, and whether the missile hits him or
he pulls the plug to save his butt, the result is just as
good. Maybe having a jittery radar operator ready to
flip the switch at the slightest hint of a missile on the
way is even better, in terms of degrading the defenses.

Also in the challenger's corner, of course, are a pair
of equally threatening heavyweights, the F-4E Phantoms, weighing in at a well-conditioned 58,000 pounds
and loaded with four CBU-52 that will scatter 250
grapefruit-size bomblets over an area the size of a soc-
cer field, each one detonating and sending shrapnel pel-
lets for more than a half-mile at rifle bullet speeds. The
thin skin of the SA-2, the Fan Song, and the Firecan are
no match for these tag team partners of the Weasel. It's
going to be a helluva fight.

IT DIDN'T TAKE LONG TO get thrown into the battle. A
couple of days later I found myself teamed with Larry
Cary as the killer element going to a target along the
Red River, just a few miles up from Hanoi. The lead
Weasel was Lucky Ekman, and he had a new arrival to
the Weasel squadron on his wing. Larry had a prior tour
and a MiG kill as a backseater in the F-4, Lucky had too

many North Vietnam missions to count accurately, and the "new" Weasel was only new as far as this tour was concerned. All told, the front-seaters of the four-ship had a combined mission count of more than 500 trips to North Vietnam. Throw in the bears and GIBs and you got close to 750 missions. We were either overqualified or overdue for disaster. How many times can you tweak the nose of the dragon before you get burned?

The plan was simple. We'd enter the target area just ahead of the strike package. We'd interpose ourselves between the bomb droppers and the most likely threat sites. We'd root around in the area doing whatever was necessary until the last bombers finished, and then we'd either follow them out or continue to search for SAM sites until we hit "bingo" fuel or ran out of ordnance. Somehow it made sense when Ekman was briefing it, but when I begin to ruminate on the scenario, it occurred to me that it was a bit like playing several consecutive innings of Russian roulette.

As the killer element of the team, Cary and I had a full menu of jobs to handle. We'd be there with the Weasel pair as they followed their detected radar signals to find SAM sites. If the Weasel detected a missile radar, we would attempt to see the impact of any Shrike or Standard that he fired, then attack the site. If the SAM fired at us, we would follow the signature smoke trail back to the site or look for the dust cloud on the ground that marked the launch. We would attack the site. At the same time, we were also a mini-MiGCAP for the Weasels. If enemy aircraft attacked the F-105s, we would engage the MiGs. When the strike package was on its way out of the area, we would take the lead of the flight and conduct armed reconnaissance to see if we could visually acquire any occupied SAM sites that hadn't otherwise been engaged. The first-in, last-out responsibility of the hunter-killer team meant that we'd be in the target area for a little more than twenty-five minutes.

With four CBU on each of the Phantoms, we would plan to dole out the munitions to be sure we had something remaining throughout our time on target. If we were engaged early, we would drop one CBU each on the site to put it out of commission. As the mission progressed, we'd drop a pair, and if we went to the end of our responsibility period without dropping, we would then dump the full four cans on the first target we could find. A nice change to the ROE was that the MiG bases were now an authorized jettison target if we had not expended on a SAM site.

During the briefing, the lead bear spent some time going over maps of the area surrounding the day's target, pointing out sites that had been active recently. Some of them had fired missiles in the previous couple of days. Others had been detected by their radar emissions and plotted on the map, seeking intersections of plot lines that might disclose a location. The bear distributed several black-and-white recce photos, all dated within the last two weeks of known SAM sites. We would each get a little time to study the photos in the hope that we could correlate what we saw on the ground during the mission with a picture, and thereby find an occupied site. Before he finished he gave us a ten-minute, fall-asleep-in-your-chair, technical lecture on Soviet radars and their frequency bands, along with the presentations he expected to see on his equipment. We were now saturated with an overload of S-bands, megahertz, and pulse recurrence frequencies. We might have asked the time of day, but we'd just been told how to build a watch.

Ekman cut the bear short. "Here's the real plan," he explained. "We're going to be ahead of the strike off the tanker. We're going to favor the right side of the track inbound to keep between the bombers and the threat. The first radar that comes up solid on us, we're gonna get rid of the blivet—the Standard ARM goes as early as possible. I don't like flying an asymmetric load, and when the 450 wing tank goes empty, the Standard will go shortly thereafter.

"We're going to root around looking for these briefed sites. Keep your head on a swivel and listen to the bear. Your RHAW gear will tell you some stuff, but we've got better info. If he tells you 'no threat,' believe him. If he calls a launch, get ready to take it down. If he says 'take it down,' then you'd better be heading for the dirt and getting the burners cookin'. If they shoot we'll attack the site, and the F-4s will assume the lead for the attack while the Weasels cover you against an attack from other sites.

"You F-4 guys are the MiG cover for us while we're looking for sites. If we get a Fan Song signal up solid, we're gonna close on him and stuff a Shrike down his throat. We'll call our shots and you can try to follow the missile to the site to hit him with the CBU. If we haven't expended you with ten minutes left on station, I'll let you guys assume the lead and visually search for the sites in those pictures. You might want to put the coordinates of one of them in your INS for a little help. As soon as we get clear of the target area, the -105s will reassume the lead and take us to the post-strike tanker. Any questions?"

We all nodded our approval. It was time to head back to our separate squadrons for the final discussion of Phantom ops by F-4 guys and Weasel stuff between Weasels.

Larry Cary and Hank Scheible, riding in his backseat, headed to the 469th building with Slockbower and me. We took just a few minutes to review our notes and confirm basics about our formation positions, hand signals, attack sequence if and when we committed on a SAM site, and the handling of any emergencies in the F-4 element. We were ready to go.

We beat the crowd to the parachute shop and were already suited up and heading out the door when the rest of the package started filing in for their equipment. We would be starting engines, taxiing, and airborne before the rest of the flights. The heavy load of the F-105G, particularly the asymmetric tank configuration of the lead aircraft, made it necessary for him to take off on the hot summer day with the centerline tank empty. We would hit an extra tanker to top off before merging with the rest of the strike on the main tanker cells.

OUR CALL SIGN IS CROW. The hunter-killer flight call signs are always bird names. The bombers today are Dallas, Sixgun, Carbine, and Laredo. The escorts from Korat are Racer and Pine. The MiGCAP is Buick and Chevy. We'll have jamming from Buzzer 21 and Buzzer 41. Disco is an EC-121 Super Constellation, orbiting near the North Vietnam border and overseeing the area with radar. Red Crown is a Navy destroyer in the Gulf of Tonkin, with more radar coverage and a TACAN station aboard. The tankers are on Red and White tracks, with a high and low cell of four tankers on each. There are a lot of players in our bunch, and that doesn't begin to consider the chaff package, which is only a bit smaller and will precede us by twenty minutes. We also have a pair of Jolly Green rescue helicopters and a four-ship of A-1 Sandies, in case someone gets shot down.

The tanker rendezvous for the package goes as usual, with swarms of airplanes approaching from every direction in a meshing of machinery that would strike terror into the heart of anyone who hadn't seen it before and raises a twinge of apprehension even in those who have done it fifty or more times. It is an awe-inspiring air show, which only years of going against the same targets with the same airplanes and the same aircrews from the same bases for the same mediocre impact on the war could create. Like clockwork the fighters join with the tankers, perform the mystical act of coupling with the boom to suck fuel into the tanks, then unwind from the orbit to proceed in a parade to the north of Laos for drop-off and the start of the strike. Few radio calls are made among all of the airplanes, except for the singular frustration of one flight lead with a wayward wingman who missed a channel change signal and has failed to check in.

Then we are inbound. Ekman and his partner push up the speed of the Weasels until we are reading 540 knots on the ground speed indicator, 9 miles a minute. Cary looks my way, then gives a pushing signal with his hand to tell me to move out into our tactical spread. He eases the nose of his airplane up slightly, and we climb above the Weasels to an oversight position, about 1,500 feet higher and spread almost half a mile to their right. The climb drops us back a bit, until we are on the pre-briefed line 30 degrees back from line abreast. Above, offset and slightly behind, we can watch the Weasel work against SAM sites without getting in his way while remaining in a position from which we can quickly move to attack any missile site that should threaten us. In my backseat Slockbower is setting up the radar, the radar warning receiver, and the weapons computer to deliver CBU. He flips the switch for the ECM pod, and a slight buzz comes through the headset while a light flickers on the panel of the RWR.

"Crows, cut your noise," comes the irritated call by Ekman's bear. Damn, we forgot that the ECM pod interferes with the Weasel's detection gear. Everyone else in the package might be using electronic jamming pods, but those of us with the SAM-killing mission have to forego the protection that the pods offer. We've been briefed, and Socks forgot. He flips the pod back to standby. I don't say anything but I'm glad he'd checked the pod, that it worked, and that he knows where the switch is. If we need it later, there might be no time to go hunting for the control.

It only takes fifteen minutes for the centerline tank to start thumping, indicating it's almost empty. I switch to the outboard tanks and reach down to break the safety wire on the jettison switch. A rapid double-click of the microphone switch from Cary alerts me that he's starting a pull-up to blow the tank. I'm ready and we both get rid of the gasbag at the same time. The -105s will take a few minutes longer before they'll be dumping their centerlines.

There is something about proximity to bull's-eye that affects intensity of radio chatter. At tanker drop-off, little is said. When the force changes from refueling frequency to strike primary, there is nothing but the check-ins, in order specified in the morning briefing. Then, as the miles roll down on the way to the heart of North Vietnam, the intensity of everything accelerates. The pulse goes up, the respiration rate rises, numerous sounds vying for attention and the overall pitch and volume of the many voices all intensify. The RWR starts buzzing and snarling. The noise of airflow over the canopy increases with descent into the working environment. Over the interphone, the background of straining, gasping, and wheezing increases as we maneuver, but we can't cut the volume for fear of missing an important call. The flow of information from the many input sources is critical, and we can drown in it if we aren't at the top of our game.

"Crow, Dallas. You guys inbound?" The mission commander wants confirmation of the Weasel support. We can look hard left back at our seven o'clock and see the smoking trails of the bomber flights. He could check his radar, but for some reason doesn't. "Buick, Dallas is inbound." He wants all his support in place and you can't blame him, but it adds to the noise.

"Crow's inbound. All's quiet," the lead bear soothes.

"Buick and Chevy are on station, Dallas," is the reassurance from the CAP flight. The escorts must be comfortably in sight, since there is no request for stroking from the close-in guys. The RWR indicates an early warning radar beep every few seconds, and now the buzz of a couple of Firecan gun director radars. It's almost as if they hear the radio chatter and want to check in as well.

We are nose low and descending through twelve thousand feet as we pass the Black River. The mountains disappear ahead of us, and the flats of the Red

River delta spread to the horizon. It is a sight that brings chills to the spine of anyone who has ever been out here before. The tranquil countryside can change to a firestorm in a heartbeat. It is filled with guns and SAMs, radars, and MiGs. It is the baddest of the bad places that one could be in.

"Crow lead, tanks away in ten," warns Ekman. It doesn't affect me or Cary, since we already have dumped our centerline, but the number two Weasel will avoid the possibly soaring tank from his leader when he blows it. On several occasions the big 650-gallon tank on the F-105 has been seen climbing to more than three thousand feet above the aircraft that jettisoned it. "Ready, now," is the call, and then the big white tank separates. Today it chooses to drop clear and fall immediately.

"Crow's got light activity. Some early warning, some Firecan. No threat." It is reassurance for the bombers as they get closer to the target.

"Dallas, let's green 'em up and start your music." The bomb flights will be setting their switches for the drop and making sure their ECM pods are on and ready to respond to any radar probes. We've come a long way from the days of pure noise jamming. Now the pods are supposed to do a lot more magic with the enemy radar. They create repetitive targets in response to a radar ping, or they might steal a range cursor and drive it off the enemy's display scope. It is magic of the highest order, and one only hopes that the engineers who have never had that heart-stopping moment of panic as a SAM goes roaring past a maneuvering airplane before detonation have done their job right. Claiming the cash on a money-back guarantee might be a bit difficult.

"Crow lead's got a steady contact. Early warning. No threat." He was serious about looking for the first strong signal to launch the Standard. "Crow's coming right. Stand by." Our element checks into the turn and stays out of the way. "Crow's gonna be shotgun in ten . . . Shotgun!" is the call, and then the flash and bright white smoke trail as the AGM-78 goes blasting off the wing. The missile looks bigger than ever as it separates from the airplane, then zooms ahead of the flight and almost immediately takes a turn upward. It disappears ahead of a white smoke trail, looking as though it's headed for the moon. No radars that way. Wonder what the gremlins aboard are thinking?

"Dallas, SAM, SAM . . . disregard," the apologetic call of a tense wingman comes in seconds. It happens with some regularity. Nerves wound tight will trigger a reaction even when warned. A missile is a missile and a missile can kill you.

"Dallas, this is Crow. All's quiet. No threat."

"SAM, SAM. Bull's-eye two five zero at thirty-five. Time zero seven two five Zulu. This is Disco on Guard. Disco out." The comedy continues. No one has ever figured out that the EC-121 picket airplane that surveys the battle area with its airborne radar and monitors all the radio frequencies is always out of synch. They hear a flight call a SAM or a MiG, then relay the call over the emergency frequency to all the airplanes airborne, totally oblivious to the fact that the airplane that made the call was the one that was threatened, and the ones that didn't make the call didn't really need to know thirty seconds or a minute after the fact. Warning is early, but replay is yesterday's news. We are right where Disco called the threat, and we know it was our own missile.

We are in the flats now. Lucky is on his old familiar stomping grounds, obviously nosing toward a particular favorite target, keeping his speed up, changing directions regularly but clearly headed somewhere. His wingman stays just slightly back from line abreast. Cary keeps our element back about a mile and offset. We are going faster than the F-4 is really comfortable, but that is necessary to stay with the Weasels that seem unconsciously to creep toward the 600-knot mark. We keep the throttles well forward, and as long as we stay smooth, we don't need afterburner.

"Sixgun lead's got strobes at one and two o'clock. Three ringer."

"Yeah, Carbine's showing lots of SAM activity too."

"Crow's got no threats. Crow's got lots of quiet. Steady, guys." The bear isn't going to be stampeded into scaring the force. His job is to keep things comfortable and sort the real from the imagined. "Crow's got a couple of lookers but nothing serious."

"Dallas two, move it up a bit." The chatter is rising. Now the need to get everyone perfect in their leader's view is beginning to overcome radio discipline.

"Roger, Dallas lead. Two's got some guns up at one o'clock. They're shooting out there."

"Dallas has the target coming up in about fifteen miles. Dallas three take spacing." The flight manager is getting things in order for his attack.

"Sixgun flight, let's [*bzzzzzz*] . . . ine *break*. Break left . . . MiGs at [*bzzzzzz*]. . . . " Suddenly things get real noisy and transmissions are covering each other. There are squeals of radios stepping on other radios. And the messages are garbled.

"Slock, was that . . . " I start to ask, but Bob's not waiting for anything.

"I don't care, *break, break,* goddamn it *break*." He wants action now and I don't argue. I slam the throttles into AB, kick full left rudder, and bang the stick to the left so hard I can feel the slap of it hitting his leg. We're over into 135 degrees of bank to the left, and I've got six G on the airplane straining to see if there's a threat behind us.

While we're in the turn I can't see anything unusual, and I keep my voice slow and steady as I continue my question, "Did you hear who that was? Was that for us? You see anything?"

"Thanks. No. Sorry. I guess it wasn't us. Thanks." He's panting, but apologetic for the brief moment of fear and grateful that I acted. I don't ease up, but feed in right rudder and reverse while still maintaining a lot of G on the airplane. I pick up Cary slightly low at my one o'clock. We've fallen behind with the break turn, but it's better to be safe than sorry, and I'm not going to jump on Socks for reacting first and asking questions later. It's the essence of survival. We may not find out who was breaking for what until debrief or maybe not even then in the quiet of the air-conditioned command post listening to the tapes. It doesn't matter. Right now I've got to get back up where Cary can see me and I can support him.

"Dallas is up. Dallas lead is in." The first bombers are on the target. The RWR is showing a gyrating spider at the center of the scope, but the Fan Song lights aren't flashing, and so far there aren't any missiles airborne. Maybe it's a MiG day. There's a lot of light antiaircraft fire coming from our left as the batteries of 23mm guns start spraying into the air. Tracers and tiny popcorn airbursts fill the sky as the first bombs detonate on the ground. Grayish black clouds erupt to define the target area, about ten miles from our position. We've still got no SAM sites threatening. In seconds, the remainder of Dallas flight is on and off the target. Sixgun, Carbine, and Laredo still to go, then we can get out of here.

"Crow's got nothing but guns. Nothing but guns, guys." Well, one man's nothing is another man's stark terror. Guns are still the greatest threat. The SAMs may be frightening, but it's usually the guns that kill you. There's an awful synergy to the defenses. The SAMs chase you, faster than you are and smaller than an airplane, with a blast that doesn't have to hit you directly to bring you down. They force you to operate lower to gain the benefit of terrain masking to break the radar lock that guides them. That puts you right in the heart of the gun envelope, and the lower you go, the more guns there are to shoot at you. Closer to the guns means less lead, and there's little that you can do about them except suck it up, keep your speed high and keep moving the bird. The MiGs are just a nuisance; a nuisance with a brain and a man at the controls, dedicated to ending your mission for the day.

"Crow two, lead, you want to move forward a bit and see if you can get a shot at some of these Firecans?" We're halfway through the time on target, and Ekman would like to kill something. Getting a Shrike in the air can maybe cut down on some of the radar-directed gunfire, and it might keep the SAM radars quiet as well. Cary's got our element high, back, and offset from the Weasels. We cross from side to side each time the Weasels give us a bit of turn, trying to use the geometry to cut off the fast-moving F-105s. We're always close to 500 knots, and I like the way Larry is keeping the energy level. I've never been too fast in a situation like this, and I know it's easy to get too slow.

"Roger, Crow. Two's got a contact right, one o'clock. Looks like I can shoot in about thirty seconds. Stand by." The Weasels are nearly line abreast now. "Crow two's got activity. Crow two's got activity" is the notice that suddenly a missile site has joined the party. My RWR begins to light up, and the tiny spider of signal vectors at the center of the scope suddenly grows a menacing arm out toward the nose of the airplane. The lights on the threat display flash both Firecan and Fan Song indications. The yellow activity light flickers twice, then stays on bright.

"SAM, SAM! Take it down, Crows! Crow's got a launch at one o'clock," Ekman's voice cuts through the howl of the RWR that has just lit up with a bright red launch light and a steady squealing launch tone so distinctly different from the buzzes and beeps that have been on since the border that it demands instant action.

"Crow two's Shrike away!" I see the fire-off of Crow two's wing as the missile comes off the rail. Both Thuds roll right toward the launch signal and bring the noses down as they dive for the ground. Cary starts right, and I follow into a descending right turn. I hear Socks grunting as the G loads increase and he tells me he's flipping the ECM pod into active. I'm watching the ground in the direction that the RWR vector tells me the threat is coming from. Two missiles erupt from a tiny village in a cloud of bright orange smoke and brown dust. They rise several hundred feet at about a 45-degree angle, then transition to nearly level flight. They're headed on an intercept that appears to cross our flight path somewhere ahead of us. It looks like no threat.

"Crow three, Crow three, heads up. We've got another missile airborne at left nine," I hear Socks eliminating the middleman and yelling at Cary over the radio. He's been looking out while I've been concentrating on the first two missiles. This one's come from another site and is a well-coordinated effort to bracket the hunter-killer flight with two missiles to distract us while a visually guided launch comes up from behind to slam the door. I roll left to check the new threat and pick up the bright white exhaust from the sustainer rocket. It's close and it's heading for three.

"Crow three, break left! Break left!" It's going to be close. Cary hears me, and I watch his airplane snap into a reversal. The nose swings up violently, and then the entire top of the airplane goes white in a condensation cloud as the controls bite into the humid air and disrupt the airflow over the wing surface. The plane seems to snap through the first 60 degrees of turn almost instantaneously. The missile passes just under the nose and detonates in a bright flash of fire and smoke. Cary's airplane emerges from the trailing edge of the blast and doesn't seem damaged. I'm lagging well behind his turn and now roll over to slice across the circle and cut him off to get back into position.

"Crow three, four's on your left, high and closing. You okay?"

"Uhhh, yeah. I think so. I think I've got a major over-G here." I'm not surprised. I've never seen an airplane change direction like that before.

"Crow three, this is lead. You need to take it out of here?" Lucky's level voice displays a serenity that indicates he's been through this at least a hundred times before. "If you guys need to head out, you're cleared off. Crow two will stay with me for a bit longer."

"Crow, roger. Crow three's headed outbound. Crow four, let's go bulls." Cary calls me over to the squadron discrete frequency so he can tell me his condition without interfering with the rest of the strike package comm. I acknowledge the change and Socks flips the channel.

"Crow four check."

"Four." We're almost to the mountains, and Larry

starts a climb. I've closed to about fifteen hundred feet and line abreast. I'll need to get closer to take a look, but we don't want to give up our tactical spread as long as there's an enemy threat.

"Roger, Crow three's okay. It looks like the G meter's pegged. I musta pulled something over ten. The airplane's flying alright, but one of the generators dropped off. It reset okay, so everything's working. Wanna close up and give me a look over?" We're well into the foothills now, and I close to tight formation. I stop on the right wing and look carefully over his airplane for damage. There are no apparent leaks or fluids streaming. The skin looks okay, with no wrinkles that would indicate a structural failure. I drop low and ease back under the tailpipes. The engine nozzles both match, and the lines of the keel look straight. There are some panel fasteners popped, but all the panels are apparently in place and secure. I come up on the left wing and check that side. Despite the more-than-ten-G maneuver, the airplane seems intact. I give Cary a thumbs-up.

"Crow three's gonna dump the CBU here to get the weight down a bit, but we'll keep the outboards. Looks like we've got enough gas to make it back to home plate without a tanker. You can keep your CBU if you've got enough gas." I ease wide and watch as he pickles off the four canisters. Larry looks at me and gives me a push-away hand signal to move out into a route formation. We head to Korat.

The mission is complete. More sorties on the statistics sheet. More tonnage on targets. It is a good day for the Air Force and a bad day for the Navy. We bring everyone home. The sailors lose a pair of airplanes near Kep. Tomorrow the ratio might swing the other way. And who knows about the day after?

◆ ◆ ◆

HANK SCHEIBLE AND I WERE sitting on the left side of
the CTF bar sucking on cold Budweisers and debating
whether we should head over to the club for some dinner. It took less than a couple of weeks to exhaust the
menu choices. There was gray meat with gravy, gray
meat with a bone, gray meat ground, gray meat with
tomato sauce, and gray meat chunks masquerading as
stew. You could get a soggy foil-wrapped baked potato,
or lumpy mashed. For variety there was an invention
from one of our WSOs, chili-cheese-rice-and-onions;
an artery-clogging, heartburn-inducing calorie load designed to coat the stomach for a long night of poker
playing and beer drinking.

Hank's eyebrows rose in the sort of conspiratorial
grin that he regularly displayed. "I've got an idea. Let's
grab a taxi and go downtown." It was an idea of dubious
merit. Korat city hadn't been high on the list of tourist
attractions during my last tour. Other than one or two
visits to Veena's for a squadron party and a couple of
pass-throughs to contract a Mercedes and driver for a
couple of days in Bangkok, there hadn't been much
reason to go downtown.

"I dunno," was my first reaction. "What's to do?"

"We won't know unless we go. C'mon. We'll go
down to the rub 'n' scrub for a massage, then get something to eat." He was enthusiastic. I was reluctant. He
pressed. I wavered. He got up to leave. I followed. We
headed over toward the BX, where there was a taxi
stand and bus stop. The bus cost two baht, a dime. The
taxi was twenty baht, a dollar. Scheible and I were combat aircrew and big spenders. We popped for the taxi.

The tiny Datsun, with its ripped vinyl seats and
sweaty driver, boasted a "certificate" stating that it was

approved by the base for operation on the airbase and throughout Korat city. That must have meant something with regard to operational safety checks, hygiene, lack of criminal potential, and knowledge of all the good spots for sex, drugs, and rock and roll. Or maybe it just meant the guy driving was a cousin or son-in-law of one of the Thai air force officers on the other side of the base who issued the certificates. There was no way of telling whether the document offered guarantees of anything other than a thrilling ride.

The taxi chugged in a cloud of blue smoke down the flight line road to the west gate. A wave of the hand by the Thai guard sent us off toward Friendship Highway, the four-lane from Bangkok to Korat. We circled around the departure end of the runway, blew through the stop sign in front of Veena's Farm, and accelerated to frightening velocity toward the city. It was only about ten miles, but it seemed a lot longer with the hot blast of air through the open windows, the careening and bouncing on worn shock absorbers, and the blatting of the engine through a rotted-out muffler as the driver churned up and down through the gears.

"Where you go?" was his only question, as he turned around to look into the backseat. At the speed we were going, it seemed prudent to keep the answer brief and get him looking forward again as soon as possible.

Scheible volunteered, "Korat Baths." He must have been there before, because he sounded authoritative. I was just along for the tour.

The scenery was Asian classic architecture, from the "unfinished" school of design. The essential simplicity would have made Mies van der Rohe proud. Buildings all seemed to be incomplete concrete or cinderblock slab structures, with open storefronts on the ground level and living quarters, usually without window glass or doors apparent on the second and third levels. I would find that regardless of the time of day or night, the lights were always on and the access at ground level was always wide open. A very limited number of the businesses seemed to have rusty accordion gates that expanded across the front, but most were open air and stayed that way.

The buildings were set back from the highway, and the unpaved dirt frontage area was often puddled with mud and trash. Sidewalks seemed to be an undiscovered nicety. Lighting was dim sixty-watt bulbs, hanging unshaded from bare wires. Most wiring appeared to be an afterthought, stapled to the walls' connecting fixtures with large, round switches screwed in at random. The occasional bright stores were most often small restaurants with fluorescents overhead and white tile walls. The brighter lights and tiles did little more than exaggerate the dinginess of the surroundings and the dirt on the tables, chairs, and counters. Mangy dogs were commonplace, slinking around near the fronts of almost every building hoping for a handout, but probably subsisting on trash and crawly things growing in the puddles.

As we approached the business sector, the buildings got closer to each other and to the highway. More of the stores seemed to aspire to western standards, with display windows and actual doors indicating they could be air-conditioned and might even possess something inside worth safeguarding. The road narrowed, and traffic congestion increased. Thankfully our driver fell in with the flow, which mixed taxis, diesel-belching trucks, buses filled to more than reasonable capacity with both

Thais and GIs, and bicycle based samlors.[1] Sidewalks were intermittent, curbs were nonexistent, and muddy stagnant ponds were everywhere.

Almost as a surprise, we turned a corner and were unquestionably in the commercial part of town. The street was lined with neon signs touting the attractions offered within, mostly in English. There were bars, strip joints, tailor shops, shoemakers, jewelry stores, and gaudy souvenir shops. The walkways beside the street, occasionally concrete, occasionally wooden duckboards, usually hard-packed dirt, were filled with people. Most of the males were Americans. Most of the females were Thai. The men were obviously GIs, some black, some white. All with close-cropped hair and between the ages of twenty and thirty-five. The girls were short and heavily made-up, wearing tight clothes and giggling brightly as they clutched at the men. Cheap perfume, aftershave, stale beer, diesel exhaust, and klong stench hung heavily in the humid air.

The taxi veered left down an angled street, past a well-lighted bus stop shelter currently hosting a gray-and-red bus that was disembarking another load of American military from the base. We bounced down a much darker side street for a couple of blocks, then took a hard left and pulled up to a large canopied storefront. The hand-painted lettering outlined with red neon on the white sign announced that we had arrived at the Korat Baths. A smiling doorman in white pants and a Hawaiian

---

1. Samlors are said to have been invented in Korat in 1933. The Thai version of a pedicab puts the cyclist in front and seats two small people or one large American. They usually offer a collapsible convertible top for inclement weather and have some battery-powered lighting for night.

shirt held the taxi door as we tipped the driver for graciously not killing us and stepped onto the street.

We entered the bathhouse and were greeted by a robust, jolly Thai woman who bade us enter and directed us through the lobby past a small standup bar toward a large glass window. The darkened room had one full wall of picture window that allowed customers to view the bath attendants. The dim reddish glow of the room made the brightness of the bull pen the focal point of attention. Behind the window was a small arena with three levels of benches, each occupied by eight to ten Thai girls. They were uniformly dressed in pink, one-piece waitress-style dresses, each with an octagonal red plastic badge above the left breast bearing a gold number. The girls were oblivious to the window and clustered in small groups of friends, laughing and chattering among themselves. Some showed an expanse of leg, with skirts hiked up, and others left a button or two open at the top of the dress to display a bit of cleavage.

"You see something you like?" the mama-san asked. "You wanna get good massage, you maybe wanna have numba' thutty-two or numba' sebenteen." She was either seeking our particular sexual proclivities or trying to drive business toward a girl having a slow night. I tried to see what thirty-two and seventeen looked like. Thirty-two was cute and smiling, actively engaged in some sort of disagreement with twenty-four. Seventeen was a homely farm girl sitting in the corner, trying to distance herself from the rest.

"Where's fourteen?" Hank wanted to know. I had been right. He'd been here before. Mama-san evaded the question with a semi-shrug and proposed that number twelve might be nice for him. A quick glance at the suggested masseuse and Hank nodded assent. He was led briskly toward the bull-pen door while Mama-san barked an order into a microphone.

The clear starlet of the second level was number thirty-five. She had four other girls around her as she animatedly recounted a story, probably regarding some eccentricity of a recent client. She was a bit taller than most, had a nicely rounded figure with bulges in all the right places, and a classic Eurasian face. Her huge brown eyes looked as though you could fall in and drown. Her wide mouth seemed permanently set in a welcoming smile, displaying beautiful white teeth and stretching across her face almost to the width of her dark eyes. She would be a beauty anywhere in the world, and clearly stood out from the group. Could she give a good massage? Frankly, Scarlett, I didn't give a damn.

"Number thirty-five." Mama-san nodded approval at my choice and went through the microphone business again. In seconds I was heading down the dark hallway behind a purposefully striding, but nevertheless arousing, butt in a pink dress.

The room was reasonably large, with a massage table in the center and an Asian-style square stone bath along the far wall. A rack of fresh towels was on one side of the deep tub. The girl immediately started the water, then signaled me to disrobe as she spread towels over the massage table. She was all business as she prepared my bath, pulled a cassette from a small bookshelf, and plugged it into the portable stereo on a nearby table. Then she shrugged out of her pink dress to stand expectantly before me, clad only in white panties. "Nights in White Satin" played softly and, quite appropriately I thought, in the background.

The water was pleasant as I stepped over the high

side into the tub. The girl lathered a small sponge and proceeded to wash me, directing me to stand, turn, immerse, rinse, close my eyes as she shampooed my hair and generally handled me like a six-foot, two-hundred-pound baby. The regular grazing of my back, chest, arms, and face by her now wet and soapy breasts kept me properly responsive to her ministrations. With a final rinse, she motioned for me to leave the tub and head for the table. I reached for a towel, but she indicated that wasn't necessary. She would handle everything. I was more than ready for everything to be handled.

I lay down on the table only to be directed to roll over onto my stomach. At this point, that took a bit of care and positioning. I managed as she giggled. She finished toweling me dry, then sprinkled me lightly with talcum and went over my backside with the towels again. Then she softly took one hand and extended my arm straight out from the table. With a bit of baby oil to lubricate, she began at my fingers, gently rubbing, stroking, flexing, and pulling. One by one she worked the fingers then progressed to the palm, the wrist, and the forearm. By the time she got to my elbow and upper arm, I was beginning to feel a total relaxation that started from one corner of my body and was an indication that when the whole process was over, I'd not have a physical care left in the world. Just to ensure that she could get the proper leverage and angle to knead my arm while keeping it straight, she placed my hand between her breasts. Each time I edged to the left or right from the designated spot in the center, she giggled and firmly replaced the hand in the neutral spot. Rather than frustrating, this kept the sexual tension high.

After the second arm, she started at the toes. The same procedure as the arms, up the back of each leg, eventually reaching my back and shoulders. It was incredibly relaxing, but I wondered what would happen on the front side. I didn't want the back to finish, but couldn't wait for the front to start. All too soon, but not as soon as I wanted, I got the order to roll over. Rampant on a field of white terry cloth, I lay. More giggling as she draped a towel over my pelvis, creating a small but erect tent. Then thighs, chest, neck, and even face were ministered to. I got massages in places I hadn't known I had muscles.

Previously unnoticed, on the table next to the portable stereo, a white oven timer rang. "Time a'mos up," the girl announced. "You wanna nudda hour? Hundred more baht." She was a master of her trade. I'd been prodded, kneaded, loosened and tensed for the proper period of time, but the expected conclusion of the ministrations wasn't going to come during the first period. If I wanted to see whether the implied was actually going to be delivered, I would need to double my investment. The sudden realization of what I should have known all along, that this was a business proposition first and foremost, put considerable slack in the terry-cloth tent. I decided I'd rather head for dinner, since it was inconceivable that I could take much more massaging and the other activity wouldn't take anywhere near an hour. I shook my head in the negative and rolled off the table.

By the time I got dressed, I heard another door down the hall being opened. I emerged from my chamber just in time to see Scheible emerging two doors down, buttoning his shirt. "You all cleaned out?" he asked.

"Not quite. But close enough. You got a place in mind to eat?"

"Let's go to the KR Club. It's a disco in the Korat Hotel. I hear they've got a Filipino band, lots of girls, and a restaurant." It was apparent that Hank was a pretty well-trained tour guide.

"How'd you find all this out?" We headed out the door and jumped into one of the waiting cabs. Hank hadn't been at Korat for more than a week or two longer than I had. He was obviously a quick study on the local culture. He must have fallen under the leadership of an older and more experienced front-seater immediately upon arrival.

It took just a few minutes to get to the white stucco, neon-lined doorway of the Korat Hotel. It was everything that Hank had been told. A dark, smoky, candlelight disco with a loud band and lots of young Thai girls sitting two by two at tables set for four, and a brightly lighted restaurant just beyond the nightclub entrance. The hotel aspect of the place looked like it primarily rented rooms by the hour. The food, however, was pretty good.

Yeah, I thought to myself, Sherman was right. War is hell.

7. BAHT CHAINS AND BUDDHAS

What they could do with 'round here is a good war. What else can you expect with peace running wild all over the place? You know what the trouble with peace is? No organization!

—Bertolt Brecht, *Mother Courage and Her Children* (1941), Act I

IT WAS EASY TO GET to the Korat Hotel. It was one of the three or four major destinations for the base taxi drivers. There was the bathhouse, the KR Club at the Korat Hotel, the SP Club at the Sripatana Hotel, and probably a couple of Indian tailor shops. By seven or eight o'clock most nights, lines of people waited at the base taxi stand for the trip to town. Get dropped off at either of the two hotel clubs and you were within walking distance of all the sins that any young American fighting man could want. Whatever you sought, you could find it within minutes. I didn't know what I was looking for, so it took me a little longer.

The club at the Korat Hotel offered a lot of small tables, waitress service of watered drinks or icy Singha beer, and a smorgasbord of powdered, perfumed, and willing Thai girls hoping to meet a free-spending GI for a couple of hours, a couple of weeks, or a lifetime.

There was a slightly off-key Filipino band that played covers of American and British rock albums; not songs but whole albums learned rote from start to finish. When they started Santana's *Abraxas,* you could expect to hear every note in order, just as on the original record. "Oye Como Va" was always right after "Black Magic Woman," every night starting just a few minutes after ten. They weren't good, but they were loud.

It took me about three trips to connect. So much was going on in my head, ranging from overcoming my uptight Catholic sexual upbringing to sublimating the macho idea that paying for sex is somehow unmanly. When you spend your days looking for people trying to kill you with missiles, a little bit of commercial sex in the evening seemed like a pretty minor sin, after all. I certainly had plenty of sinning company in Korat city, and while American mores might not find the behavior acceptable, America was a long way off. The Thais seemed to view sex as natural, and the opportunity for folks to make a reasonable living at the business of pleasure was simply icing on the cake.

A certain level of caution was required, since the sex industry was an equal opportunity employer. There were cute girls and hardened girls. There were older girls and younger girls, some of whom were way too young. And there were some girls who weren't girls at all. The *katoi* was always a possibility. They might be called transgendered or transvestites or maybe just female impersonators. They occasionally were quite obvious, but most of the time they were beautiful and looked every bit a desirable partner for the flower of American manhood. The Thais didn't seem to pay much attention to them and probably got a lot of laughs from the surprise when an American thinking he'd conquered the loveliest woman in the bar discovered his error. It wasn't uncommon for coworkers, whether officer or enlisted, aviators or maintainers, to aim a new guy in town at the "sweet young thing" all alone at a dark corner table.

I visited the KR Club a couple of nights in a row. I danced self-consciously with one or two girls and usually wound up heading back to the base near midnight. In the dark of the nightclub it was difficult to see who you were meeting, and the blare of the band made it impossible to talk, even if a language difference didn't exist. Then one night I noticed a quiet girl sipping a Coke in a far corner of the room. She wore a flowered print dress that was attractive without looking whorish. She had a cute smile and deep dimples, huge dark eyes, and mid-length shiny black hair. She wasn't on the main route to the dance floor, the dining room, or the bar, so she was overlooked by most of the predators in the room. I watched an occasional GI approach her, but she seemed quite selective in whom she danced with. She accepted my offer, and then I sat with her and bought her another Coke. About two hours later I went home with her.

We took a taxi ten blocks or so down the main artery of Korat city, past the Sripatana Hotel and down a lighted side street to a small restaurant and grocery building. The driver dropped us off, and she took my hand, leading me across the street into a dark area that contained a half-dozen two-story teak buildings, each apparently a single-family dwelling. The grouping was alongside a small klong, and pools of stagnant water filled the spaces between the houses. The door was open downstairs, and the lower level was mostly empty space with a small Asian "bombsight" toilet and shower on a side room off the open living area. She led me up the stairs to a large bedroom with a low king-size bed, a small dresser, a nightstand, and a lamp. A Japanese oscillating fan sat on the floor, waiting to be summoned into service. Open unscreened windows on three sides allowed for comfortable tropical breezes to cool the room. She turned on the fan, lit a small mosquito-repellant coil, and placed it atop a can on the floor near the dresser. Visions of a hospital stay racked with malaria came immediately to mind. She disrobed and all worries about mosquitoes left my mind.

THE HUNTER-KILLER MISSION BECAME SECOND NATURE. Every day the same group of Weasels met with the same small group of Phantom drivers to follow the same routes to the same targets. We were always first in, last out, shielding the force on the side of greatest threat, letting the Weasel poke his nose at signals, then firing his missiles, sometimes at real missile sites and sometimes at ephemeral electronic will-o'-the-wisps that maybe were caused by sunspots or the phase of the moon. We blustered about "Dr. Pepper" situations, a euphemism for missiles surrounding you at "ten, two and four" like the clock on the soft-drink bottle. We expressed hope during briefings that maybe we could get them to fire at us so that we could find them and attack, but I confess that my hope was that the SAM operators would be taking the day off for some national holiday of which I wasn't aware. Everyday we had the same call signs, birds of prey. We were Eagle, Condor, Crow, Hawk, Falcon, and everyone in the force knew who the

SAM killers were. It became routine on the post-strike tanker, as we headed back to Korat, to hear flight leads check in on our frequency with a "thanks, Condor," acknowledging that maybe we had helped to make their job for the day a bit easier.

Strangely, every Linebacker specialist group pointed at someone else that had it tougher. The bombers thought the SAM killers had it rough. The hunter-killer teams thought the laser illuminators who orbited the target while waiting for a bomb to fall had to be special. The illuminators gave the nod to chaffers who held formation, straight and level through the worst of flak and SAM country, to lay the corridors of radar-baffling foil to protect the strike. The chaffers freely gave credit to the MiGCAP troops who chased and engaged enemy aircraft, dueling one-on-one to the death with missiles and guns against a highly experienced enemy. Few ever said their job was the tough one. Someone else always had it worse.

The target for the day was the Viet Tri military storage area again. It was right on the banks of the Red River, a stone's throw from the MiG base at Phuc Yen and well within range of all the SAM sites that surrounded Hanoi. The good news was that it wasn't far from the mountains and didn't require a long transit across the flat rice paddies of the delta. Exposure for the bomb droppers would be intense but of relatively short duration. For the hunter-killers there would be ample opportunity to excel. We would shield on the Hanoi side, fly past the target, shield on the Phuc Yen side, fly around the target, and shield some more. First in, last out.

We were Eagle today. Ed Cleaveland was lead

Weasel, with Dave Kennedy, a first-tour Weasel with talent and the courage to make it work, on his wing. I had Bill Feisel in my pit, a bulky guy with a big grin and wry sense of humor who never seemed too tense about anything. Charlie Price was flying my wing with Bob Dowden. Cleaveland, who had been in the Weasel business for a long time, followed the standard practice when the briefing room door closed of talking about what we were going to do rather than repeating the cover-your-ass details that everybody knew but was required to repeat so that the higher-ups who weren't flying the mission couldn't be blamed when an accident happened.

We'd let the Weasel snoop and feint at signals, call the warnings when necessary, stuff a Shrike down a radar's throat when possible, and point out SAM sites if seen. The F-4 element would chase a Shrike if we could, follow a SAM launch plume back to the site, and if nothing happened by the time the bombers were working the target, visually recce the area east and around Phuc Yen to kill any sites that had been too timid to come up and talk to us. If we didn't expend our CBU by the time the strike force was outbound, we'd dump on the airfield at Phuc Yen or Yen Bai as we headed outbound. It was Dr. Pepper time.

A light rain was falling as we preflighted, but the refueling track and the target area were forecast to be clear. The radar trail departure worked as advertised. The Weasels rolled with thirty seconds' spacing, then I rolled down the runway. Well before liftoff, Feisel had the two Weasels on the radar. The second blip followed the first with about two miles of spacing. As lead turned right, he drifted off the centerline to be followed in a few seconds by two. A quiet buzz of the RWR told me that Charlie had locked onto my aircraft and was following the parade into the clouds. We held a constant airspeed, playing follow the leader and climbing until we broke out into sunshine at just over twelve thousand feet. We closed to fingertip formation and headed for the tanker.

We got gas, the tankers extended their track up to the 20-degree north drop-off point, and the strike package headed to the target. I had the element on the right side, spread about six thousand feet and riding about 30 degrees back from line abreast. Visibility was good. We blew the centerlines as soon as they emptied, and I wasn't a bit surprised when Eagle lead announced that he had a Bar Lock early warning radar and might be getting rid of the Standard. Mike O'Brian, Cleaveland's bear called, "Eagle lead, shotgun," and the huge missile took off roaring ahead of the flight, then turning upward as if it had aspirations to become *Apollo 20*. Ah, the power of the warrior, to so easily turn a million dollars of taxpayer investment into a fireworks display for a very small audience.

We cruised onward, peering toward the Red River delta and waiting for the rest of the show to start. The air was clear, the sun was bright, the airplane was comfortable. "Look out!" The scream was urgent. I snapped my head left just in time to see a flash by my wingtip, a white body hurtling straight down from who knew where. Who was that? What was that?

"Eagle three, did you see that?" It was Charlie's voice.

"Sorry about that, Eagles," O'Brien said. The Standard had come back, falling well short of its lunar aspirations and apparently deciding that the shortest distance to whatever radar it might be seeking was directly through the middle of our flight. I knew how to evade SAMs. I knew about fighting MiGs, at least I thought I did. I didn't know what to do about errant radar-hunting missiles that didn't differentiate between friend and enemy. Straight up was not a place I normally expected the threat to come from.

We eased down from altitude until we were in the flats, just east of Phu Tho, headed toward Hanoi at about five thousand feet over the ground. The headset was filled with the buzz of Firecans, and the center of the RWR scope was a green amoeba with tendrils extending randomly to the outer edges of the display. An occasional Fan Song rattled through the noise, but nothing sounded like a real threat. The launch light flickered on and off but never came to full brilliance. "Pretty quiet, Eagles. Guns only." The Weasel confirmed what I thought.

"Okay, Eagles, we've got some activity now. Looks like it's coming from near Phuc Yen. Heads up." His equipment was telling him more than mine. I didn't have anything serious going on. I asked Feisel how Charlie looked. "He's okay, holding near line abreast. Looking good." There was a lot to be said for flying with the same guys regularly. I glanced right and saw him exactly where I would be if I'd been on the wing. We angled northward toward the airfield.

"Launch. We've got a launch out of Phuc Yen. Eagles, we've got a launch."

The RWR was screaming now. The rattlesnake of the Fan Song and the steady wail of the launch tone made it unnecessary to look at the scope. The twin orange trails of the missile boosters did a good job of showing where the site was without an electronic vector as well. The missiles arched upward, one after the other, and headed toward the Weasel. I eased right, away from the -105s, waiting to see if the SAMs tracked them or us. I checked the master arm switch on, even though we had set the weapons switches right after we'd dumped the centerline tank. "Eagle Three's got the site," I called to let Charlie know we were attacking. "You ready, Bill?" It was an unnecessary question: he knew his job.

The missiles leveled off and flew past lead, oblivious to the airplanes and either dedicated to some other flight in the area or now ballistic as the SAM operators realized that they were in the crosshairs. "Eagle three's up," I pulled up slightly and rolled left, almost inverted until I could get the nose back down onto the bulldozed area that marked the launch site. We were low and close. This must have been a new installation, because the camouflage wasn't yet in place and the site was obviously naked. "Three's in."

The missile site was in the reticle. The radar scope showed a lockup, and as I let the pipper drift up onto an olive drab missile on a transporter truck, I crushed the pickle button. We pulled four, then five G and almost missed the radio call as Price called onto the target and warned of a missile passing us from another site. We were tight, but this guy wasn't going to shoot anymore today. Coming off the pass, the place was buzzing with 23mm tracer, interlacing yellowish trails trying to sew us up in a tight little bag.

I pulled off to the right and saw Charlie coming off the target, and could tell immediately that he had me in sight and was cutting the corner to get back to line abreast. "Eagle four, let's get out of here," was my unneeded radio call. We twisted the airplanes to the north, then checked left to look back at the results. The sparkle of CBU detonations was covering the site. Price and I were line abreast, four thousand feet apart, and jinking left and right in a rhythm like two experienced ballroom dancers doing a tango. We were just past the end of the MiG base runway, barely a thousand feet above the ground.

"Eagle three, you've still got CBU."

It wasn't what I wanted to hear. I glanced at the weapons control panel, and the glowing lights told me that I hadn't gotten a release. There wasn't any clue in the way the airplane handled, but Price's visual check had seen the weapons still hanging on the racks. "Eagle lead, three. We're northbound along the ridge. Say your position." I wasn't sure what the next step was, but if I still had ordnance, we might be needed against another site.

"Eagle lead's outbound, just west of the target. The force is outbound in the clear ahead of us. We're climbing, heading two four zero. We'll meet you at the tanker."

It wasn't uncommon to come out of the target area as two separate elements. Occasionally we would do it when one element had excess fuel remaining or, more often, as in today's situation, when we got split up while attacking or defending against a missile site. I flashed a wing left to indicate a left turn, and saw Price cut hard left and pass behind me. I completed the 90 left and found us aimed straight at the Yen Bai runway. "Eagle four, I'm going to dump on the runway ahead. Be off left outbound." I reached down and rotated the weapons mode switch to direct and salvo to get rid of all the CBU in one quick pass. No dive toss on this one. I popped just slightly and pulled down on the broad greenish expanse of concrete that formed the only visible part of the MiG base. I would have loved to see some airplanes on the ground, but they were either heavily camouflaged or out of town for the weekend visiting relatives in China. The airplane shuddered slightly as the canisters came off. I pulled left, picked up Price on my left side, and looked back at the runway. The canisters hit about two thousand feet from the far end, exploding like 500-pound bombs on the concrete. They hadn't had time to open after coming off the airplane.

We climbed out over the Red River, Feisel hunched over the radar scope searching for aircraft ahead of us. "What happened, Bill? Why didn't we get a dive-toss release? How come the cans didn't open like they're supposed to? Huh?" I didn't like it when stuff didn't work.

"I don't think the system had time to work. You were in pretty close. Shit, I could see guys running on the ground. I think you must have been inside the computer solution, so it simply wouldn't let you drop." Bill had the answer. It wasn't the equipment's fault. It was mine. We'd been too tight, too low, too close to the target for the computer to let me release. It was casting the deciding vote on whether I should be allowed to endanger myself and my airplane by dropping a bomb where it might kill me as well as the enemy. The electronics had a veto. Unseen behind my oxygen mask, I grinned at a flash of HAL 9000 overriding its human masters in the movie *2001: A Space Odyssey*.

"What about the runway?"

"Too low to allow the radar fuse to function and open the canisters. Low-order impact was probably just as good. We had them set to open 1,200 feet above the ground, you released at about 600." I shook my head without comment, wondering what poor Feisel must have been thinking as I pulled this stuff. He'd shown a lot of confidence that I wasn't going to get us killed, but I wasn't sure, at that moment, if it had been deserved. "I've got contacts. A pair at eleven o'clock, looks like about fifteen miles ahead, slightly high," he finished the weapons delivery debrief and the rejoin contact without taking a breath.

We caught up with Cleaveland, got our gas on the post-strike tanker, and received the usual expressions of gratitude from other flights on the frequency. Eagle was appreciated, and we had a good SAM kill for the day. Just north of Korat, we contacted approach control to hear that the weather was twelve hundred feet overcast and two miles' visibility in rain. It didn't sound like a major problem. "Eagle, Korat approach. Command post advises that you divert to Takhli because of weather."

Cleaveland acknowledged and we checked right about 30 degrees, headed for the approach fix at Takhli. Low clouds covered the countryside, but we had a TACAN lock immediately and our INS showed the heading and distance to the airfield. "Takhli approach, this is Eagle with four for landing," Ed called for clearance.

"Roger, Eagle. Takhli is eight hundred overcast, visibility a mile to a mile and a half in light rain. Cleared high TACAN one approach to runway three six. Call departing the final approach fix." Great, just great. Some wing weenie at Korat was protecting his butt by diverting us from home plate to a field with worse weather. Eagle lead rocked his wings, and we all closed up the formation. We started our descent into the murk. I knew Cleaveland well enough to know he was holding the exact same thought regarding the fool at home.

We descended in four-ship and turned to align with the final approach course. Lead called departing the final approach fix, and Takhli approach asked for our landing sequence. Cleaveland moved us into right echelon and told the tower, "Eagle's got four for initial." It was a classic fighter pilot act of defiance. The weather was crap, we'd been diverted from home, and if this was a good place to divert, then we'd fly a visual approach and land out of an overhead pattern. Screw 'em all!

EAGLE IS UNDER THE CLOUDS now. We're aligned with the final approach course, and in the murk and rain we can see below us but not very far ahead. Ed waves and breaks left. Five seconds later Kennedy breaks. I take spacing and roll crisply into a hard left turn, in and out of the cloud bases. I can just barely see the runway. Gear, flaps, time to turn. "Eagle three, base, gear check." I can dimly make out the flashing approach lights in the rain. I receive landing clearance and touch down in a spray of water. We roll off the runway, dump our drag chutes, and taxi into parking in a Thunderbird display of four-ship chutzpah.

We park the airplanes shoulder to shoulder along a blocked-off taxiway. There are at least twenty airplanes from Korat in a long line. Blue vans arrive and whisk us away to maintenance and then intel for debrief. A few of the flight leads get on the phone back to Korat to determine when we can return. The answer seems to be sometime in the morning.

A blue school bus arrives and takes us to a large rambling hacienda sort of structure that houses aircrews on temporary duty. The one-story teak building rambles in all directions with wings and ells housing two rooms here and four rooms there. A central lounge area has been converted to a bar. The place is filled with diverted aircraft; some from Ubon and Udorn, a big contingent from Korat, and then the recently arrived deployed crews from the States. There are F-4 crews from Seymour Johnson, Holloman, and Homestead Air Force Bases in the States and a detachment of newly arrived F-111 drivers from Las Vegas. A lot of guys know a lot of guys, so we quickly renew old acquaintances and claim an empty bunk for the night. It doesn't take long before everyone is reassembled in the bar with a cold beer.

One beer leads to another, which leads to some whiskey, which then leads to singing bawdy songs, telling raunchy stories, engaging in infantile games like dead bug, in which someone shouts "dead bug" and everyone flops on their backs on the floor with arms and legs in the air. Last guy to hit the floor buys the next round. Arguments ensue about who's last, and inevitably someone refuses to buy. It hardly makes a difference, because all the diverted Korat crews don't have wallets or personal items in their pockets on combat missions, so we don't have any money anyway. There's wrestling and arguing and physical contests and more drinking. Slowly the party begins to wind down. Individuals drift off to rooms and shed sweaty Nomex flight suits to crawl into beds. The dwindling crowd in the bar compensates for loss of numbers by increasing the volume. Little sleeping occurs.

Lights flick on to greet thumping headaches and camel-dung mouths. My wristwatch says three o'clock. "C'mon. We gotta go." Cleaveland's bear is gathering the hungover remnants of Eagle flight. "Command post needs the airplanes back to load for a ten o'clock go.

We've got an hour to get airborne."

Doors slam and curses fill the halls. Pilots and WSOs, Weasels and bears stumble out, pulling on flight suits and dragging G suits, survival vests, and helmet bags. The damned blue bus is sitting in front of the building, softly belching exhaust as we careen down the walkway. One of the other Weasels is sporting a gradually swelling black eye. He's been punched by an F-111 pilot while starting to urinate on the swing-wing driver's bed. The night's revelry has taken a toll, and it is apparent that many regulations regarding crew rest and drinking have been abandoned. The stupidity of the divert is compounded by the predawn return.

We launch. The flight to Korat takes barely twenty minutes. We land in the first glow of a rising sun and turn the airplanes over to the maintenance crews. Little is said in debrief, and we simply disappear down the road to our individual hootches. The day will be spent sleeping and recovering. Someone else will be going to Hanoi today.

THE GIRL'S NAME WAS SOPIN. It was a nickname, used by Thai and *farang* alike in preference to the long polytonal and multisyllabic formal names of most Thais. The girls in the O club dining room, the taxi drivers, the bartenders, all had short names, easy to pronounce and remember but not very distinctive. There were literally dozens of Nits and Noys, the brief adjective that indicates small or tiny. At Korat we had a Pom and a Jeed and a Dang. I didn't know of any other Sopins.

She was cute and vivacious. She spoke understandable English, indicating a series of relationships with

Behind the bar in the Crew Training Facility (CTF) in her 34th Tac Fighter Squadron party suit is one of several local girls who kept the place organized.

RIGHT Bob Slockbower finished his year-long combat tour at Korat and was reassigned. Within a few short weeks he was deployed with his new squadron back to Thailand, where he continued to fly combat through the Linebacker II campaign. *(Courtesy of Dr. Ed Parker, flight surgeon of the 469th TFS)*

LEFT Dee Lewis introduced me to combat in the F-4E and helped me to appreciate the value of a good partner in a two-place airplane.

Unless otherwise stated, photos courtesy of Ed Rasimus.

Despite two gear-up landings and a tendency to fly sideways, Arnold the Pig seemed to make the schedule every day. Here's Arnold taxiing with a full load of twelve Mk-82 bombs.

An H-43 "Pedro" rescue helicopter hovers nearby as an F-4E engages an approach end barrier in an emergency landing.

A moment of distraction nearly cost Tiger FAC Charlie Price his life in the low threat environment of Cambodia.

An F-4 about to launch. The Navy was a heavy player, both day and night, from carriers in the Gulf of Tonkin.

Charong waiting for a customer relaxes for a few minutes. The samlor drivers practically lived in their vehicles through all kinds of weather.

Beside a small Christmas tree, during the brutal days of Linebacker II, Barry Johnson relaxes with a drink and some small talk with one of the club's waitresses.

Returning from a mission with empty bomb racks, this F-4E of the 469th TFS displays the Korat shark-mouth paint job. *(Courtesy of Don Logan)*

The author leans against a bomb-loaded wing before launching on a Linebacker mission.

RIGHT A quick wit, a broad smile, a disk-jockey's baritone voice, and exceptional skills as a fighter pilot made Gyle Atwood (right) a valuable member of the group. Here he checks out a magazine in the squadron lounge before a briefing.

LEFT Hank Schieble catches some sun on the lawn in front of the CTF.

A pair of F-105G Wild Weasels and their F-4E Phantom partners from the Hunter/Killer team. Here they ride the wing of a tanker midway through a rescue effort. Note the bombs remaining on the Phantoms, but most missiles have been expended by the Weasels. *(Courtesy of the U.S. Air Force)*

> HERE LIES
> ROSCOE
> CAME TO KORAT IN 1965
> DIED HERE ON 13 SEPT 1975
>
> "I SPENT ALL OF MY LIFE WAITING FOR MY MASTER. BUT HE NEVER RETURNED FROM NORTH VIETNAM. NOW WE ARE TOGETHER, AND I AM HAPPY TO SEE HIM AGAIN. ONLY GOD CAN PART US NOW."
>
> PRESENTED TO WING ONE ROYAL THAI AIR FORCE FROM 44TH TACTICAL FIGHTER SQUADRON (F-15) COMMANDO WEST II 1 DEC 1986

A deployed F-15 squadron at Korat, eleven years after Roscoe's death, installed this poignant memorial to the dog that was a friend of every fighter pilot, but most especially to Ray Lewis, his original owner. *(Courtesy of the U.S. Air Force)*

My back-seater for a large part of the year, Kirby Carlton, never wanted a fighter job but did what was asked without question.

Sopin is part Lao and part Thai and moved comfortably between the back streets of Korat city and the finest hotels and restaurants of the capital. She showed me the best that Thailand had to offer.

Roscoe in repose. This photo from the Korat base newspaper was published with the faithful dog's obituary in 1975. *(Courtesy of the U.S. Air Force from the* Sawadee Flyer *newspaper)*

Sopin strikes a pose at the Rose Garden, a theme park near Bangkok, which featured half-scale replicas of major palaces and historic buildings of Thailand.

Spike Milam, the Raven FAC, is in his working clothes and accompanied by his faithful steed. He is clearly not meeting USAF uniform standards, nevertheless, he is fighting in this strange war. *(Courtesy of Spike Milam)*

Americans over the six or seven years of the war being fought from Korat. Sopin knew her way around town and was willing to be my guide, my dinner companion, my interpreter, my lover, and, she hoped, maybe my wife someday. All for a hundred bucks a month. She became my *tee-lock,* or hired wife. I became a regular rider of the two-baht bus to town several evenings a week, returning by bus or taxi in the wee hours to grab a shower and shave, then show up for briefing. When I saw Mama-san she began to greet me as Butterfly, the Thai metaphor for one who samples the sweetness of many flowers.

Sopin introduced me to Charong, a samlor driver. He might have been her brother or maybe a cousin, or maybe just a friend. He was definitely her protector and guardian angel. He was darkly tanned and, watching the bulging muscles of his legs as he peddled his vehicle down the streets of Korat, you had no doubt that he could hold his own in any street fight. When Sopin and I went to the KR Club, Charong was our transportation. When I came to town, he was waiting at the bus stop, turning down other fares and available only to me. When I spent the night in the teak bungalow, he slept curled up in the passenger seat of his samlor on the street in front of the house. If I needed to get up at three in the morning to get back to the base, there was no need for an alarm clock. Charong whistled a wake-up call from outside the window, ready to drive me to the bus stop or taxi stand. While with him I would not have my pocket picked, my watch stolen, or my meal tampered with.

Local protection was one thing, but everyone in Korat city knew what we did and what the risks were. Air Force fighters had been operating at the base and flying combat since 1964, nearly eight full years. We had long ago given up efforts to deny what was going on. Sopin had corralled a fighter pilot and she didn't want him harmed. That meant I would need a little bit of long-range protection, something more than Charong could provide on the back streets. Sopin hadn't heard about St. Christopher, but she knew that Buddha could help. I would need a Buddha if I was to survive. It had to be a special, powerful Buddha, not the cheap plastic or tin versions available on every street corner. It needed some extra pizzazz not available in the off-the-shelf Buddhas that every Tom, Dick, and Hanuman might be carrying. She told me to bring ten bucks and get to town by eight o'clock Wednesday night.

Charong met me at 7:30 at the bus stop. He laughed and waved me into the samlor seat, then rose in the pedals and took off down the street at a brisk pace. As we went, he gestured at an unusual number of saffron-robed monks headed down the road, all seeming to be late for an important event. Glancing over his shoulder, he pointed at me and signaled that I was "same-same monks." Headed toward a nightly shack-up with my *tee-lock*, I didn't see a lot of parallels with the celibate holy men.

Sopin was dressed and ready when I arrived. She pointed across the street from the bungalow at the open front store where a group of Thais were lined up, apparently waiting to enter the small tea house and restaurant. There were at least forty people, some monks, some women, even some children, all waiting. "Let's go," she pointed at the end of the line. Apparently this was the event for the night.

Initially I felt conspicuous as the only six-foot

farang, but the smiles and waves of the neighbors soon made me feel part of the family. A number of the people spoke their few words of English, helping me to understand what was going on. "Buddha-man come. Very holy. Make happy, make safe." Some must have had some Christian missionary exposure, as they described the event. "Buddha priest. Big blessing man. Holy man."

This was a long way from a Jimmy Swaggart revival. There wasn't any hand waving or hymn singing. No blues band played the introduction, and there wasn't any fall-down-with-the-spirit sort of healing going to happen. This was a small, frail, shaven-headed man in a standard saffron robe, in a small room in a side-street family restaurant. He sat cross-legged on a woven mat on the floor, and spoke quietly to the people who came forward in ones and twos to receive his wisdom and his blessing. He didn't lecture on sin and punishment or fire and brimstone. He simply listened to people, and then touched them on a shoulder and whispered something to them. They got what they needed and learned about a simple way of life. He asked nothing, but apparently provided much to the people who came to him.

When we got to the head of the line, Sopin signaled for me to remove my shoes and place them by the doorway. By example, she motioned for me to kneel and enter the presence of the monk on my knees. We approached, and he showed no surprise at the arrival of an American. Sopin spoke briefly to the monk, and he smiled at me. He turned to a small canvas knapsack behind him and rummaged briefly through the contents. He retrieved something, then extended his hands to me.

Sopin mimed, returning the two-handed gesture. I reached forward and the monk placed a small stone square image of the Buddha between my palms, then pressed them together with his hands and softly intoned a brief prayer in Thai. It took about twenty seconds.

"It is yours. Buddha protects you now." The monk spoke some English. I brought my hands, holding the stone between them, to my forehead in a *wai*, the gesture of Thai respect so similar to the folded hands of my Catholic childhood. The monk did not return my *wai* but bowed his head ever so slightly toward me. Sopin quietly signaled that we must leave, and to back up on our knees out of the room. I somehow felt I'd had a very special experience. We left.

Charong smiled as we approached. Sopin chattered away at him, describing the monk and the ceremony. He turned backward in the saddle of the samlor and *wai*'d toward me. Apparently I had gained considerable esteem. "Must get you chain now. You wear Buddha every day. Okay?" Sopin wanted some assurance that I understood the importance of the whole thing. I was just cogitating on the fact that I thought I had now succeeded in violating each and every one of the Ten Commandments. I'd been passing up the Sabbath for a while, I'd been disrespectful to my parents a bit, I'd been in the business of killing folks professionally and recently had taken to habitual adultery. Now I was carrying a strange idol in my pocket and was about to package it in gold and wear it around my neck each day as I went into battle. Isn't life strange?

We headed toward the old downtown section of Korat city. Here was the original village square and the commercial center of the second largest city in Thailand. This was away from the bars and neon of the GI-infested newer section. There were clothing shops and hardware stores, plus a row of about twenty glittering, brightly lighted gold shops. Each shallow storefront had the same decorations of red-enameled signs, gold filigree display cases, and row upon row of gold chains. The gold was sold by weight, and the craftsmanship of the chains was simply a bonus. Chains were weighed in baht, the weight of the basic coin, about the size of the US nickel. A baht weighted about fifteen grams. A one-baht chain sold for about thirty-five dollars and was typically about the size of our standard dogtag chain. A two-baht chain could be longer or the same length, but with thicker links. It weighed twice as much. Chains ranged up to four, five, or more baht. The gold was nearly pure, twenty-four karat, so soft you could scratch it with a fingernail.

My Buddha required a two-baht chain and a gold sheet case to hold it. We negotiated with the merchant not for the cost of the gold, which was fixed by the market, but for the style of the case and the type of links for my chain. I could pick up the case tomorrow, ready to wear. I would henceforth be protected.

8. MIXED MESSAGES

Four brave men who do not know each other will not
dare to attack a lion. Four less brave, but knowing each
other well, sure of their reliability and consequently of
mutual aid, will attack resolutely.

—Charles Ardant du Picq, 1870

ARNOLD NEEDED A FRIEND. NO one liked Arnold. Everyone in the squadron, it seemed, tried to avoid Arnold. It
wasn't his fault. He'd been abused, and the scars of that
abuse couldn't be erased. He just couldn't go straight.
He wandered to the left for a while, then to the right.
Most of the time he just went a little bit sideways. All
this meandering took a lot of energy, and the result was
that Arnold consumed a lot more than those around
him. Arnold was known as "the pig," after the family
pet on the *Green Acres* television show. I decided to
stick up for Arnold.

It was the two gear-up landings that had warped
Arnold beyond what the best maintenance people could
straighten. They could align all of the reference points
in accordance with the tech orders and certify the airplane for flight, but Arnold still remained out of whack.
Trim the airplane to center the ball in the turn-and-slip

indicator, and he'd fly along for about a minute, perfectly coordinated. Then, with a barely perceptible nudge, the ball went off to the left and Arnold slewed through the air in a skid again. Trim one more time and it would last for seconds before he skidded in the other direction. The result was that Arnold was always flying sideways and consumed more gas than any airplane in the flight. Arnold, tail number 69-7267, was one of only two airplanes in the 469th that had a name. The other was Marcia, 69-7551, who bore the ignominy of being named after a female maintenance officer. She was a bit temperamental—the airplane, not the maintainer.

Pilots and WSOs were being assigned aircraft, and no one wanted Arnold. I'd had my name on airplanes before, and it wasn't a very big deal to me which one it was. I'd be leading most of the time, using less fuel, and if I wasn't, I still felt that I could be smooth enough to compensate for Arnold's gluttonous appetite. I agreed to take Arnold. Socks was within a couple of weeks of completing his year tour, so although his name would be on the back cockpit he didn't object because he wouldn't have to ride the pig very often.

It was an election year, and the campaign was heating up. President Nixon was in a battle with George McGovern about who was going to end the war more quickly. We'd been Vietnamizing for several years, drawing down the American presence with the goal of letting the people fight for their own freedom. That didn't quite explain what we were doing in Thailand every day, where the bombing packages seemed as large as ever. No one wanted to be the last person to die in a losing cause, yet we all continued to fight as though we were about to win.

On August 29, the president announced that we

would be down to 27,000 troops in South Vietnam by the end of the year. Seemingly within hours of the announcement, we got called into a squadron meeting. The 469th Tactical Fighter Squadron was to be deactivated by the end of the fiscal year. Within thirty days we were to box up the memorabilia of eight years' worth of flying and fighting, and ship everything that said 469th to the archives in St. Louis. Folks within sixty days of completing their tour would leave immediately. Others would transfer, along with the squadron's airplanes, to merge with squadrons at Udorn. A few crews would be chosen to remain at Korat and become part of the 34th, which would become an "augmented" squadron, larger than most fighter units. I was one of those chosen to remain at Korat. Warped old Arnold would stay as well, but Socks would go home immediately.

The crews chosen to stay were all dedicated Linebacker crews. Most of us were hunter-killer specialists, and only a few weren't on their second combat tour. There was a brief flurry of paperwork as supervisors finished performance reports on those who worked for them, transfers were formalized, statistics were compiled, and packing boxes were inventoried. Plaques, flags, photos, and filing cabinets went off to some dusty warehouse back in the States, where maybe years later historians would mine the data to find out who had fought and died in the service of their country in a land far away. Those of us who stayed at Korat threw out our green party suits and went to the tailor to order black ones.

In the last week in September, moving trucks arrived in the hootch area. Most of the 469th crews headed for

Udorn packed up their belongings, clothes, cameras, stereos, personal effects, and carved teak elephants to be shipped. In the morning they flew to Hanoi, then recovered at the end of the mission at Udorn. Simple, efficient, and inexpensive. They would be moved from one duty station to another by "government transportation." No reimbursement required.

Back at Korat, our 34th was a tight ship. The commander, George Dornberger, was a leader by example. He flew the tough missions and was respected by all. The operations officer and his two assistants were equally strong. Paul Dwyer, the ops officer, had a prior F-105 tour, as did the assistant Mike Thomas. Jon "Luke" Lucas, the second assistant ops, was a fighter pilot's fighter pilot. He knew more about flying and fighting in the Phantom than most of us would ever learn. All four of them bucked the trend of staff officers or cross-trained bomber pilots that seemed to permeate so many fighter units during the war.

With nearly a hundred F-4 qualified crewmembers on the base, the 34th was definitely a supersize squadron. We would fly all of the hunter-killers, most of the MiG escorts, and a regular helping of bombing sorties in support of Linebacker. We'd also continue to do night sorties with bombing in Laos, South Vietnam, and the North. We even did some B-52 protection during their night bombing in the southern panhandle of North Vietnam, providing the big bombers a security blanket against MiGs and SAMs by our mere presence.

The SAM-killing mission was one that continually evolved. It was a very serious cat-and-mouse game that brought new tactics and new equipment into the equation whenever it was available. The SAM operators fought for their lives and to defend their country, while we fought to protect our friends flying the tasked missions and, hopefully, to someday recover the hundreds of our lost comrades who languished in the POW camps of the North.

The SA-2 had been around for a long time, and we often wondered why the air defenses hadn't begun to incorporate some of the newer missile systems that the Soviets had fielded. We had seen the shoulder-fired SA-7 deployed with ground troops, primarily in the South, but it didn't mean much to the fast-moving jets. The little missile had short range and couldn't catch us. It was a threat to helicopters and forward air controllers, but we didn't worry about it. There were big missiles that hadn't made an appearance. They had different radars that our electronic countermeasures might not jam so effectively, and the radars operated in frequency bands that might not be so clearly detected by our radar warning receivers. When would the SA-3 show up? And would we encounter the SA-4?

Tom Coady and Sam Peacock were in a two-ship of F-105G Weasels, supporting an unusually small strike that someone had determined would not merit a full hunter-killer team. They had wound up across the Red River, just west of downtown Hanoi headed well out into the flats, where there wasn't much protection from SAM launches. The normal buzzes and beeps of the radar detection systems told them they were expected if not necessarily welcome. Suddenly a Fan Song came up loud and clear, with a full three-ringer-plus display, so strong that the radar strobe extended out beyond the edge of the etched calibration rings and meant that they were very close and the radar was very powerful.

It didn't take long to get a reaction. The SAM crews

could tell what a Weasel's attack pattern looked like, and when they got one nearby headed toward them, they knew they were on the bubble and had to shoot first or die. Tom watched the launch, the SAM rising almost in slow motion from the site, then arching into a pursuit curve toward him. He lit the burner and started the airplane down, watching as the missile closed on him. He waited, patiently waited, watching the closing weapon track him through the descent. Wait, wait, just a bit longer. Then, at the last possible moment, pull up and inside the missile's arcing flight path. The high speed of the missile and the stubby wings grab for air but can't make the turn, and it passes just off the left wing of the airplane and detonates fifty to sixty feet away. The rattle of shrapnel against the fuselage can be heard above the roaring of the airflow over the canopy and the noise of the engine.

The radar is still on them and the radar warning receiver is still howling. Coady looks back at the orange cloud where the missile came from and sees the second one coming from almost the same site. This one is following a different path. It has leveled off low and is coming at them in an almost ground-hugging path. The F-105 has dissipated a lot of energy in the hard turn to evade the first missile, and now he's forced to go down even lower to try to regain energy. The SAM starts up, and the missile is on a collision course. Coady rolls inverted, trying to keep the SAM in sight while still desperate to regain some serious maneuvering potential. He turns hard right and the missile follows the turn. This isn't an SA-2. Guidelines don't turn like this. Coady is descending, and the missile is virtually flying formation on him. They're frozen in time; seconds seem like hours as the scenario unfolds in extreme slow motion. It's as though there were someone on-board the SAM thinking through the cutoff angles, working the energy, just as a fighter pilot might maneuver against another airplane. The missile seems to be aimed quite consciously at the rear cockpit. This isn't SA-2 behavior. It closes on him frame by frame in a very detailed movie.

The SAM is black. We've been seeing white SA-2s for years, and lately we've begun to see camouflaged missiles, often in mottled olive tones. This one is clearly black. The forward control fins are larger than typical and not aligned with the rear ones, as on the SA-2. The exhaust is different than the orange nitric-acid oxidized booster of the SA-2, or the white flare of the solid sustainer. The smoky trail is dark gray and discloses the jerky control movements characteristic of a digital flight control system. Bang-bang full deflection of the fins makes things look rough, but it also means near instantaneous direction changes. The maneuverability is incredible.

The missile passes the Weasel at almost a 90-degree crossing angle. The proximity fuse explodes the warhead within six feet of the tail. The airplane shudders and shakes, the controls go mushy, and one of the hydraulic systems immediately goes to zero. Defiantly, Coady bends the airplane back right one more time to put the nose on the SAM site and fire off a Shrike, hoping to put the radar off the air. They turn and keep the afterburner engaged as they start heading toward the mountains. They reach the relative safety of the high country and make for a tanker. The tanker extends well beyond his authorized northern limits to pick up the wounded airplane, far into the upper reaches of Laos. The external fuel tanks are all punctured, the tail section is peppered with warhead fragments, and the rear looks like it's encountered a serious duck hunter with a large-bore shotgun. They manage to nurse the bird into Udorn.

Intelligence folks want to know what happened. Coady and Peacock relate the details of the "Black SAM." No one seems to know what they've encountered. In shape and configuration it looks a bit like an SA-4, but the smoke trail and jerky control movements don't fit the profile that we've got for the missile. Cubes of jagged shrapnel are harvested from the tail of the damaged Thud and shipped off to higher headquarters for analysis. The messages come back from Seventh Air Force that it isn't really something new. It's simply an upgraded SA-2 with a bit better turn capability. The Weasels are told that the missile wasn't a surprise, but they should downplay the unique nature of their experience. Within days, several more crews report sightings of "fat, black, smoky rockets," and the word spreads that maybe something new is on the scene. Then, without much explanation, the Black SAMs disappear.

THE 469TH IS GONE. THE history they made as an F-105 squadron and then the first F-4E unit in Thailand during Rolling Thunder is crated and shipped off. Without fanfare, parade, or thank you from a grateful nation, the squadron is retired. The war is winding down, and soon there won't be much of America left in Southeast Asia. So why are we still going to Hanoi? Why are we still bombing the same old targets? Why are we being asked to fight and die?

Word comes in that Seymour-Johnson has extended the deployment of their squadrons of F-4s to Ubon. My squadron is gone, but more airplanes are being moved into the war. There are some F-111s going in as well. Wait a second: we deactivated a squadron in place, and now we move two squadrons of F-4Es from the eastern United States? Are we really withdrawing? We get a squadron of F-4Ds at Korat from Korea. The 35th TFS from Kunsan arrives, and the activity at the officer's club bar picks up. A half-dozen F-4C Wild Weasel aircraft from Kadena, Okinawa, add their weight to the flight line. The Phantom version of the Weasel has been in development for several years but hasn't yet been tried in combat. Now it looks as though they will be getting their chance.

The daily *Stars and Stripes* doesn't tell us much about the peace negotiations. They've finally decided on the shape of the table. Great! They've decided to recognize the Vietcong as well as the North Vietnamese. Makes sense to me. Quite clearly this war has been about VC and NVN and SVN and USA. Any agreement is going to have to have all four of the parties sign on. We get a bit more information in intel during the daily flight briefings. Not a lot more, but some insight into what's going on. We read in the newspaper that Kissinger reports a "light at the end of the tunnel." We get briefed before the missions that the "State Department" has suggested that we shouldn't abort for bad weather. We should get to the targets and not cancel missions if at all possible. We will exert maximum pressure on the North even if it requires extreme risks and tactically unsound moves.

Yeah, right. When was the last time Henry the K was dancing with SAMs between the cloud layers? And if this is so important, why aren't we hitting the big stuff?

We get still more airplanes. The 354th Tactical

Fighter Wing will be arriving in a few days with three squadrons of A-7D fighter bombers. Three squadrons' worth of airplanes, aircrews, maintainers, suppliers, vehicles, and more. They dribble in slowly over a week and a half. The influx taxes the facilities at Korat, and pavement for parking airframes is in increasingly short supply. The people are housed to the west of the main base in a fairly primitive Army facility called Camp Friendship. They use our operations area, our command post, our shops and munitions support, our bars and chow halls. They are comrades in arms and they have come to do a job, but what is the job, and isn't the war ending?

I'VE CHANGED MY TACTICS SINCE the dive-toss failure. I never know how many of the CBU I'll want to deliver in the mission. We always carry four cans and may want to drop one, two, or all four. With dive toss, the decision has to be made before the attack. When the pickle button gets pressed, it has to be held until the weapon releases. Another release needs another complete cycle of radar lock, target designation, and pulloff. If I choose "direct," I can simply press the pickle button as many times as I need to get the desired number of weapons on the target in a single attack.

It's impossible to predict what the dive angle will be, but I discover that a single manual sight setting can be used if I vary the release altitude above the ground. There's a simple relationship, and it ensures a dive-bomb pass that won't leave me and my airplane scattered among the remains of the SAM site. For every degree of dive during the attack, I release 100 feet above the ground. A 10-degree pass requires 1,000-foot release. A 20-degree means 2,000; 40-degree, 4,000, and so on. It works. It's basic, and I don't wind up hanging my precious pink body out in harm's way to get no release of my weapons.

The size of the squadron and the armada of airplanes that we've assembled mean that not everyone is flying every day. On days off we spend some time in the squadron handling paperwork, but most of the time gets wasted lying around in front of the CTF working on our suntans. The round-the-clock schedule means someone is always getting off work, so there's always a beer in someone's hand. We read books, talk tactics, swap stories, and discuss the best places in Korat and Bangkok for sport and recreation.

Roscoe, our mascot, has taken to sleeping under an oleander bush near the front door of my hootch. He is getting old and is a bit overweight. Years of steak chunks and ice cream mooched from the continual stream of fighter pilots have taken a toll on the faithful old hound. But he shouldn't be quite so weary. I mention to Doc Zimmerman, our squadron flight surgeon and commander of the base hospital, that Roscoe doesn't look too good. He agrees and says he wants to check some things out.

Korat is big enough now that there is a base veterinarian, but his function is to inspect food for the dining halls and clubs, not to treat pets. It's been traditional, since Roscoe first came to Korat, that the squadron flight surgeon takes care of the dog. That has usually meant keeping inoculations current and occasionally spraying a bit of antibiotic on a scratch or wound encountered in some amorous adventure. Now Doc Z is being asked to perform more critical treatment. The blood test comes back that Roscoe has heartworms. The first question we all ask is if it's treatable. Doc isn't sure, he needs to find some vet medicine books.

A few days later the Doc requests an aircrew meeting. This is unusual. Hospital commanders, even if they are also unit flight surgeons, don't call aircrew meetings. Luke Lucas, the assistant ops officer, approves of the request and we assemble at the CTF at five o'clock the next afternoon. Roscoe is in attendance.

"Okay, guys, here's the story," Zimmerman starts. "You've maybe noticed that Roscoe has been a little bit lethargic. He's sleeping a lot, he pants when he walks, he doesn't seem too eager to jump on the truck to go to briefings. I've managed to get some blood work done on him and it looks like he's got heartworms. This isn't like intestinal worms, it can kill him." Diagnosis must be the bad news. Is there going to be some good?

"There's a treatment, but it isn't easy," he continues. "If we don't do something, Roscoe is going to die. But the treatment can kill him as well. The way they take care of heartworms is by administering strychnine. It kills the worms and they are then expelled. But, the strychnine can kill the dog too. Too much and it kills the dog, too little and it doesn't kill the worms. I need a decision from you guys on whether to treat him. I'm not going to make the decision without a unanimous vote to go ahead. I'm not going to be known throughout the Air Force as the guy who killed Roscoe."

He continues to detail the treatment plan. If we agree, he'll calculate the dosage, then give him the medication. If it works as described in the books, he explains, the worms will be killed and then come out of the heart muscle into the bloodstream. From there, typically, they move into the lungs, where the dog will be able to cough them up. Two treatments will be required, roughly a week apart. The first one will kill the mature worms, the second will take care of the remainder that may hatch after the first treatment. If it works, Roscoe should regain his vigor and have many good years left. If successful, Doc's reputation in the Air Force will be intact. If it fails, Roscoe will be gone in a few months. If it really fails, the strychnine will kill Roscoe in a week. Poor Roscoe sleeps, blissfully unaware of the discussion going on about him. He's simply comfortable surrounded by all his friends.

"If you guys give the okay, I can start tomorrow. Now, here's the hard part. When I give him the first dose, we've got to have someone with him until the treatment is over. Who's the RCO?"

The Roscoe Control Officer has traditionally been the junior backseater in the squadron. It has been a soft job with not much required, more joke than job. If Roscoe disappears for a day or two, someone calls for the RCO to find the dog. If Roscoe needs his annual rabies shot, the RCO is the guy tasked to find him and herd him to the doc. Most of the time the RCO hasn't even known he has the job. Now we have to check among several WSOs to see who has the junior date of rank. It turns out to be Paul Waterman, a soft-spoken navigator who's come through the training pipeline so quickly that he arrived at Korat still a second lieutenant. He's only been on base for a couple of weeks and pinned on silver first lieutenant bars little more than a week ago. Paul raises his hand to admit that he's probably the guy we're looking for.

"This is the tough part," Doc continues. "After the

injection, within a day or two the heartworms start to come out of the muscle and travel through the bloodstream. When that happens, Roscoe has to get up and move to expel them. If he's allowed to sleep or lay around, he'll choke to death. So, the RCO and whoever is willing to help him needs to get Roscoe up every two hours and walk him around the block. Day or night, every two hours for a week. No breaks, no forgetting. Can you do that?"

Waterman looks like he's just been told his girlfriend is pregnant. He's wide-eyed and slack-jawed. He's not sure what he's just been told is official, as in a military order that a lieutenant colonel gives a first lieutenant subordinate. He looks to his flight commander for some guidance regarding whether a doctor can command a line officer. He looks around at the rest of us, who are all staring at him. He nods his head slowly. "Yessir, I can. At least I think I can." He looks again at the group, seeking some help. Lt. Colonel Dornberger nods his head, adding the imprimatur of the squadron commander to the direction of the doctor.

"Okay, guys, what'll it be? Do I go ahead? And do you agree to share the responsibility if something goes wrong?" We look at each other. Everyone loves old Roscoe, and it looks like we don't have a choice. We exchange nods around the room. A formal vote is taken and we agree to treatment.

Roscoe has a collar, but no one is sure if there is a leash on base. Someone suggests checking with the security police to see if they have one for a working dog that we can borrow. No one knows if Roscoe has ever been on a leash. Roscoe isn't talking.

Twenty-four hours later, Doc stops in at the CTF

early in the evening. Treatment has begun. Roscoe has been injected and introduced to a leash. Paul Waterman has had five stitches in his left hand for a small bite incurred in the process of explaining to Roscoe exactly what a leash is for. Paul has two alarm clocks next to his bed and a new roommate, a golden, seven-year-old, mixed breed dog. It's going to be a rough two weeks for Paul, but when the bags under his eyes show up after the second night of trying to sleep in two-hour increments and walk a recalcitrant dog around the block every time he wakes up, the rest of the lieutenants set up a schedule of shift watchers to help. Roscoe lives three more years.

"YOU HEARD ABOUT THE NEW barber shop?" Hank Scheible is sprawled on a nearby web-back lawn chair. I can tell by the tone of the question that there's going to be more to the story. We've been watching the new facility being built, halfway between our hootch area and the officer's club. It's a large square building that is going to be a big step up from the two-chair clip joint that has been in the back of the club by the cashier's office. There are a pair of fenced-in tennis courts and a basketball area next to the building. I haven't seen the inside yet, but I've heard there are to be two or three racquetball courts and a weight room, along with a sauna and the barber shop.

"Nope. Is it open yet? You tried it out?" I offer the expected curiosity.

"It may be too late," he volunteers.

"Whaddayamean?"

"Apparently they opened up a couple of days ago. They brought in a couple girls from downtown to cut hair. One's a real cutie, I heard." Subconsciously I run my hand up the back of my neck to see if maybe I could use a bit of a trim. Hank continues, "You know how the barbers at the club used to give you a back and shoulder massage as they finished up? The old guy used to loosen you up and then give that little pop to your neck that kind of hurt a bit, but then felt real good?"

"Yeah, I was never sure if that was good for you."

"Well, it seems like one of the new girls takes the massage a couple steps further down from the shoulders. First guys to get their hair cut got the full treatment. Looked like it was going to be standing room only at the barber shop, with guys waiting for a haircut and a 'special' massage. But then the wing commander went in for a trim, and when she went for his zipper he shut the place down. Won't be any more haircuts there for a couple of days until they find a new barber. Too bad." Scheible grins and shakes his head.

Every day is just a little bit different. Some days there are SAMs. Some days there are MiGs. There is always flak, but it doesn't have the intensity that it did during the early days of the war. Maybe our interdiction has taken a toll. Or maybe they just decided that guns aren't the best answer. Some days we can get to the targets, and others we're assigned to secondary areas to reconnoiter roads or strike dirt road chokepoints. Weather during the fall begins to progressively worsen over the North, as the monsoon pattern begins to shift the storm emphasis from central Thailand to the Red River Delta. Some days we get to Hanoi, but more often we are sent to alternate targets in the panhandle of North Vietnam or the plains of northern Laos.

Targets are truck parks and suspected storage areas. The threat is relatively low, with no SAMs or MiGs and just an occasional flurry of gunfire. There are sorties to

South Vietnam to support ground troops, and even some level drops under radar control from a ground station or on the wing of a LORAN-equipped pathfinder airplane. The war is becoming mundane, almost boring. There are too many airplanes and not enough missions of meaning. The threat seems to go down. But there is always the chance to do something stupid.

A slow and steady rain has been falling all night. The mission for the day is a simple two-ship, loaded with twelve Mk-82s into the Mu Gia pass area. It's low threat, just a few dozen guns, and should be fairly straightforward. No mass briefing, no great tactics, nothing exotic going on today. We pick up the maps and get a weather briefing at the command post. I explain to my wingman about formations, refueling procedures, what to do in an emergency, and what I expect in terms of radio discipline. "Two, bandits, and bingo . . . that's all I want to hear from you." Acknowledge channel changes with your number, call out enemy aircraft, and tell me when you reach a low fuel state. It's a cliché among fighter pilots, but it reinforces the fact that wingmen should shut up and simply fly the missions as briefed.

The F-4 has a design deficiency. When the canopy is opened in the rain, the water drains inevitably down the Plexiglas and drips onto the flat consoles on each side of the cockpit. In many areas it makes no difference, but the radios are notoriously intolerant of moisture. The mission proceeds normally until takeoff. My wingman joins up below the clouds, and we then climb together until we break out on top at fourteen thousand feet. I kick the rudder back and forth to signal with a tail wag that I want him to move out into tactical spread formation. He doesn't go. I look at him and see him signaling with his left hand. He moves his hand fore and aft next to his ear, then up and down in front of his oxygen mask. It's the signal for radio failure. No receiver, no transmitter. I call for him on the radio. No response. I give him a push-away hand signal and he moves out a few ship-widths to route formation, where he can relax and I can decide what to do.

It's a basic rule. You don't go into combat without a radio. No comm, no war. You have to be able to communicate with each other in case of emergency. You have to be able to warn the other guy if something happens. You have to be able to talk to the controlling agencies. You have to acknowledge targets and advise about fuel states and describe problems if they arise. You don't always need to talk, and you should shut up as much as possible, but you have to have the capability just in case.

We've taken off at maximum gross weight, 58,000 pounds of airplane, fuel, and bombs. The cloud layers below us mean we can't find the visual jettison range to get rid of the bombs. We'll have to land with them. That means we'll have to do an approach-end barrier engagement, and we'll have to reduce our weight to maximum landing weight, which is considerably less than takeoff weight. One of the important numbers we pick up from a chart each day at briefing is the allowable fuel-remaining weight for an emergency landing with ordnance. Today we have to burn down our fuel to 4,000 pounds remaining. That's about fifteen minutes of flying time left. Long enough for me to fly an instrument approach with my wingman, let him see the runway and land, then continue around a quick GCA back for my own landing. He will catch the barrier to stop, then be cleared by the ground emergency crew. The barrier will be reset and I'll land. It's simple, straightforward, and we brief the procedures on every mission.

I give him a hand signal for a channel change to Korat approach control. His radio doesn't work, but if it comes back he'll know what frequency I'm on. With two hands side-by-side, I signal the intention to fly a formation approach for him to land. With a thumb extended downward, I mimic a tail hook and he responds by lowering his hook. He understands. We're cleared to the instrument holding pattern, where we will orbit for about half an hour to burn down fuel.

Gyle Atwood is the supervisor of flying. He's sitting in the Korat control tower, where his job is to provide emergency assistance for F-4s that have a problem in flight. He's got telephones and radios to talk to the fire department, the runway barrier crews, the approach controllers, and anyone else that might be needed when a problem arises. Gyle is one of the pilots from the squadron and one of the best we've got. He's one of the younger captains, short but muscular, with a disc jockey's baritone voice and a movie star smile under his black, flowing, bulletproof moustache. We've flown together a lot. It doesn't look like I need much help, but he checks in on the radio frequency for an update and to let me know that the weather is holding at about eight hundred feet and two miles' visibility.

At altitude, the weather is clear and the sun bright. We cruise in lazy circles, burning gas and getting lighter in preparation for the landing. The outboard wing tanks go empty and now we've got 12,000 pounds of fuel remaining, 4,000 in the wings and 8,000 in the fuselage tanks. We can dump the 4,000 out of the wings with the flick of a switch. I start to dump, and a pair of contrails appear behind my airplane as the fuel starts flowing out the two dump masts on the trailing edge of the wing on each side, at the wing fold. My wingman follows my example. Within minutes we're down to 8,000 pounds, only four to go to landing weight.

With 5,500 pounds remaining, I ask Korat to start our instrument approach. I wag the wings to signal my wingman into close formation, and we descend into the clouds. The stratus is not exceptionally dense and there is no turbulence. This is going to be easy. As the radar controller turns us onto final, I signal for lowering the landing gear, and then the flaps. Gear is good, flaps are good, hook is down. We're steady on final. On glide path. On speed. At two miles, we break out of the base of the clouds and see the approach lights. We ease down the glide path, and as we reach the overrun, I point forward and let my wingman continue to his landing and barrier engagement. I push the throttles up and raise the gear.

Back in the clouds, I reach the end of the runway and hear the radar controller report, "Carbine lead, your wingman has successfully engaged the barrier. We'll be running you around a short box pattern back to landing." Great, I've got 2,800 pounds remaining, about twelve minutes.

"Carbine lead, Korat approach. Fire chief advises your wingman has blown a tire. Should be clear of the barrier in about eight minutes." Not good news. Still, we've got about eight minutes to get around the radar pattern. Should work out okay, with 2,200 pounds remaining. I'm doing the math in my head on how long a typical radar approach will take, how much fuel we've got, and how accurate the barrier crew estimates usually are. We're still in the ballpark.

"Uh, Carbine lead, fire chief now advises that your wingman has blown both tires. This is going to take at least twenty minutes to clear the runway. Say intentions."

Damn! He must have been so worried about landing with the heavy bomb load that he landed with the wheel brakes on and locked up. Probably the first time he's done this. Now we've got a problem. I'm at 2,000 pounds of gas, what would normally be minimum fuel for landing, but that's without 6,000 pounds of bombs on the airplane. I'm rapidly running out of ideas and options. We're rapidly running out of gas.

"Carbine, this is Phantom four, say fuel." Atwood's jumping in now. He knows exactly what the situation is and is trying to consider the alternatives.

"Roger, Phantom four, we're at 2,000." We're already a bit below that, but I pad the number a little. Maybe he can hurry up the barrier crew.

"Carbine, Phantom four. The DO recommends you divert to Takhli." The deputy commander for operations has been called on the phone, but his information is a significant couple of minutes out of date already. A good idea five minutes ago isn't an option anymore.

"Negative. Carbine doesn't have enough gas to make Takhli. See if you can get the runway cleared." Usually we would have the parallel taxiway for landing in a situation when the runway is blocked, but there are no barriers to stop the bomb-laden airplane, and the seventy-five-foot-wide taxiway offers a lot less margin for error in case of a blown tire. The instrument approach won't line me up with the taxiway either. Climbing clear of the base and aiming the airplane away from Korat city for a bailout is becoming a distinct possibility.

"Carbine, this is Korat approach control. Turn right heading zero four five, climb to and maintain flight level two zero zero. SOF advises he has a tanker for you." Wow! Gyle may have just bought us a reprieve. I've got 1,600 pounds of gas remaining and am not even sure I can make it to 20,000 feet. Gingerly I push the throttles forward, not wanting to squander a bit of fuel on an overenthusiastic movement. We turn and climb. The gas gauge seems directly connected to the altimeter. As the altitude rises, the fuel quantity goes down.

"Carbine, contact Lion control on two three four point four. Your tanker is White Four One. Good luck." I acknowledge and change the channel.

"Lion, Carbine, through fourteen thousand for flight level two zero zero. Squawking ident."

"Roger, Carbine. Radar contact. Your tanker is on your nose at 165 miles. This will be a tanker turn-on rendezvous. My control. We'll get you some gas." The controller's confidence isn't enough enthusiasm to convince me that I can stretch my little remaining fuel for 165 miles. There's no room for error, and the drag of the bombs is incredible. The controller is going to run us straight at the tanker. Done perfectly, the tanker will start a 180 reversal at 27 miles and roll out less than a mile in front of us. That's the way it's displayed in all the manuals. Nose to nose, slightly offset left, then when the controller calls the turn, I continue straight and the tanker turns. I don't think I've ever seen it done perfectly in several hundred tanker joinups.

We're below 1,000 pounds now. My backseater has got the tanker on the radar at 80 miles. We seem to be closing way too slowly. I punch on the autopilot, judging that "George" can be smoother and maintain altitude while I look at the radar and fuel gauge, milking the throttles smoothly to keep airspeed. Lion doesn't chatter, but gives me a range update every 20 miles. He verifies my own radar picture. It's going to be very close.

We're almost at the turn point, and I can see on the radar that we've got a second tanker in trail with the first. We're covered if there's a boom failure or something goes wrong with the first tank, but I'm certain we won't have time. We've got to get gas from the first jet, and we've got to get it on the first try. There are no second chances.

The tanker's turning. I can see him, wing rolled up in a left sweeping bank. It looks like he's too far in. He's going to be behind us. No, he's okay. He's coming around and holding steady in the windscreen. He's got 45 degrees to go. We get the radar turned off, the refuel receptacle open, the autopilot off. The tanker rolls out less than 1,000 feet in front of us. Lion, baby, I love you, man! The boomer has the boom extended in welcome and waves it up and down like an elephant's trunk. I slide into position with 400 pounds on the gauge. Incredible. The boomer reaches out and grabs us. Two quick pokes, and I hear a clunk as the jaws of the boom engage our receptacle. We're taking gas.

We ride the boom, comfortable for the first time in the last half-hour. We've screwed up, but somehow a lot of pros came together and saved us. We managed to make a mistake and live through it, because we had the right guy on duty as supervisor of flying, the right controller on the scope at Lion, the right tanker crew who could fly the intercept perfectly, and the right boomer who didn't screw around when he needed to poke an airplane and pass some gas.

It's been a lucky day, and I've learned a valuable lesson. There's an old saying in the fighter business that the three most worthless things in the world are the sky above you, the runway behind you, and the gas you left behind. Landing an airplane loaded with bombs isn't that tough. You have to get down to the maximum allowable landing weight, and that involves reducing your fuel load to the minimum. But I didn't have to reduce my fuel, since I wasn't the guy going to land on the first pass. Had I kept my internal wing fuel and simply let my wingman dump his, I would have had an extra 4,000 pounds of JP-4 and plenty of time to orbit waiting for the runway to clear or even to divert to Takhli. Hours of boredom punctuated by moments of stark terror, the perfect description of tactical flying. The snake is always waiting to jump up and bite you.

I'M IN THE CLUB AFTER dinner, standing along the teak railing of the bar talking with Barry Johnson. Like so many of us, Barry is on his third combat tour. Although this is his first fighter assignment, he previously dropped iron on Asia as a B-52 pilot and a forward air controller. Now he's an F-4E pilot, and we're often teamed in the hunter-killer mission. Like me, he's got a "meaningful relationship" with a beautiful young Thai girl who works as a waitress at the officer's club dining room. It seems to explain why he always knows when the apple pie is fresh and the vanilla ice cream is still frozen. He even gets the occasional steak cooked the way he likes it. We're sipping on a cognac after dinner. Just one, to finish the meal and then get a good night's sleep.

A couple of A-7 drivers have migrated over to the bar from their quarters in the Camp Friendship area. There are two types of A-7 pilots, and neither of them are held in much regard by the F-4 and -105 crews who have been in place at Korat, going north. The A-7 is a new airplane in the inventory, and it holds the panache of being single seat and single engine. It is the classic "fighter" but doesn't have an afterburner and is notoriously slow. It has great endurance and can carry a remarkable load, but it is an unproven system. The crews seem to be either older fighter pilots, predominantly from the F-100 community, or young lieutenants right out of pilot training who graduated at the top of their class. The old guys have little or no experience going against the heavily defended targets of the Red River Delta, and the young guys seem to be overly impressed with their good fortune in being assigned to single-seat fighters. The old guys tell the young guys how good they all are, and the young troops stroke the old guys' egos in return.

I glance at Barry and he looks at me. We both then look at the young lieutenant who is recounting a tale of derring-do over a nondescript chunk of jungle near Danang. We eavesdrop shamelessly, knowing that in a minute we are going to impart great aeronautical wisdom to the young pilots. I wave to Jimmy the bartender and ask him to set up four shot glasses with cognac and bring me a book of matches. Johnson knows what's coming. "Oh no. Not again!" he laments.

"Hey, Lieutenant," I turn toward him. "Have you guys seen a SAM yet? What are you going to do in that puny little airplane of yours when you've evaded your first missile and you don't have any afterburner to get some smash back?" It's a pretty cheap shot, but that's what barroom brawls are supposed to be about.

"SAMs? I'm not afraid of SAMs. I've never seen one, and I'm not scared of something I haven't seen. They don't seem to bother you guys. Why should I be afraid of SAMs?" His bluster seems ill advised, to say the least. I've never found the slightest problem with being frightened by something I haven't yet encountered. A little pre-encounter fear has always seemed to me to be a prudent approach.

"Well, my young aviator, you should be afraid of

SAMs because they are going to try to kill you. They are going to sneak up on you and chase you at nearly three times the mach, and then when you are down in the weeds, the guns are going to finish the job the SAMs started. And you'll be looking around and see the Phantoms and the Thuds with afterburners blazing, climbing up to the safe altitudes to evade the next barrage of SAMs while you wallow around getting the crap shot out of you. That's why you should be afraid of SAMs. Without an AB, you guys won't stand a chance." The setup is now nearly perfect.

Now I turn toward Barry and nod. We each pull a shot of cognac toward our position at the bar, and we each strike a match. We light the surface of the cognac, and in the dim darkness of the bar the blue flame atop the shot is impressive. We watch it for a few seconds for effect, then slowly and deliberately raise the flaming glass, and in one smooth movement drink the flaming liquid down and replace the empty glass on the bar with the blue flame still licking softly at the residual drops of liquor. "That's an afterburner, son, and you need one."

"What?" The lieutenant knows what's coming and isn't sure if he'll be up to it. "How'd you do that?" He hopes there's a secret and we'll tell him what it is before he has to attempt the trick himself.

"Simply light it and drink it. Don't blow it out; that's what trash-haulers and bomber pukes do. Don't wait too long or the glass gets hot. And you've got to keep the flame in the glass when you finish. That's the afterburner part." We tell him all he needs to know.

"Okay, set 'em up." He gains stature by not hesitating. He lights the cognac, raises the glass, and as it approaches his mouth he quickly blows the flame out and tosses the shot down.

"Nope. You cheated. Here, we'll show you how it's done." This is a mistake, but I'm too far into the game to realize it. Barry and I light, look, toss, and set the properly afterburning glasses back on the bar. "Your turn."

It takes a half-dozen rounds before the lieutenant and his partner get the technique down. By that time we've become close friends, even though he still won't acknowledge the wisdom of respecting enemy defenses. He will survive nevertheless, and the A-7D will prove remarkably capable in the coming months.

Barry and I will survive the night, but won't be sure the next morning if our survival was the best outcome. Barry has a duty tour to pull in the command post. I'm not on the flying schedule, so I drop in to see how bad he feels, hoping that he is more hungover than I am. I stop off at the Coke machine in intel and chug down an icy cold one, hoping the blast of sugar and near-frozen liquid will quell my nausea and headache long enough to tease Johnson. I muster my reserves and enter the darkened control room of the command post where Johnson is holding his head in his hands, slumped over his desk. "Hey, guy, how you doing?" I feign cheerfulness and hope to hide my misery. He looks pathetically up at me and shakes his head. The night has taken a fearful toll. I have no doubt that I feel worse than he does; it would be impossible for him to be experiencing the hangover that I have, but I don't acknowledge the misery. I slap him on the back and tell him I'll see him at the CTF later that evening. I saunter out, then, as the door closes behind me, slump and seek more aspirin. Maybe a nap for a couple of hours will help.

9. PAUSING AGAIN

About night flying:

a. Remember that the airplane doesn't know that it's dark.

b. On a clear, moonless night, never fly between the tanker's lights.

c. There are certain aircraft sounds that can only be heard at night.

d. If you're going to night fly, it might as well be in the weather so you can double count your exposure to both hazards.

e. Night formation is really an endless series of near misses in equilibrium with each other.

f. You would have to pay a lot of money at a lot of amusement parks and perhaps add a few drugs, to get the same blend of psychedelic sensations as a single night weather flight on the wing.

—Frank Chuba, "Fighter Pilot"

NOT AGAIN. IT DIDN'T SEEM possible. It was an election year. Nixon was viewed as pretty much of a sure thing. There was still a lot of protest about the war back in the States, but nearly everyone who thought much about it came to the conclusion that he was getting the US out of Vietnam and Kissinger had been making progress in Paris. Why then, just a week and a half before the presidential election, was it happening again? The president announced a limitation of our bombing campaign to south of the twentieth parallel.

I had a new backseater. With bombing restricted to more permissive areas such as Laos, Cambodia, or South Vietnam, the squadron could mix new, inexperienced crewmembers with more seasoned people, generating a larger pool of fully qualified folks if we had to return to the Red River Valley and leaving the squadron better prepared for whatever the future might hold. I was crewed with Kirby Carlton, a good ol' boy from Moultrie, Georgia, who made Jim Nabors's Gomer Pyle look like an urban sophisticate. Kirby had been a C-141 transport navigator who'd gotten caught up by the Palace Cobra snake and transitioned to the F-4. He intended to do his duty, but wasn't going to set any records for scarf-in-the-wind fighter pilot aggressiveness.

Kirby had a nearly constant smile and an almost naïve innocence in his approach to life. He seemed to take it for granted that I would look out for him and not get either of us killed. That probably seemed like a good bargain. We began to pick up a variety of missions. We dropped bombs on meaningless targets that didn't shoot back. We made toothpicks out of big jungle trees and probably took a big chunk out of the monkey population, but it wasn't much more challenging than getting the airplane airborne, finding a tanker, and not hitting the ground during the bombing pass.

We began to fly some nights. I didn't like night flying. Never have. I wanted to see what was going on around me, and the dark skies of the combat zone, unpunctuated by the lights of towns or villages, left me disoriented and uncomfortable. The airplane didn't know whether it was day or night, but I did, and despite the luminescent glow strips on the fuselage, rudder, and wingtips to aid in formation flying, I never felt secure. The cockpit lights could be turned down to a minimalist glow, but even then there were control panels and bulb covers with scraped off paint that let random light slivers into your peripheral vision to distract and disorient. If you flew at night, you'd always have a small chunk of duct tape stuck to your G suit leg to cover lights and glows. Even then, turning your head could cause a jumble of reflections from the cockpit or canopy to scramble your balance and leave you mentally tumbling end over end into the blackness of night.

IT WAS A TWO-SHIP, LOADED with wall-to-wall air-to-air missiles. Our job was to defend a series of three formations of B-52s out of Guam that were attacking a military storage area near Vinh from MiGs. Since there hadn't been any MiG attacks on B-52s during the entire war, it seemed that the mission would be fairly benign. Snapping our fingers to keep the elephants away. Snap, snap. No elephants here. It must be working.

Vinh was a good-size city near the coast in Route Pack II. It had been known over the years for harboring a lot of guns and occasionally, when bombing near the capital was on hiatus, for a fairly aggressive attitude with SAMs. Now, with the Linebacker campaign only recently suspended, they probably hadn't yet moved much missile defense this far south. It was a serious target for fighters during daylight raids, but wouldn't be much threat to the heavy bombers dropping their strings of ordnance from 35,000 feet or higher. There hadn't been much SAM activity recently, the guns wouldn't reach even halfway to the BUFFs altitude, and the probability of a MiG engagement was right down there with the Second Coming.

The plan was tactically sound. We had a directed orbit point about ten miles to the southwest of the target area. We would arrive on station ten minutes before the first flight of B-52s, and then stay on orbit for a bit over an hour as the successive flights of bombers did their job. If MiGs showed up, we would drive them off with a combination of missiles and magic. The orbit was a twenty-mile-long racetrack, and we would put one airplane on each side of the holding pattern so that one of us would be facing to the north, ready to engage the MiGs at all times. While I was heading north, my wingman would be southbound. When I turned south, he would head north. We could keep track of each other with our radars and maintain a 2,000-foot altitude separation just in case. Most of the flying would be done on autopilot.

The surreal nature of the night was emphasized early, as St. Elmo's Fire came aboard during refueling. The tanker had found a canyon among the towering clouds to keep us in the clear, but the flashes of lightning from the storms kept the area loaded with static electricity. As I closed on the tanker's wing, the canopy bow of my airplane began to fluoresce. It was a ghostly green glow at first, then a flickering of light crawling up the sight head and filling the space above the glare shield with greenish flashes. It was as if the radar scope had split and spilled its contents out into the cockpit, where they flowed, unconstrained by gravity, wherever they wished. I tried to focus on the tanker, but the dancing of the glowing lights kept distracting. As I moved into position behind the boom, the green balls of ectoplasm ebbed and flowed in the nose area of the cockpit. It wasn't supposed to hurt me, but I couldn't be sure the ghost knew that. I couldn't wait to finish getting the gas and getting away from there.

I watched my wingman getting his fuel and wondered if he had the same phenomenon. And what about my backseater? "You getting any of this in back, Kirby?"

"What?" he asked.

"Can you see this stuff in the back?" I wondered if it was bright enough or persistent enough for him to see what I was seeing. I wondered if he had the same phantom fire in the rear cockpit.

"I don't see anything," he answered. "I've just been sitting back here, watching the tanker and killing some Millers."

That seemed out of character for straight-arrow Kirby. "You brought beer on a mission?" I was incredulous.

"No, not beer. Millers! You know, those pesky brown moths. Isn't that what you call them?" I'd fallen victim to a Southern colloquialism. I'd never heard the insects called that before. It seemed a better explanation than the image of redneck Kirby sitting in my backseat sipping on a can of beer.

The orbit area was clear, but black as the halls of Hades. There were few lights on the ground and only a few visible stars penetrating the light haze at our altitude. We cruised in the midst of an inky black ball with pinholes of light equally dispersed all around. The inertial nav showed us at the orbit point, and I cleared my wingman off and turned into the first northbound leg. The reddish glow of the instrument lights was as low as I could get it and still be able to monitor our flight condition. The radar scope was adjusted to a similar low state. I could barely see the sweep of the antenna and the golden hairlines of the range and azimuth marks on the scope bezel. The first radar missile was selected, but the master arm switch was off. It wouldn't do to trigger off a missile by accident during the boredom of our orbit. I punched on the altitude hold mode of the autopilot and set the throttles to hold us at 350 knots indicated.

It wasn't long before Kirby called radar contact on the first cell of bombers. They were about forty miles out and showed a string of three clear blips marching down the scope. "Don't lock on to them, Kirby, they don't like that," I warned him. The heavy drivers got real upset when radars lit them up, and their electronic defensive operators could make our radar do funny things. I had seen them make the scope bloom with a flurry of false targets or simply steal the range gate and run it off the side of the display. It made you wonder if they had that much power or your radar was simply acting up. I didn't like people messing with my system.

THE TIME PASSES SLOWLY. DARKNESS seems to weigh upon the hands of the clock, slowing them so that the period will never end. It takes effort to focus, to keep the situation picture in my head. I am here, the bombers are there, the Gulf of Tonkin is over there, my wingman is just passing my left wing, Vinh is over there, and that bright white light is where there wasn't anything important just a second ago. The light is no star, and it isn't supposed to be there. The dim glow of the red launch light on the radar warning receiver is almost too low to see. I've got the audio too low to hear. Is it . . . no it can't be. It's a SAM. I hit the paddle switch below the stick grip to disconnect the autopilot and grab the stick as I push both throttles forward, not into afterburner but just to military power. No need to light up the whole world with a pair of big AB flames. I roll left into the light and let the nose down. The light follows me.

We're half-inverted descending through 18,000 feet, and the airspeed is building toward 500 knots. The light is no longer rising; it's following my descent. Kirby hasn't said anything but now wants to know what is going on. I'm not really sure. The light is doing what I might expect a SAM to do, and I'm doing what I think it takes to frustrate the SAM's intentions. I'm going to grit my teeth until I can't bear it, and maybe if I can see the full missile I'll be able to evade it. The light goes out. Has the sustainer burned out? Is the missile ballistic? Without the flame I can't see a thing. I start a huge barrel roll. I've got four, now five G on the airplane.

"Hang on, Kirby. If we're alive in ten seconds, we'll be okay." I owe him a bit of explanation. The missile can't follow me through the roll, and the self-destruct timer should blow the missile ten seconds after burnout of the rocket. At least that's what they say in the manuals. The light is gone, the roll is over. There's nothing. I'm gasping for breath and trying to regain some composure. We're alive.

I climb back to our orbit altitude. "Did you see it?" I want some confirmation from Kirby that I'm not having some sort of paranoid hallucination. "Did you see the missile?"

"Ah seen that light. It sure did look like it was follerin' you. Was that a SAM?" It dawns on me that he's never seen a missile and probably doesn't recall everything they taught him in WSO school about SAMs. The faith of the backseater in the infallibility of the nose-gunner continues to amaze me. He never questions, he trusts completely, he lives or dies on my competence. Amazing.

"I don't know. I think so. You okay?"

"Yep. That was scary. How much longer we gotta do this?" It's exactly the question I have. I've used up pretty much all the fun for the evening and definitely want the boredom to resume if we have much more time on orbit. I glance at the clock and see that we have about ten minutes more before we can be released to go home. It can't come fast enough. I climb back to the orbit.

The time is up and I call to my wingman to turn out-bound. We'll trail him out and close up before we get to the Laos border. Cruising along, we make small talk. "Kirby, you know that if we have to go back downtown, you're crewed with me." I'd better break the bad news to him.

"Whaddaya mean?" It's one of those meaningless questions that aren't necessary but keep the conversation going. Sitting in tandem in a dark airplane at 3:00 a.m., you don't get nods and smiles and conversational feedback unless you say something on the intercom.

"I'm one of the hunter-killer specialists. If they decide to resume the bombing of Hanoi, I'm gonna be going. You're my crewed backseater. That mean's you're going too. You're going to be a primary Linebacker crew. You might not have to go if you're crewed with someone else, but there's no guarantee. If you're crewed with me, it's definite. You okay with that?" It is as clear as I can make his options. I have no problem with Kirby's skills, even though he is a brand-new WSO. I just want to be sure that he's ready if the mission takes a bit more than the relatively low threat missions we've been flying.

"Well, I guess, that's what I'll have to do then," he expresses resignation at his fate. "I guess you're probably as likely to get me through it as anyone else. Count me in."

RACE RIOTS TORE AMERICA APART during the late '60s. Places like Watts and Newark became part of the language of race relations. The military was supposedly colorblind, but there had been riots at air force bases in Texas, and now there was one aboard the carrier *Kitty Hawk*. Officially we were integrated, but realistically we were as different as black and white. If American society still had not totally accepted the concept of civil rights, assuredly the testosterone-fueled young males who came from the suburbs and the ghettos, the redneck South and the elitist North were not going to leave their prejudices behind.

At Korat there was equality on base and mandatory race relations training, in which we were taught the nuances of offensive language and actions. The goal was to foster understanding of ethnic differences and promote empathy, but inevitably the result was a broadening of means of insulting someone. Now you could learn the things that individuals were sensitive to and bring them to bear with great precision. You might not have known before the training what words were used in different U.S. regions for insults, but now you had a much wider vocabulary.

In town, equality was waived. When the bus stopped, the whites and blacks went their separate ways. There were separate bars and separate restaurants. There were massage parlors and prostitutes that catered to specific groups. Bars featuring country music were all white; those playing the blues were black. You could train and educate, but you couldn't mandate societal change. Crossover was rare, and even if you believed in racial equality, it was generally assumed by both whites and blacks that you didn't.

Tailor shops catering to Americans offered custom outfits that made even the garish clothing of the psychedelic rock bands look dull in comparison. Whites ordered safari jackets and tuxedos with red satin lining, "just like Johnny Carson wears." Blacks brought in magazine clippings from the States with pictures of the dashikis and caftans that they wanted. Shoe shops custom-made virtually any shoe or boot you could find a picture of in whatever leather you could name. Whites got elephant skin "dogger" heel cowboy boots, and blacks specified four-inch platforms with their initials engraved on the heels. Bad taste was on prominent display everywhere.

In uniform the resistance was subtle, but it was always there. The race relations training told us about pseudofolliculitis, the tendency of the beard hairs of African-American men to curl back into the skin, leading to inflammation and discomfort. That led to a rush to the hospital for doctor-authorized shaving waivers so that blacks could grow their beards longer. In response, white supervisors regularly demanded presentation of the paperwork permitting the beard. Rather than understanding, the knowledge increased conflicts.

Haircuts were everybody's problem, with whites trying to let their sideburns grow to match the rest of seventies' society, and blacks wanting to blow out full and flamboyant Afros. There was no hiding the sideburns, but the Afros could be slicked down during the day to look compliant with the haircut regulations, then "picked" out when off-duty and in civilian clothes. The transitions were often remarkable.

At the post office, there were gatherings of whites in one area and blacks in another. Obstruction of walkways was a passive method of protesting the other side. Try to check your mailbox and you might have to wait for half a dozen airmen exchanging the ritualized evolution of a handshake called a "dap." Each would have to tap, pat, shake, wave, snap, and finger-jive a choreographed series of moves that must have been distributed through some sort of underground newspaper and then practiced in front of a mirror for hours before public attempts. When the greetings were completed, a surly salute was rendered and the walkway cleared.

Only on the flight line did the team solidify. Maintainers, operators, specialists, bomb loaders, all worked shoulder to shoulder to get the job done. The sole criterion for acceptance was how well you did the job, not what color your skin was, how long your hair was, or what kind of clothing you preferred. In the support specialties it wasn't quite as dedicated. Personnel, finance, civil engineers, security police, supply, all varied in their susceptibility to race problems. It lurked below the surface and could erupt almost anywhere.

10. CHRISTMAS CARDS TO
JANE AND HO

This story shall the good man teach his son;
And Crispin Crispian shall ne'er go by,
From this day to the ending of the world,
But we in it shall be remember'd;
We few, we happy few, we band of brothers;
For he to-day that sheds his blood with me
Shall be my brother; be he ne'er so vile,
This day shall gentle his condition:
And gentlemen in England now a-bed
Shall think themselves accursed they were not here,
And hold their manhoods cheap whiles any speaks
That fought with us upon Saint Crispin's day.

—William Shakespeare, *Henry V,* Act IV, Scene III

IT WASN'T ST. CRISPIN'S DAY, it was about six weeks later, near the end of December, but those of us who were there will remember it with nearly the same reverence as Henry's warriors recalled their moment of glory. Whether gentlemen abed in the United States held much envy of us is debatable, but for those who were there, we will take it upon ourselves to hold their manhood cheap. And we do.

Jack Van Loan[1] had been in jail since 1967, and it was now 1972. Recently I asked him about the view from his cell; he related this tale:

It was a quiet afternoon without too much going on when here comes a raid of some kind which everyone in the room was ignoring. We had about 35–40 cons in the room and down at one end playing bridge was Jim Young, an F-101 Recce driver and three other guys. The raid went on and finally it became apparent when the guns stopped and the SAMs stopped that the MiGs and the F-4s were dogfighting right over the top of the prison. One of the tricks used by both our guys and the bad guys was when you got an adversary trapped at dead six, drop down to tree top level and haul ass right over the center of the city. That got everyone with an AK shooting straight up and guess who got shot?? Of course, the number two guy—the chaser. Well anyway, I am sitting there when all of a sudden there is a brief whistling noise and then this F-4 goes by going super plus and there is an enormous clap of noise with stuff lifting off the ground, including me, and over where Jim and his guys are playing bridge this huge piece of plaster about the size of a blanket breaks loose and down it comes right over Jim. He doesn't even look startled but has blood running down his face from some cuts on his head. Without skipping a beat or even acknowledging the boom, the blood or the blasted plaster, he leans forward and with no emotion says, "four hearts." That's when I realized we had been there too long!!

It's impossible to comprehend, no matter how many times you sit and listen to the stories, the perspective of the war for the POWs. They were captured in late 1964, and '65 and '66. They came from F-100s and -105s, F-4s and A-4s, F-8s and A-6s, from the Air Force and the Navy and the Marines. They went to war when patriotism was a virtue and courage expected. They did what was asked of them without for a moment questioning whether their country would come to get them when things went awry. They were tortured and paraded, beaten and interrogated, but most of all they were disappointed.

It must have been a support for their hardships as each day they heard the sound of freedom overhead, jets attacking the critical targets in the North Vietnamese homeland. They got reinforcement to face their captors by seeing airplanes and listening to the bombs and the defensive reactions. They got occasional news through the tapping on their cell walls as they resisted with every fiber of their being their torturers' demand not to communicate with each other. Then, in the late summer of 1968, it got quiet. This had to be crushing to morale. What had happened? Why wasn't the war going on anymore? Was anyone thinking of them or trying to gain their freedom? Were they abandoned? They had faith and confidence, but there had to be doubt and discouragement.

Three and a half years—*years!*—later, there were airplanes overhead again. There was jet noise again, and bomb blasts and SAM launches and flak barrages.

There were new arrivals with news of America. In April and May of '72, it must have seemed that at last there might be hope of freedom. For six months they were hopeful once more. Pressure was being placed on the North Vietnamese, and maybe victory would come soon. Then, in late October, it stopped again. What now? Is it more cruel to dangle freedom and withdraw it without explanation than simply to never offer the slightest hope?

I was scheduled to be the F-4 supervisor of flying, a shift from six in the morning to six in the evening, carrying an FM hand-held "brick" and roaming the flight line in a pickup truck, on call to assist in launches and recoveries of my aircraft type. The SOF was a jack-of-all-trades, expected to handle anything that came up during the day, from weapons loading to weather watch to in-flight emergency assistance. I showed up on the morning of December 18, 1972, to pick up the radio and start the duty day.

Lt. Col. George Bowling, operations officer of the Weasels, met me at the door of the command post. He was grinning from ear to ear. "Raz, you're not going to believe this. C'mon in to intel and I'll show you something."

He led me into the quiet area of the intelligence section and pulled a small notebook out of his flight suit pocket. "Take a look at this. We're standing down today. Everything has been canceled and we're starting a max effort tomorrow. Here's what's going to happen tonight." He didn't say the specific words, almost as though he was apprehensive that the command post might be bugged and speaking them would divulge the awesome secret. He flipped the notebook open and displayed a list of call signs under the bold, all-caps heading "B-52s—THREE SHIP CELLS." I counted the call signs and multiplied by three. There were going to be 150 BUFFs tonight, all targeted within Route Pack VI.[2] It could mean as many as fifteen thousand bombs all in the Hanoi area in one night. This might be the beginning of the end.

"Holy shit! They're going to send 'them' into Pack VI? They're gonna get eaten alive. How are they going to do that?" I was conflicted between exaltation that we might finally be getting serious about ending the war and the fact that we might, in a moment of incredible naiveté, be sending a lot of vulnerable airplanes into an environment that maybe the SAC folks didn't clearly understand. We had been told for years that SAC had electronic warfare magic that made them survivable even in the most intense defenses of the Soviet Union. The alibi for not using them was that they would compromise this magic if they used it to win the war in Vietnam. That had always seemed like a load of crap to justify years of avoiding the dirty part of the war, as they flew meaningless sorties dropping thousands of bombs on jungle that didn't shoot back. They were certainly going to see someone shooting back tonight.

"We went to Guam a couple weeks ago to brief them on hunter-killer operations. I went with Tom Coady and Luke Lucas to talk to the SAC folks about what we do against SAMs. They liked what we had to say. We told them about our capabilities to detect the radars and hit them with Shrikes and about the F-4s killing the sites. They ate it up. They said that with Weasel support they can get the job done." I listened to Bowling tell about

_____

2. The actual sortie count for B-52s on December 18, 1972, was 129.

the briefing, but knew that it wasn't going to be that simple.

"So, we're going to be doing hunter-killer for the BUFFs?" It might be a good mission. It would certainly be an opportunity to put some serious hurt on the enemy. The SAMs would be looking at those big juicy targets, and we could really do a number on them. But the strikes that he had just shown me were tonight, not tomorrow.

"They said they absolutely won't go without Weasel support," Bowling continued. "But, they also won't go except at night."

There it was. The deal-breaker. The very essence of hunter-killer was visual. You had to see the missile site to attack it. You had to see the Shrike heading for the radar. You had to see an impact if possible. You had to see a missile come off the launcher. You had to see smoke. You had to see missiles in flight to evade. You had to be in the clear in daylight. You had to! At night, you would certainly see the missiles. I'd done enough night work to know that guns and missiles could light up the night sky. Tracers and muzzle flash and missile plumes were no problem to see in the dark. But after you see the bright flash, you get a phenomenon called after-image. See a flashbulb go off, then look away. The bright spot is centered on your retina, wherever you look. Seeing a missile fired at night would be no problem. Finding the missile site after the shot would be the problem. It sounded too much like being a defenseless target.

I picked up the FM radio and the keys to the truck and headed over to the squadron. There was already a bustle of activity. Dornberger and Mike Stevens were huddled in the scheduling area laying out names against expected tasking. We were the only game in town for killer support in the Weasel teams, and now we'd be operating at high volume both day and night. Those of us who had been dedicated Linebacker SAM killers weren't going to be able to do the whole job. A lot of guys who hadn't been downtown were suddenly going to get an opportunity to excel. We needed hunter-killer flights to support chaff drops for three waves of B-52s. Then we needed H/K teams to support the bomber wave itself, killing SAMs, avoiding missiles and each other, and staying out of the way of thousands of falling bombs. Finally, we needed H/K for two major strike packages during the day tomorrow. Chaff and bombers and MiGCAP and escorts and who knows what else. Yeah, a lot of guys were going into the barrel tonight.

I was lucky. Because I had the all-day SOF duty, I would miss the night and by default be on the day schedule tomorrow morning. I looked at the names tentatively penciled in. Most of the regulars were on the day schedule. The night killer elements were a mix of experienced crews who had been flying escort and bombing missions, along with brand-new folks who had arrived in October and November and not yet been to the tough spots. The day killers were guys like Larry Cary, Charlie Price, Luke Lucas, Paul Dwyer, Mike Mahaffey, Mike Thomas, and me. I hoped it was a conscious awareness that the day killers might be able to do the job, and the night killers would be filling the square to make the SAC guys happy that someone was there below them snapping their fingers to keep the elephants away. Snap, snap . . . no elephants. Still must be working.

On the Weasel side of the equation, it was different.

The Weasels could acquire radars, warn of threats, and fire ARMs at night. Evading SAMs would be dicey, but we had all done it enough to be able to handle it in the dark. And firing your own missiles might require the discipline to close your eyes or look away to avoid being blinded by the flash coming off the wing. But it could be done. The Weasel squadron was splitting the dedicated Linebacker hunters between day and night. There would be a need for strong experienced leadership at night as well as during the day. The wingmen of the hunter element would be young Weasels who had been doing support in lower threat areas. Additionally, there would be the baptism of fire for the F-4C Weasels, now getting their first opportunity to try out their equipment in a high-threat situation.

There would have to be a schedule distributed early during the day to let crews get ready for the night missions. They'd need some sleep, maybe a chance to talk about tactics for doing something they'd never done before. Some might even need ten or twelve hours to sober up. There was going to be a ten o'clock briefing for all crews. The duty officer was calling the hootches to round guys up and get them in to hear about the effort. I told him not to bother with mine. Mama-san had been taught always to answer the phone with a single message: "Hallo, he no here." Socks had trained her, and she often denied a presence well before the request for an individual had been made. I would stop by and knock on the doors personally.

The briefing room was packed. It was rare to get the entire roster of aircrews together at one time, and if there had ever been any doubt that the 34th was possibly the largest fighter squadron ever created, this would dispel it. There were nearly one hundred assigned and attached pilots and WSOs. The agenda was short and to the point. We were going back to Hanoi. It was to be a max effort. It was scheduled for three days, maybe longer. Expect to work twelve-hour shifts, and expect everyone to be on the Pack VI sorties. Don't go downtown. Don't call anyone. Don't discuss the missions on any unsecure phones. Check the schedules twice a day. Make sure you're always available. Get to the briefings early, and plan like your life depends on it. There will be no weather aborts. Tonight's schedule is posted. If you're on it, get into crew rest.

As the briefing broke up there was a mix of cheers and laughter, some nervous and some triumphant. Maybe this was finally it. Maybe we were going to wrap this thing up. Maybe after more than eight years of playing patty-cake we were going to finally kick some ass. More than a hundred B-52 sorties in one night was going to really get someone's attention. Merry Christmas, Ho!

The quadrangle bustled all day. Crews rushed between the weapons shop, the command post, and the various squadron buildings. The day schedule for December 19 was going to be every bit as impressive as the night ops. The three A-7 squadrons of the 354th Wing were going to launch and go unrefueled with bombs. The Weasels and hunter-killers would be interspersed, supporting chaff strikes and waves of bomb droppers. Escorts would be covering bombers from Korat as well as the other Thai bases. The EB-66 jammers would be on station constantly. Even the EC-121 radar pickets and C-130 airborne command post airplanes would be merged. Coordination of engine starts, taxi sequence, communication checks, maintenance loads, and even crew bussing to the aircraft had to be arranged. Getting the airplanes checked at the end of the runway and through the takeoff checks would have to be choreographed. An abort or emergency on the runway could not be allowed to screw up the launch. Procedures to clear the runway, get out of the way, step aside for the folks behind, all needed to be firmly established, rebriefed, and confirmed.

The sun set early, and the noise of the jets didn't start until just after dinnertime. The F-111s from Takhli were going to hit the MiG bases, single ship, low level. Then the chaff droppers laying their corridors. There would be Weasels and MiGCAPS and jamming from EB-66s. Then the big show, the first wave of B-52s. Those of us waiting for the day schedule on the 19th weren't going to be sleeping much. The club was empty. The CTF had only three guys sitting at the bar, sipping on warm cans of beer. The poker game was suspended.

The slamming of truck doors and cranking of engines signaled the first predawn assembling of crews for the day missions. I rolled out of the room and took a seat in the back of one of the trucks, taking time to lace up my leather boots. Only leather boots for trips to Hanoi. The cloth, nylon reinforced jungle boots might be all right for wearing around the base, but if the mission went to Pack VI, it had to be the leather boots. My Buddha was tucked into my flight suit collar. I was ready.

The traffic in and out of the command post area was heavy. The day crews shuffled into the planning area to grab maps and target photos and start the detail work of copying sequences, code words, call signs, and refueling track info. The night crews were funneling through intel debrief, chattering wide-eyed about what they'd seen on the missions. The adrenaline rush wouldn't abate for hours. A couple of the Weasel pilots stopped to talk to the day crews. The tales were impressive. Fireworks, firehoses of flak, SAMs everywhere, B-52s coming apart and falling thousands of feet. Beepers from parachutes. Bombs by the thousands lighting up the landscape. Impressive.

Intel started the briefing with an update on the night's operations. There had been three waves of B-52s, and they had lost three of the big bombers. Charcoal one had been downed in the target area in the first wave. Peach two, in the second wave, had been able to nurse the damaged airplane south into Thailand before the crew bailed out. They were recovered by Marines from the base at Nam Phong, north of Korat. Rose one, in the third wave, crashed just south of Hanoi. An F-111, Snug 40, was missing and presumed lost. The latest report was of an A-7 from the carrier *America* downed while attacking a SAM site just before the briefing started. All of the other supporting tactical aircraft returned unscathed. We were asked to be alert for emergency beepers and radio transmissions from downed crews as we worked the target areas. It was better than we'd thought, but worse than we'd hoped.

The target list was not significantly different. There were only so many items of military significance in the small area of the Red River Delta. There were all the usual suspects, the bridges and rail yards, the military storage areas and the familiar industrial areas around Thai Nguyen. There were a few unfamiliar but welcome additions. Radio Hanoi had been struck last night, and it was on the list for a day attack as well. What was unusual was the fact that there were so many strikes in the package. There were targets at Phu Tho and Viet Tri, at Phuc Yen and Kep, on the northeast and northwest rail lines. It seemed that if there was something of value, it would be visited.

There had been resistance to the war for at least five years. Protesters had fled to Canada, burned draft cards, gone limp in the streets, and made noise throughout the nation since 1968. It was hard to believe that what was occurring on the flight line was being done by the youth of that nation. The work being demanded of the crew chiefs, maintainers, bomb loaders, and specialists was nearly overwhelming, yet there they were, nineteen- and twenty-year-olds, grinning from ear to ear as they met the crews, prepped the airplanes, and readied the strike. Some had been on the flight line all night. Many had to be ordered to the barracks to get some rest, since they would be needed again for another night of maximum effort. Yet they stayed, and helped and worked and smiled.

It was, after all, the holiday season. It was a time of Christmas cheer, and finally, even on the flight line without the benefit of classified briefings and target listings, they knew this was the real thing. We were finally, after more than eight years of tepid, halfhearted, politically driven war, going to take the war to a conclusion. So it was only appropriate that these youngsters, slaving on the flight line, would send their greetings and wishes to the enemy. They had created Christmas cards for delivery by their pilots. The huge white centerline fuel tanks, sure to be jettisoned on the way in to the target areas, were festooned with red and green spray-painted sentiments for Ho Chi Minh, Jane Fonda, and Ramsey Clark. Some were traditional Christmas sentiments, sent sarcastically, and others were more ribald. There were scatology and insults aplenty, surrounded by artfully sprayed green Christmas trees and red Santa's sleighs. Some tanks were works of remarkable talent, and others were crude scribbling, but every tank on every centerline on every airplane that was going to Hanoi was painted.

It didn't take long for the word about the painted tanks to get to the wing commander, Colonel Vojvodich. The idea of defacing government property wasn't one that he could tolerate without demanding some answers. Where did all this spray paint come from? Whose idea was this? Who was in charge of government issue spray paint? The answer came quickly. It was Turk Turley, the field maintenance squadron commander. Turk, an F-105 hundred-mission veteran from my first tour, was now flying the F-4E as a maintenance squadron commander attached to the 34th Tac Fighter Squadron. It was FMS that owned the paint locker, and therefore Turk's responsibility. "Get Turley in my office, *now!*"

"I think he's flying, sir," the wing king's exec responded. "I'll track him down as soon as he gets back."

The wing boss knew Turk well. Turk had volunteered to fly his wing on any Pack VI missions, not only as a way of keeping the wing commander alive—the boss's experience in fast jets was mostly related to reconnaissance—but also as a way of keeping young lieutenants isolated from "the man" and out of harm's way. Turk knew he could take care of himself, and might even be able to put himself in place to get a MiG if he had to pull the boss's chestnuts out of the proverbial fire.

Turk reported to headquarters smartly as soon as he got the word. "Yes, sir. What seems to be the problem?"

"Turk, what's this about your flight line troops misusing government paint and putting all that crap on those centerline fuel tanks?"

"Beats me, sir. I heard something about some markup going on, painting on the bombs and centerlines."

"You know that's prohibited. What the hell do you intend to do about it?"

"Well sir, I think I'm going to have to order more paint." Turk saluted smartly and withdrew.

The skies were clear over Hanoi when we got there. Tendrils of smoke drifted up from targets that had been hit during the night and still smoldered. There was always tenseness as you left the foothills and got out into the flats, but today there was little going on. The A-7s were hitting targets to the north and west of Hanoi, while the F-4 bomb droppers were dealing with bridges and storage areas closer to bull's-eye. Only one or two SAMs were fired, and little was seen of the big guns. A MiG engagement had taken place during the chaff drops, and the contrails of the missiles formed a tic-tac-toe game overhead, white against the bright blue sky. The air defense was either overwhelmed from the previous night or had made a conscious decision to hoard their resources and wait for the BUFFs to return. Either way, we had a light day.

The second night of the campaign, the B-52s returned with three more waves of bombers.[3] Recce photos showed both the damage and the precision of the campaign. Bomb strings from the huge aircraft walked

---

3. On day two, the B-52s flew 93 sorties. Day three brought 99, and by day four, with most targets destroyed, the B-52 effort was scaled back to 30 sorties per night. A Christmas day recess provided opportunity to reconstitute the bomber force, and 120 sorties were flown on the twenty-sixth, then 60 each night until the end of the campaign on December 29.

across the targets and carefully seemed to sidestep residential areas or designated off-limits compounds. Intelligence information on probable POW compounds was put to good use, and while we may have joked about dropping one on Jane Fonda, we were well aware that a lot of our friends had front-row seats for the battle that was going on.

Jack Van Loan and many of his friends had been moved out of Hanoi early during the Linebacker campaign. They had been transported out of the city in mid-May to a new camp they dubbed Dogpatch, near the Chinese border. Some said it was an attempt to break up the cadre of senior resistance leaders among the POWs. Guys like Jack Van Loan, Robbie Risner, Paul Galanti, Larry Guarino, and others had been well organized, and with the commencement of Linebacker, they were working hard to integrate the new arrivals to the POW camps into their organizations. Maybe it was breaking up the leadership, or maybe it was a way of protecting the North Vietnamese bargaining chips at the peace talks. Either way, they were going to miss the show.

Dave Mott, on the other hand, was still in the center of town.[4] He had been at the Hoa Lo prison, the infamous Hanoi Hilton, from shortly after his capture until early December. Then he was moved, in apparent anticipation of a possible rescue effort similar to the 1970 Son Tay raid, from Hoa Lo to the smaller Plantation in the northeast section of Hanoi. With rudimentary hand tools, they were ordered to dig bomb shelter trenches in their cells under their rough board beds, large enough

---

4. Capt. David P. Mott was shot down in South Vietnam on May 19, 1972, near Quang Tri, while flying an OV-10 Bronco with a Marine artillery spotter. He was captured, transported to North Vietnam, and interned at the Hanoi Hilton.

to crawl into in the event of attack. The similarity in size between a sheltering trench and a man-size grave was not lost on the prisoners.

With the first strikes, it quickly became apparent to POWs in the capital that things were coming to a conclusion. The bombing intensity, the night defensive reactions, even the flaming wreckage of the big bombers that had been hit overhead, all served to let them know that someone at last was getting serious about ending the war. The bombs were close, but everyone in the prison compounds knew the business. They knew that we knew they were there, and they knew the difficulty of hitting targets when the defenses were up. Photos of suspected POW camps were posted in intel, and several of us took coordinates on missions and made attempts to overfly the camps and maybe get the message through that we knew where they were and wouldn't hit them.

From the Plantation, Mott could only see outside by standing on the boards of his rough bunk and straining to reach a corner of the high, small window. From there he could see the flashes of the airbursting flak and the bright fire trails of the SAMs. From there he could catch the tumbling fireballs of the B-52s that were hit, and see the flames' reflections in the chutes of descending crewmembers who were able to eject. There would be company in camp in a day or two.

Ted Sienicki was at Hoa Lo when Linebacker II kicked off.[5] It didn't take long before the camp's propaganda operatives were broadcasting statements from Americans over the radio, complaining about the

---

5. First Lt. Ted Sienicki was shot down on May 3, 1972, in an F-4E on a fast FAC, "Wolf" mission near the DMZ.

"nearness and intensity of the bombing." The prisoners couldn't tell the source of the statements, whether they came from the few collaborators among the otherwise tight-knit POW community, or maybe from an American politician or antiwar activist, but the reaction was immediate. It couldn't possibly be close enough or intense enough.

Our dream was to someday soon hear silence, peer over the glass-embedded, stone-capped high walls, and see the Gulf of Tonkin, 'cause the city was fucking bombed away. We laughed at that statement for the rest of our tour, and it became the phrase of choice to indicate when somebody was whining or being a baby, poor sport, whatever. Oh, dear, the bomb is too near and too intense.

One day, a bomb exploded closer than ever. We weren't hurried in from outside, as we usually were; the raid was a surprise with little warning. A softball-sized jagged piece of shrapnel flew by me at great speed, and bounced along the cobblestone and slate floor. Impressive. It was nice to finally feel like a ground troop.

Sienicki's reaction wasn't fear, but hope and enthusiasm. "I never worried about bombs being too close. Neither did anybody I knew. But one guy, upon learning from a B-52 crewmember who arrived in camp that SAC was using the Hilton as an offset aim point, wondered aloud how many times he or others simply forgot to press the offset button!"

Night three was bad for the bombers. Six were lost. Quilt three, Brass two, Orange three, Straw two, Olive one, and Tan three; the names read like a litany of bureaucratic indecisiveness. Dull colors and inane nouns, each one a label for a huge chunk of American prestige and military might. Each one a last ride for a half-dozen men, asked to fight and die for a war that only a few Americans cared about anymore. When we arrived for the predawn briefing of the day three missions, we wondered if it would get worse or if there would be a turning point.

Target photos on the intel wall showed results. A top down view of Radio Hanoi showed a multistory blockhouse surrounded on all four sides by revetments to shield the building from near misses and shrapnel blasts. A three-shot series of black-and-white 8x10 glossies showed the facility before the first strikes, then with a row of Mk-82 craters across the building with one impact atop a revetment but the core unscathed, and finally with a dead center hit by a laser-guided Mk-84 dropped by one of the Ubon F-4s. There'd be no propaganda broadcasts from Hanoi Hannah for a while.

I had Kirby Carlton in my pit. As I'd predicted, he was going to bull's-eye. As we dropped off the tanker, the APR-36/37 began its chirping and buzzing. By the time we got to the North Vietnam border and edged along Banana Valley, the Firecan light was fairly steady, and the center of the scope showed a gyrating bug with dancing green legs to indicate the direction of various radars that were ticking across us. I could hear Kirby's breathing in the intercom and, though he didn't say anything, I could tell his apprehension was building. I watched the radar scope and saw him routinely scrolling the antenna up and down to search in front of us. The inertial nav showed he had the orbit point we'd selected as an anchor as we would search for SAM sites.

We were using bull's-eye today: the center of Hanoi. We still had fifty miles to go when the RWR showed the first launch light and a stuttering launch tone. "Launch light," Kirby announced, although it wasn't necessary. Bright red lights in the cockpit have a tendency to garner my attention.

"That's not a launch, Kirby," I tried to calm him. "See the light flickering and not real steady? Listen to the tone. It's kind of broken up. That's not a real launch. You'll know it when we get one for real. I'll tell you when it's real, then check the vector direction and start looking that way for the missile. Call it for me when you see it." We'd been through most of this in our crew briefing before the flight, but I knew that the first time was always tense.

"Okay." He was holding up well. He'd do all right.

The sun coming up reflected off the Red River and showed the lakes scattered through the city. We were almost to the orbit. The launch tone cut through the radio chatter from the strike flight, and the difference was distinctive. "Here we go, Kirby. That's the real thing."

ALMOST AT THE SAME TIME, the Weasel calls the launch. "Eagle's got a launch. Take it down, Eagles."

"Missile at one o'clock, Raz." Kirby proves himself adept at following instructions. His voice rises in pitch just a bit, but he's doing a pretty good job of covering.

"Okay, got it. Hang on, we're taking it down right." I roll the airplane, light the burners, and descend into the missile. Larry Cary, flying four today, checks right and stays with me. We're both headed down, side by side, about three thousand feet apart. The missile climbs on a bright orange smoke trail, still in the booster phase and therefore not yet guided. A puff of smoke indicates booster drop-off, and the white flare of the sustainer starts almost immediately. The missile levels but is already above us, passing well clear to our left. Once past us, we don't care where it goes. We've got the site.

"Eagle three's got the site. Let's check right for a left roll-in and off to the north. Looks wide open, let's drop all four cans." The missile site is in the clear. Apparently the battery has just moved in and hasn't yet gotten their camouflage in place. They are on the southeast corner of a good-sized lake, just to the south of the Red River. Missile launchers and the radar are easy to see, and as I pull up to roll in, I can see rows of olive drab trucks carrying more missiles ready to replenish the launchers.

"Eagle three's up." I pull up only slightly, then roll inverted to ease the nose down and aim at the missile launchers. Barely four thousand feet above the river, I'm looking at the fattest site I've ever seen. Rolling back upright, I put the pipper on the first launcher nearest the river. Pickle once. I raise the nose just a bit and see the radar van. Pickle, pickle. Roll just slightly right, then pickle. I feel the tiny lurches as the CBU cans come off at each punch of the button atop the stick. I pull off momentarily to the left, then slam the rudder and stick back to reverse right. A stream of 23mm tracer arches up off my nose, but I'm turning away. I look back over my right shoulder and see the first of the sparkles as the bomblets start to light up the site. Puffs of smoke over the missiles identify where the CBU cans have opened.

In a split-second the area is covered with bomblets detonating like hundreds of flashbulbs at a presidential press conference.

Cary follows and performs the same ballet. He's experienced enough and cool enough under fire to know what to do. His CBU pops, and soon his bomblets are adding to the fireworks show. I watch his airplane come off the pass and can tell by the cutoff angle that he's got me in sight. But it's just beginning. Now there's one, no two, now three missiles coming off the launchers. They haven't been launched, they're simply exploding. There are more missiles coming off the trucks. No Soviet designer ever built a transporter to shield against CBU, and the flood of shrapnel has pierced fuel tanks and set off chemical reactions causing missiles to skitter across the ground, lurch into the air, or simply explode on the backs of their vehicles. We clear the area to the north, then come back toward the southwest recrossing the Red.

"Eagle three and four are Winchester," I pass the word that we've expended our ordnance. Eagle lead still has Shrikes aboard and will cover the strike flights that are already outbound. As I look back over my left shoulder, there is a tower of bright orange smoke rising from the lake. It's nearly a mile high now and still billowing upward. Flashes within the cloud base tell me the site is still cooking off. There'll be one less threat to the BUFFs tonight.

On the tanker for post-strike, we get congratulations from strike flights that were in the area. One flight lead reports that the orange column of smoke was passing fourteen thousand feet as he was on his way out. "Nice job, Eagles," is the best paycheck we could ask for.

◆ ◆ ◆

THE MISSION BRIEFING ON DAY six brings new orders. If there was ever any doubt that the military is nothing but an extension of national foreign policy, it is dissipated that morning. The intel briefer starts with a classified message from the secretary of state. The message is terse and to the point. Negotiations in Paris are at a critical juncture, and it is absolutely critical that maximum pressure be maintained on the North Vietnamese government. There will be no weather aborts for any reason. The normal background chatter that buzzes under the drone of a routine briefing goes eerily silent.

We have learned the hard way over the years that there are certain things you simply do not do if you want to live. One of the most critical is that you never go into SAM country if you can't see the ground. At the very least, if you have to fly over a cloud deck you keep a minimum of ten thousand feet of clear air between you and the underlying weather. You have to see a SAM to avoid it. You need a minimum interval to find the missile and then maneuver to get out of its way. If you can't see the launch and can't see the missile, you can't do much to protect yourself.

You need some clear airspace around you to watch for MiGs. When the MiGs come to play, they are under control of ground radar sites and they don't need to see a thing. All they need is to follow the ground controller's instructions, close undetected to within missile range, then fire and escape. You'll be dead before you know there's a threat.

Guns aren't much different. The big flak batteries in Route Pack VI are often radar directed. I learned back in my F-105 tour that ducking into a cloud is no way to escape a malicious flak battery. They simply keep shooting without the slightest indication that they are aware of any clouds. For Dr. Kissinger to be telling us that there will be no weather considerations regarding getting to the target is a demand for suicide missions. If you lose the authority to make prudent judgments about where you go and what visibility is required to get the job done, you sacrifice your tactical control. There's a bit of mumbling about whether Dr. K has shaken the stick of an individual's particular jet to indicate he's taking control. It isn't his butt on the line.

The targets, once again, are right around the capital. The hunter-killer flight is simply going to anchor an orbit at ground zero, bull's-eye. If we can see the ground, we'll recce the area and look for sites. If we get shot at, we'll kill them. If they look at us with radar, we'll Shrike back at them. Standard routine. Nothing new, except the weather won't make any difference. I have visions of cruising in close formation in gray murk waiting for the flash of a SAM hitting the flight.

We get to the target area and, as the weatherman predicted, there is solid undercast over the Red River valley. Tops of the clouds are around four thousand feet. We spread out, in the clear, just a few thousand feet above the layer. The inertial nav system winds down to zero, telling me we we're over the center of Hanoi. We set up a racetrack holding pattern. It isn't quite the holding you would do waiting for an instrument approach to the airport at Hometown USA. It's a bit faster. Make that quite a bit faster, with us holding between 450 and 500 knots. We are spread somewhat wider, and we aren't constrained by airspace limitations of an air traffic control agency. But, it's a holding pattern.

Fifteen, then twenty, then twenty-five minutes pass. We are sitting over the center of Hanoi flying predictable circles, three thousand feet above a solid undercast in SAM country! Nothing! Absolutely nothing happening. The bombing flights come and go, dropping on LORAN coordinates with a pathfinder aircraft or seeking holes in the cloud layer to the north of Hanoi with alternate targets. But we stay on station and see no SAMs, no MiGs, no flak. Maybe we've won. Maybe they've run out of missiles. Maybe the war is over.

A hundred and twenty miles to the northeast of our orbit, Jack Van Loan is in trouble in Dogpatch. He is senior in his group of POWs, and his captors hold him responsible for behavior. One of the guards is upset and berates Jack on the lack of respect shown by one of the prisoners who did not stand up when a guard entered the courtyard. Van Loan shakes his head and sees just one more day of confrontation to add to the years of resistance. The guard tells him to dress for an interview with the camp commander, the "Rat."

There have been years spent with the Rat. He has been with them through the long interrogations, the periods of solitary confinement, the beatings and "rope tricks" and propaganda shows. The Rat introduced them to the Cuban and the pacifists and the movie stars. He has been the architect and the overseer of years of torture. When bad things happen, the Rat is usually nearby.

Jack dons his "dress reds," the canvas red-and-white-striped pajama outfit that has been worn for so many beatings, parades, and propaganda photos. The Rat yells about the disrespect and bad behavior of Jack's prisoners. Van Loan reminds the commandant that standing and bowing hasn't been required for years. "What the hell is so special now?" he inquires. A crowd of guards and camp occupants hear the commotion; they gather at the open windows of the office. The Rat responds, "B-52s bomb Hanoi!"

"I don't believe you." In fact Van Loan definitely does believe him, but he's learned to try to get more information whenever he can. He hopes to work the Rat's frenzy into an advantage that will let him discover more about the situation.

The commandant turns to his desk and picks up a newspaper. Across the front is a series of pictures of six American crewmen, all from a B-52 downed over Hanoi. He yells that there are hundreds of new Yankee air pirates captured, and now prisoners of the Vietnamese.[6] It's a gross exaggeration, but it tells Jack that the war has entered a final phase. The tirade goes on as Jack is warned and threatened about the bad attitude of his charges, and how he must teach them to show proper respect.

Jack returns to his room and releases the news that B-52s have struck the center of Route Pack VI and they will all be going home soon. It's a relatively merry Christmas for the POWs. The bombs bursting in air and the rockets' red glare have a new and very intense meaning for the prisoners. Something is very definitely being done on their behalf.

THE AMERICAN FLAG FLIES FROM the flagpole in front of the command post in the quadrangle. The deputy com-

---

6. During the entire Linebacker campaign, 36 B-52 crewmembers were captured. A total of 43 POWs from the Linebacker II campaign were released, 33 from B-52s and 10 from USN/USAF tactical aircraft types.

mander for operations building flies the 388th Tactical
Fighter Wing Flag, and each of the squadrons flies a
flag depicting the squadron patch. The 34th squadron
proudly displays a string of small white flags beneath
the squadron banner, each with a bright red five-
pointed star depicting a MiG kill. They don't date back
to the Rolling Thunder campaign; there would be a lot
more flagpoles needed. These are Linebacker kills, and
it's the nature of fighter pilots to want aerial victories. It
would be nice to have some sort of similar flag to display SAM kills, but there aren't any flags for missiles,
and we don't paint tiny silhouettes of radar vans on the
intake or canopy rail of our aircraft. We have to live
with the fact that we've killed SAMs and there simply
aren't enough MiGs to go around.

Gyle Atwood is lying on the "beach," our grassy area
spread with lounge chairs near the front door of the
CTF. The doors are open to make it easy to wander in
for a beer, and the stereo speakers have been moved outside to provide a bit of rock 'n' roll ambience to the sun
worshippers. "Hey, Raz, you ever get a shot at a MiG?"
It's inane conversation on a lazy afternoon, relaxing after the morning trip to the north.

"Nah, I've got more MiG shots at me. I always manage to trap them at my six. Closest I ever got was line
abreast with a -17 one time. I usually try to go too fast
for them to catch me."

"Think you'll get one?"

"I've got a live-and-let-live philosophy. I've never
been hurt by a MiG, don't see no need to hurt one of
them. Now SAMs, they're a different story. I don't like
missiles. I like killing missiles." This isn't totally true,
but with few MiGs and being dedicated to a different
mission, it's a pretty good rationalization. The fact is

that MiG killing is very much a matter of being in the right place at the right time. If you're lucky, you get a MiG; if you're unlucky, a MiG gets you. Often the killed never sees the killer. One-on-one duals pitting aerial skills between fighter pilots are always glorified, but seldom the way it really occurs in the skies over Hanoi.

"Seems like the guys at Udorn have got the MiG market pretty well cornered," I continue. "They've got the goodies to get in the right place. They're supposed to be getting some sort of gadget that can tell the MiGs at a distance.[7] They've got dedicated GCI controllers to point them at the bad guys, and they even get their own radio frequency, so we don't know that they're being vectored into position. Hell, I've heard escort flights being vectored by controllers to block the MiGs or herd them back in the direction of the Udorn guys. I don't care, as long as they keep 'em off my back."

Day eight of Linebacker II and we're coming in from the Gulf of Tonkin just north of Haiphong, headed toward the capital. Bombing flights have got targets on the northeast railroad as well as between Kep airfield and Hanoi. I'm flying Condor three with Larry Cary on my wing as four. SAM firings have become increasingly rare, but being in the delta with scattered clouds and heavy haze is always sure to raise the heart rate.

"Red Crown, on Guard. Blue bandits airborne. Three two zero at ten, bull's-eye, angels five. Red Crown out." The destroyer in the gulf has radar to cover most of the

---

7. Aircraft at Udorn were being outfitted with Combat Tree—a system capable of interrogating the MiG IFF (air traffic control coded identification for radars). Ground radar stations can view enhanced blips from cooperating aircraft, but must know the IFF code of the aircraft. With Combat Tree, the Udorn F-4s could positively identify their radar contacts as enemy aircraft without the MiGs' cooperation.

area, and links to both Disco, the EC-121 airborne radar control plane, and facilities in Thailand that pick up North Vietnamese radio transmissions and even, reportedly, live intel from observers on the ground near the enemy airfields. MiG calls are coded as red, white, or blue, indicating the type as -17, -19, or -21. Positions are relative to the geographic center of Hanoi. MiG-21s are airborne ten miles northwest of Hanoi at five thousand feet. We're just coming up on the coast, westbound and descending from twenty thousand feet. The picture begins to form in my head. No threat.

The Weasels are ahead of me, about two miles and descending. I've got the element slightly offset to the right and riding about two thousand feet above the F-105s. Cary is on my right. "Kirby, the MiGs are probably out of Phuc Yen. That's about where that position is." I want him to get the picture as well.

"Red Crown, on Guard. Blue bandits, three two five at twenty, bull's-eye, angels thirteen. Red Crown out." Sounds like the MiGs are headed north and climbing. Doesn't make sense. The strike flights are the opposite direction and to the east. Maybe they think their airfield is the target again, and they're running for the border.

We're over land now, with about forty-five miles to go to the center of Hanoi. Radars are pretty quiet, with only the occasional buzz of a Firecan. We've blown the centerlines, and the toughest task right now is trying to get a bit of cutoff each time the Weasel makes a turn. The F-105s seem to unconsciously accelerate the closer they get to bull's-eye. We're doing a nice firm 500 knots, and the Weasel pulls away every time we run straight for more than a mile or two. It's a dance of continual anticipation. Try to guess which way he's going to make his next turn and aim there ahead of time, so that you cut across the corners. Guess wrong and you fall behind; get it right and you're ready to help no matter what happens. You develop a rhythm when you fly with the same guys regularly that lets you guess right more than wrong.

"Red Crown on Guard. Blue bandits, now three three zero at forty-five, bull's-eye, angels four zero. Red Crown out." They're halfway to the Chinese border now, and so high that they must be planning on a long-range weekend trip to some hot spot in China. I can see the wandering path of the Red now, and almost make out the outline of the lake where there's no longer a SAM site. I wonder for a moment how long it took them to clean up the mess we left a few days ago. Maybe they won't put another missile there. I look forward again, as Condor lead seems to be veering a bit south, probably going to point at a place down near Nam Dinh that has shot at a lot of Navy airplanes. I wonder where the MiGCAP is. Seems as though they ought to be heard from by now.

We're not seeing any SAMs, which is continuing emphasis that the enemy is conserving them for the B-52s' night missions. It also means that the MiG calls are probably correct. They won't want to endanger their own aircraft with the big missiles. I'm trying to watch the Weasels ahead of me, scan the ground for SAM sites, and look to my left, where the MiGs have been called. They're small aircraft, they don't trail smoke like we do, and they are going to know where we are, while we are probably not going to get much more detail on their position. The more places I've got to look, the less I'm really seeing in any of them.

"Disco on Guard. Disco shows blue bandits now three four zero from bull's-eye at thirty. Angels two five. Disco out." Thirty miles north of Hanoi at 25,000 feet. Now returning and descending. That's not good. It is a not-unfamiliar tactic, and if they are coming our way we will probably see them slash through us at supersonic speed. They may or may not be preceded by an Atoll missile.

The handoff between Red Crown, a Navy destroyer out in the gulf, and Disco, airborne over northern Laos, is an indicator that the whole scenario is being choreographed at a higher level, probably by the top-secret facility recently established in northern Thailand called Teaball. We've tried to learn more about what Teaball does, how they do it, and what is going on between us and the MiGs, but little detail is available. The answer we get from intel is that we don't have the appropriate security clearance. We don't have a "need to know." The idea that the American side doesn't need to know what is going on, in an aerial combat equation that can result in our death, doesn't make any more sense than the other aspects of the war, so we simply accept the judgment. The essential fact is that there is a place called Teaball. They talk to Disco and other folks. They probably talk to the MiGCAP, and they know some stuff about what the enemy airplanes are doing. If it works, MiGs get killed. If it doesn't, well, we don't worry about that too much. We don't have the need to know.

"Disco shows blue bandits now fifteen miles north of bull's-eye, descending through angels one eight. Disco out." They are closer now, lower, and suddenly I feel vulnerable. We may be the only folks out here running with our ECM pods in standby, so we're the clearest picture for any interceptor radar in the area. The strike package isn't much more than a broad smear on the radar scopes, and chaff that preceded them is making that blur even harder to decipher. The hunter-killer flight is south of the chaff, away from the bombing formations and offering a nice set of four discrete blips for the controllers.

I'm spending more time looking for the MiGs now than for SAM sites. I tell Kirby to get us looking on twenty-mile scope and start scanning slightly high and to our right. Without mentioning it, I flip the weapons switches out of bombing mode and select the first Sparrow. I wish we had Sidewinders, but there's no place left to hang them on the airplane most days. The centerline tank is long gone, but we've got the out-boards and the four CBU. Disco is doing the bandit calls now, and it is apparent from the altitudes and dis-tances that the MiGs are headed our way. Where's the damn MiGCAP? Is Teaball talking to the Triple Nickle F-4s from Udorn? Are those hotshots somewhere around here with authority to cook off a couple of mis-siles into the middle of the strike package? Sure hope they know what they're doing.

I see a flash of white smoke out of the corner of my eye, high and to the right. I check-turn quickly to the right. It might be a missile, or maybe a plume of un-burned fuel as one of the strike aircraft goes into after-burner. It's MiGs! There's a pair of -21s roughly fifteen hundred feet apart and about four miles away. They're diving and fast, headed for the -105s ahead of me. It doesn't look like they are aware of me. "Condor three's got bandits, right two o'clock. Condor four, let's blow the tanks. Three's coming right."

It takes but a split-second. I look down in the cockpit to just ahead of the throttles, to find the toggle switch to dump the outboard tanks. The stick is moving right and pulling the nose up. I need some altitude and turning room to get behind the MiGs, and I want some space if they come hard into me. I flip the red safety guard up and blow the tanks. Then grab the throttles, push into AB, and simultaneously reach over the front of the inboard throttle to hit the dogfight button on the front that will switch the radar to five-mile scope and boresight. All I'll have to do is put the gun sight on the MiG and the radar will feed the AIM-7 a lock-on. If I need the gun, a flip of the tiny switch on the outboard throttle with the pinky of my left hand will give me the Vulcan. Larry Cary is calling, "Condor four, tanks away. Six is clear. Tallyho." He's given me all I need to know to press the attack. He's got the MiGs in sight and is watching our tails for other players in the game.

My momentary glance into the cockpit takes just long enough for the MiGs to come forward, now almost straight ahead of me. This is going to be too easy. Kirby calls "system lock" to let me know the radar has acquired a lock on a target. I can't shoot until I know it isn't locked on either of the Weasels. I scan the area ahead. The Weasel is a good 30 degrees left of the nose. The MiGs are now straight ahead. The three F-4s behind the MiGs are closing fast. The what? Where the hell did they come from? I'm suddenly going to have to take a number to get a shot. I'm number four in the shooter queue.

"Condor four's got smokers on the nose," Cary responds with a visual call. I can hear disappointment in his voice. He too was hoping for a shot. There was one for each of us, my first and his second. We check-turn farther right and look for a straggler from the F-4 flight, wondering if they came as a threesome or if the last member of the flight is lagging. "Condor lead, three. Heads up. Come hard left. Bandits coming up on the right with shooters in trail." I watch the Weasels respond to my radio call, break left, and descend. The MiG pilots may never have seen their target, simply following the ground radar controller's instructions all the way. They're going to die unaware of how many airplanes are around them.

The Weasels circle back to the left, while I reverse my turn to close up and resume a supporting position. The MiGs disappear to the south, low and fast. The Phantoms chase. I don't know the call sign of the F-4s. I don't know what frequency they are on. I don't know if they are aware that Condor was threatened. We're missing a big chunk of the big picture here, and it's probably because the Air Force has decided we need to have more aces than the Navy. The F-4s are on their own discrete radio frequency, getting vectors to the enemy aircraft but isolated from the rest of the strike flights. They didn't know where we were, and we didn't know their intentions. There'll be no MiG kill for me today, but at least there's been no kill for the MiGs either.

AS SUDDENLY AS IT STARTED, the maximum effort ends. Linebacker II runs for eleven days, and before New Year's Eve the North Vietnamese conclude that it is in their best interest to return to the bargaining table. In Dogpatch, the prisoners are rounded up and loaded aboard buses. Paul Galanti is astonished at the speed with which they are returned to Hanoi.[8] The trip to Dogpatch last May over bomb-damaged roads in trucks driving blacked out at night took days. The journey back to Hoa Lo is only a couple of hours in broad day-

---

8. Lt.(jg) Paul Galanti was shot down on June 17, 1966, in an A-4C aircraft on a bombing mission from the carrier USS Hancock. As one of the earliest captured, he was among the first to be released on February 12, 1973, after six and half years in captivity.

light. He's sure, knowing about the heavy Christmas raids on Hanoi, that the trucks are going directly to Gia Lam airport for the long-awaited flight to freedom. When they arrive back at the familiar façade of the Hanoi Hilton, he's disappointed, but only momentarily. They know now that it will only be a little bit longer.

It's just days after the end of the Linebacker II push that the unbelievable occurs at Korat. We receive an inspection team from Thirteenth Air Force headquarters in the Philippines, an operational readiness inspection. Someone wants to check if we are capable of fighting a war. A small army of starched, pressed, shoe-shined bureaucrats descends upon the base armed with clipboards and checklists. They spend a week looking in file cabinets and desk drawers, walking behind maintenance troops and monitoring flight briefings. They tsk-tsk and mumble under their breath while surreptitiously jotting down cryptic notes that might be good news or bad news for the base. In a peacetime world they would be exercising war plans and assigning mission tasks to check our readiness. In the week after the biggest operation of the Vietnam air war, at a base that has been challenged to fly round-the-clock combat in a half-dozen aircraft types while supporting a second deployed fighter wing, the idea of an ORI is ludicrous.

Suspicions are confirmed when the inspection is over and the report is submitted. We fail miserably. Somehow, despite the real-world evidence to the contrary, the 388th Wing is graded as not operationally ready. At the CTF we huddle over the bar, nursing our beers and wondering if they might send us all home as punishment. Maybe they won't let us fly any more combat missions next week. What do you do with an unqualified wing in the combat zone? Paranoia runs rampant that somebody at higher headquarters is out to get someone.

At the wing headquarters, there is a brutal bloodletting. The deputy commander for logistics, a senior officer in charge of all the flight line maintenance, munitions, aircraft repair shops, and supply systems, is fired. The maintenance squadron commander, the munitions squadron commander, and the supply squadron commander are also fired. All disappear from the base overnight. We still fly missions, however, and the daily frag doesn't look any different than it did before the inspection. The deputy commander for operations, Col. Jack Chain, is shifted over to logistics. He's a tall, slender, young colonel with a ready smile, a brilliant mind, a quick wit, and respected skills as a fighter pilot. He's flown the toughest missions and, unlike many of the higher-ranking officers, has proven himself very capable in the airplane. His job is to fix the problems of maintenance and supply and prepare the response to the inspection report. There's no transition period or break-in for the job. He's got it now, and he's already behind schedule.

Chain is, by temperament and preference, a fighter pilot. He's flown F-100s in Europe and in combat in South Vietnam. He's been a forward air controller with the Army, and he's been qualified in the A-7 that is operating in our sister wing at Korat. He's been flying the F-4 with us in combat for the last six months. He's good at it. But he's also good at command and administration. He's been at the highest level in the Pentagon and learned how to solve problems from the top leadership in the Air Force. He is clearly destined for big things in the Air Force, that is if he can fix today's problems.

Two days after the bloodbath of firings, Paul Dwyer, the squadron operations officer, calls me into his office.

Chain is looking to let a junior officer look over his shoulder while he works. He wants to provide someone in the squadron with the same opportunity to learn early that was provided to him. He's looking for an executive officer to help him out, and he's offered me the job. Dwyer cautions that it will take long hours but I'll still be able to fly, and it will only be for six weeks or until the inspection response is completed. It sounds like a good deal. I agree.

Chain was a maintenance officer years earlier, but this is a huge and complex empire he has inherited. He starts the workday early and he ends it late. I quickly find I can't arrive before him, nor can I wait him out to leave. Each night I find myself sheepishly hanging into his office from the doorway, asking if he needs me for anything more. Invariably he waves me off and wishes me a good evening.

We lay out a schedule for the week. There are six main organizations subordinate to the logistics commander: two maintenance and one each avionics, munitions, supply, and administration. Each day we visit one of the functional areas to tour, talk with the workers, and see what is happening. The rotation teaches me a trick that Chain uses that invariably dazzles the troops and gains their loyalty. Before we jump in the blue staff car, he pulls a manual from the wall of bookshelves behind his desk. He finds a detail or two relating to the area that we are going to visit. If the day's tour is of munitions, he may glean some facts about fuse storage or disposal of packing crates from cluster bomb units. Armed with his tidbit, he waits, as we are guided through an area, until the appropriate time. Then he asks an NCO or supervisor a question of remarkable detail about a specific of that individual's job. The worker is amazed at the boss's detailed knowledge of seemingly every aspect of the organization.

Each afternoon there is a "standup" briefing. The commanders of all the subordinate organizations meet in the logistics briefing room. In rotation they each stand up, and with slides or overhead charts they quickly advise Chain about the work of the day. They have a short outline and must cover every item every day in less than five minutes. Here is where we uncover the successes and failures of the daily operations. We know what aircraft flew and which were grounded. We know what parts are overdue and what munitions are running low. If problems are discovered, we brainstorm the solutions.

Also at the daily briefing, we spend time assembling the reply to the inspection report. Every single discrepancy that the inspectors list must be addressed, and an appropriate corrective action must be implemented. The inspection team returns in sixty days and will look at every area to see that their write-ups are no longer a problem. There are hundreds of individual gripes from the inspection, and each one demands an answer. Some solutions are fast and easy. Others are complex and require considerable time, effort, and resources.

Turk Turley is one of the lucky maintenance commanders who has kept his job. A Thud driver with me during my first tour, now a Phantom pilot and experienced warrior, Turk knows how to keep his airplanes flying, his maintainers motivated, and his pilots happy. When other commanders at standup occasionally incur Chain's wrath, Turk usually has the answers for the boss that keep him off the hot seat. Now he's got a problem.

"Item number seventy-eight under the field maintenance squadron write-ups, sir. It says 'Aircraft not painted in accordance with T.O. 00-20A-1.' How are we going to address that?" Turk has to respond to the complaint, but isn't sure what the write-up is about. The tech order is a general description of the way Air Force aircraft are painted. It covers the colors for the camouflage, the placement of tail numbers, decals and insignia, and the requirements for touch-up and repainting. "What isn't 'in accordance,' sir?"

Chain frowns, tents his fingers in front of his face, and glances around the table. We all quickly scan around the group, then back to the boss. He obviously knows what the write-up is about, and he's probably already got his answer.

"Anybody?" No responses.

"It refers to the shark-mouth paint job. It isn't regulation." He drops the bomb.

"Turk, here's the corrective action for the IG team. One word. *Noted.* We aren't changing a thing while I'm in this seat. Korat keeps the teeth. I'll take the heat. Meeting adjourned." Here's a guy who's going places.[9]

SPIKE MILAM LOOKS LIKE A million bucks. Well, maybe that's a bit of an exaggeration. He's probably only displaying fifty or sixty thousand as he sits near the back wall of the officer's club bar. He's wearing a black safari suit, custom-tailored of silk and linen. His boots are some exotic leather, probably an endangered species, but there's no one to complain where he has come from. On his left wrist is a gold Rolex GMT-Master, but the usual gold President band has been replaced by an incredible double-width band of gold links that looks like

---

9. Jack Chain will eventually rise to four-star rank and command the Strategic Air Command.

it might be suitable for automotive use as tire chains in a snowstorm. The standard stamped clasp of a Rolex has been replaced by a thick, heavyweight latch plate that displays in flamboyant bas-relief the wings of an Air Force pilot. On his right wrist is a similar double-link identification bracelet, modeled after those we wore in high school but, like the watch, executed in twenty-four-carat gold. The nameplate is an inch wide and three inches long. "Spike" is prominent in broad letters. The clasp is another chunk of gold brick. Visible through the open collar of his jacket is a gold chain that my inexperienced eye estimates as at least four or five baht in weight. Beside his highly polished right boot is an attaché case that apparently is fashioned from black alligator. He's the epitome of mercenary excess.

"Hey, Raz, didn't know you were here." He spots me as I enter the bar. I squint in the darkness, trying to see who's calling. I head toward the table where Spike has risen to call out to me, and then recognize him. Milam was a student in pilot training a few years ago, while I was at Willy. He, like so many of his peers, desperately wanted to fly fighters but didn't have the grades or the luck of the draw to get an assignment to fast movers. On graduation, Spike was assigned to transport aircraft, and it looked as though his eagerness to get into the war would be frustrated.

Then in a serendipitous moment, a classmate with an assignment to forward air controller duty broke his arm. Grabbing at the unforeseen opportunity, Spike volunteered to fill the training slot and enter the pipeline to combat. The switch was approved, and he was off to Hurlburt Field in Florida to become a FAC. I didn't expect to see him several years later, certainly

not festooned with gold and looking like a throwback to
Terry and the Pirates.

"Spike, is that you?" I'm scrambling to bring the
meeting into focus. He reaches out a hand to shake and
invites me to sit. I defer until I can get a beer and then
join him. "What the hell are you doing here?" It seems
like a reasonable question.

"Just passing through from up-country. Gotta see
some folks in Bangkok for a few days, then back."

"Back where, Udorn?" It's the only base I think of
up the map from Korat.

"Nah, farther north than that. If I told you where, I'd
have to kill you." The throwaway line is used to cover
for a lot of stuff. In the States it usually means some
sort of classified program; here it clearly means across
the Mekong into Laos.

"How'd you get there?" I'm wondering what he'll
tell me.

"I did a tour in an O-1 with a cav unit in South Vietnam, and when I was within a couple of months of going
home, a guy came to me and asked if I wanted to extend
and go someplace more exciting. I took him up on it."

"So, what does that mean?" I don't know enough
about what he's talking about to ask an intelligent
question.

"I'm a Raven. We're out of the Air Force, civilian
contractors flying out of places in Laos. Strictly out of
uniform. Can't tell you much more. You might get a
chance to talk to some of us if you do any drops up in
the Barrel Roll. Things are pretty quiet right now. We
mostly control Royal Laotian T-28s and do a bit of our
own thing." I've heard about the program. It's an operation filled with experienced FACs who are all just a bit

on the crazy side. They can't get enough of the war in the regimented environment of South Vietnam, so they get recruited into a secret war with little publicity but plenty of action in Laos.

"What's with the gold?"

"We get to spend a bit of time in Vientiane. It's kind of a Raven trademark. Some of the guys plan to buy their freedom with it if they get shot down. The warlords up there are generally pretty greedy and corrupt, so we'll make it worth their while to let us go." It doesn't sound like a good plan to me. If someone is corrupt, they'll probably simply take your gold and kill you anyway. I don't want to disabuse him of his backup plan, so I simply nod.

"There's a couple of guys I've been flying with that you might remember," he continues. "Big Al Galante is a Raven with me, and I worked with Al Guarino when I was still in-country." Galante I recall as a bulky Italian who likes his beer and has a lot more style than most of the student pilots I worked with. Guarino is the son of one of the earliest F-105 pilots who was shot down and became a POW. The combination of an ambition to fly combat airplanes and the desire to do something to speed his father's release makes him memorable.

"Yeah, I remember them both. How they doin'?"

"Good, real good. I'll say hi to Big Al for you when I get back."

"What's on the baht chain? You wear a Buddha?" I pull mine from the collar of my flight suit and display the small gold box.

"I used to carry one, but now it's my dog tags." He reaches in and extracts a pair, not the usual stamped tin of government issue but two engraved gold plates, replicas in dimensions length and width, but heavier and thicker than standard. He pulls the chain from his neck and displays the nametags. The usual name, service number, and blood type are shown on one side. The opposite side has the simple statement for whomever may find it: "If I am dead and you are pillaging my body, screw you." It seems a reasonable sentiment.

"What are you going to Bangkok for?" I've got all the questions, and the conversation is decidedly one-sided.

"Gotta deliver some stuff to some folks down there. You ever see a four-seasons bracelet?" He reaches for the alligator attaché and puts it on the table. He snaps the two gold latches, which by now I realize are probably real gold, and displays four boxes amid a handful of tan file folders. He opens one to reveal a bracelet made with four heavily engraved gold panels, each depicting one of the seasons. I reach over to heft the bracelet and find that the panels are solid gold and the bracelet must weigh a quarter-pound. The workmanship is exquisite. Spike is a walking Brinks truck. I wonder if he's armed and assume he is.

"You want one? These are spoken for, but I'll bring you one in about three weeks, next time I make a Bangkok run. Cost you maybe a hundred dollars." I nod, slowly, somewhat stunned at the bargain.

We talk for another hour or two, recalling days in pilot training and folks we both know. He doesn't tell me much about his operations in Laos, other than that he is FACing. The stories are fascinating. Here's a collection of mountain bandits mustachioed and swathed in bandoliers, hip-slung six-guns, and machetes. They've been recruited from the most aggressive and successful of forward air controller pilots in the war, and probably graded on their suitability for return to civilization. Too high a civility grade and they don't want you.

They fly from dirt fields scattered throughout Laos. They work closely with the Lao and Hmong, some sophisticated and some primitive, all staunchly anticommunist. The airplanes are small modified prop planes, the sort that missionaries fly to remote churches or bush-pilots use to take hunters to the secret sweet spots in the backcountry. These birds are sometimes equipped with launchers to fire target-marking rockets, sometimes not, but always loaded with radios to talk to fighter aircraft and troops on the ground. There are no uniforms and few rules; they are the personification of the *Mission Impossible* force. If killed or captured, "the secretary will disavow . . . "

Despite the war stories, there are gaps in the tales. I never find out exactly where he is operating from. I come away without a clue to the Vientiane-Bangkok connection and all the gold. Years later I'll have to read the books to try to discover what the Ravens did and where they went. Some of it will only be unclassified long after we all are dead. It's one more facet of a complex war.

11. FREEDOM DEAL

> A fighter pilot is, when you get down to it, a warrior, a
> person who puts himself in harm's way, and does it all by
> himself. . . . That's what makes him bigger than other men,
> and this is something the fighter jock never forgets.

> —Tom Clancy, from *Every Man a Tiger*

THERE'S WAY TOO MUCH AIRPOWER on the ground in
Thailand, and nowhere near enough targets in Cambodia or South Vietnam. No one is absolutely positive that
there won't be a resumption of hostilities. The war has
gone on for so long, with so many peaks and valleys,
bombing pauses and resumptions, that it doesn't seem
it will ever end. Each day we brief flights to Cambodia,
where the Khmer Rouge insurgents are now the biggest
threat we can find. Flights load up with CBU and 500-
pound bombs, then go to the tankers, which now fly on
tracks almost directly above the targets. Occasionally
the flights proceed farther south into the extreme southern end of Vietnam, where the land is flat and covered
with meandering tributaries of the various rivers, creating not quite a coastline so much as a murky transition
from land to ocean.

Some areas of Cambodia require forward air controllers to guide the flights and make sure only enemy targets are struck. Other broad expanses of the country are declared "free fire" zones, where fast movers can conduct their own search for targets of opportunity and exercise their own judgment in determining what to attack. The whole operation becomes an appropriately code-named campaign. This is Freedom Deal. The implication is of some sort of a marked-down special on basic liberty, offered this week only for the low cost of just a few hundred thousand bomb craters across the jungle.

There are a few prohibited areas in which no attacks are allowed. The huge temple complex of Angkor Wat, a thousand years old, is one. The sprawling collection of pyramids, causeways, towers, and gardens was built over several hundred years and once housed more than a million people. It can be seen from the air from a long way away. It becomes common to take an aerial tour of the magnificent structures, and in doing so to verify that it now has become home to several thousand Khmer Rouge who feel quite confident in firing away at us with their 23mm guns mounted throughout the holy site. We leave them alone, demonstrating more respect for their history than the Cambodian rebels themselves.

The daily frag doesn't go into great detail. Missions are given a launch time and a tanker to contact. From that point they are simply on-call assets, waiting with ordnance for a FAC to find a target and then request air support. There aren't enough targets, there is too much air, and the inexorable fact is that while airborne, jets burn fuel at prodigious rates. It becomes common to join on your assigned tanker and find twelve or more other fighters already hovering off the tanker wings. In short order there is a frantic competition for limited supplies of gas. While one airplane is refueling, three more are pleading with the tanker for more time on the boom or they will have to divert to a nearby base without striking a target. Meanwhile, flight leads are off the tanker frequency begging the airborne command post for an assignment to a target. It becomes a downward spiral in which airplanes get only enough gas to remain airborne long enough to get a bit more gas. They don't have enough to get to the target, there's not enough left on the tanker to top them off, someone else is about to declare an emergency fuel state, and there's no apparent way to break the cycle.

Whining for gas doesn't seem to be working. Cricket doesn't seem to have any targets right now. I don't want to wait passively for something to happen. I ease my flight of four off about a mile to the right of the flock of chicks with the tanker hen. Rod Bates is riding with me today. He hasn't been at Korat very long, but probably will be crewed with me. "Rod, crank up the radar and give me a look out at a hundred miles to the west. There's supposed to be a new tanker coming into the orbit in about twenty minutes. Let's find him first."

"Roger that. Good idea." I watch my scope bloom into green blips and bars as the antenna begins its sweep. There's another flock over to our left, but I want one single airplane headed our way, somewhere sixty or seventy miles ahead. "I think I've got him. Looks like a beacon target 20 degrees right, out about 120 miles." Rod's taken my thoughts one step further and gone to 200-mile scope and beacon interrogation mode. The radar isn't accurate enough to detect an airplane at that range, but with the tanker displaying his beacon, we get a broad smear of a blip on our scope, and since it correlates with the expected position at the right time, we feel pretty confident that a fresh load of gas is coming our way.

I rock the wings and tighten up the flight into close formation. I signal to push up the throttles and then give a hand signal to change channels back to Lion control. I don't want to give the plan away to all the vultures sucking gas on the tanker we're leaving. A quick glance left and right gets a head nod that the wingmen have seen my signals. A second to let the radios rechannelize, and then I check the flight on with Lion. "Lion, this is Racer, four Phantoms departing Chestnut 21 at flight level two zero zero. I've got a radar contact with Chestnut 41, who appears to be on my nose at a little over a hundred miles. Can you confirm that and give me a radio frequency for him?"

"Roger Racer, this is Lion, radar contact. That's affirmative, you hold Chestnut four one at three zero zero for ninety-six miles. Are you scheduled for gas with him?"

"Lion, Racer. It looks like Chestnut two one is pretty close to bingo. With your approval we'd like to divert to four one and get topped off on his way to the anchor, so we can go to work." Playing the mission accomplishment card will maybe get me some preference.

"Roger Racer, that's approved. Contact Chestnut four one on two six eight point four. Are you Judy?"

"Roger, Racer is radar contact on four one. We're Judy." I agree to run my own rendezvous and let Rod get some radar practice. Lion has done us a favor, and I don't see any reason to increase his workload.

We contact the tanker sixty miles before he reaches his refueling orbit. He's eager to pass gas, because as soon as he empties his load he can go home and lie by the pool for the rest of the day. We're topped off and ready for a target by the time he arrives on station and relieves Chestnut 21. We hear some grumbling from the flock of fighters that are still wrestling for preference on the tanker and deciding how to get enough gas to be able to do anything. Racer is ahead in this race.

Cricket hands us off to a FAC working about sixty miles east of Angkor Wat in a free fire area. We've got plenty of gas, so we don't hesitate to drop to lower altitude and push up the power to the rendezvous. When we arrive, the area is covered with a low-hanging haze and smoke pall. The afternoon sun angle makes it hard to see much of anything. The FAC is a Sun Dog, from one of the small bases remaining in South Vietnam, flying an O-2 Cessna. He doesn't have a target yet and has simply been pressured by Cricket to take some airplanes and put them into action.

We're at the rendezvous station, but staying above the haze layer until we see the FAC. There have been more than a few midairs between slow-moving forward-air-controller airplanes and fast movers. We're talking on the radio trying to get a position from Sun Dog, but still not finding him. Without something immediate to drop on, his focus is primarily searching the ground for telltale signs of a target, maybe new tracks on a dirt road or jungle foliage that is a slightly different color, or even smoke from cooking fires. He directs Racer to hold near his working area and wait for him to find something to drop on.

The trick with the tanker has given us a full load of fuel, but we're loaded today with six 500-pound bombs and four CBU canisters each. That's a lot of weight and a lot of drag. We're flying circles in formation at twelve thousand feet, the sun is going to be going down soon, and we've got a couple hundred miles to go to get home. The fuel gauges go down quickly. We wait patiently for a target.

"Okay, Racer, Sun Dog three four has got a target

for you. Are you ready for a briefing?" He's found something. We'll find out what it is, where he is, and how he wants us to deliver. He'll probably use a marking rocket after he's talked our eyes onto the target, then we'll drop in sequence and get corrections from our bomb splashes. I tell him we're ready to go.

"Racer, we've got a suspected encampment of enemy troops and equipment along the river. Position is 13 degrees, 12 minutes north, 106 degrees, 3 minutes east. You can head toward me from your orbit, I'm east of the target at 6,000 feet. Target elevation is 200 feet, and the latest altimeter I've got is 30.06. How much play time can you give me?"

"Well, Sun Dog, it's getting pretty dim out here, and unless we link up visual pretty fast, we're going to have to head for home. Right now we can give you about ten minutes." I give him the rest of the mission briefing with number of aircraft, our mission number, and ordnance load. I stay at twelve thousand as we head toward the FAC. The sun has settled into the tops of the cloud bank to our west, and it's getting dark almost as though someone were turning off the lights around us.

"Racer, Sun Dog's holding about five miles east of the target. Have you got me in sight?" I peer forward through the murky dusk trying to find the tiny FAC airplane. All I can see is an orange glow of the setting sun to my left and a smoggy gray darkness to the right. If he turns at the right time, I might get a glimpse of sunlight on his wings, but right now I've got nothing.

"Sorry, Sun Dog, I don't have you. I'm coming up on the coordinates you gave me. You want to talk me onto the target or can you give me a mark?" Without a visual on his airplane, it will be difficult to see the tiny white smoke of a marking rocket. I hope he's good at describing the landmarks.

"All right, Racer. Have you got a good visual on the Mekong?" Good start. The river meanders through this section of Cambodia and is easy to find. We're paralleling that major artery as we look for the FAC. "The target is in a D-shaped bend in the river, the flat side of the D is on the west and the curved side is east. Have you got that?"

"Ahh, okay, Sun Dog, I've got the river and I've got a lot of bends. A couple of them form a D. Can you give me a little more?" One man's D is another man's B or some other letter. We're going to be dumping a lot of high explosives on a curve in the river, and I'd sure like to be positive about the target. It is really getting dark quickly. The clouds, the sunset, the haze are all pulling the shades down. "Can you put a mark down for us?"

"That's negative, Racer. I'm Winchester on smokes. If you've got my D, it's got three campfires showing. The three fires form a triangle, base of the triangle on the east side, apex pointing to the west. The triangle is about one hundred meters on a side. They should be the only fires you see in the area. Have you got it now?"

Now the D in the river is looking pretty good. I've got the fires and they are in a triangle. Everything fits. We're at the coordinates, we've got the proper shape of the river, we've got the three fires—not two, not four or five. And we're at the fuel state where we've got to seriously get to work. "Racer lead has the fires, Sun Dog. Understand no mark. We're bingo fuel and we'll have to give you just one pass. Left roll-in, from the east and off west. Lead will be rolling in in ten seconds."

"Roger Racer, understand the FAC not in sight, but

you have the fires. Racer two hold for my correction off lead's bombs. Cleared in hot, Racer lead."

I've got the flight spread out on my right wing as I maneuver to the east of the target, then roll in on the cluster of campfires along the riverbank. The airplane shudders as the six bombs and four CBU canisters release. It's gotten really dark now, and as I pull off I look back and see the flash of the CBU opening, then the red-orange blast of the bombs, now the twinkling of the bomblets covering the area. "Racer, Sun Dog, are you in yet?"

"Ahh, Sun Dog, Racer has been cleared in and am now off target. Don't you have the splashes?" This is scary. We're in a free fire zone. Everything on the ground in this region is considered hostile, but it isn't a good thing to be dropping on a FAC-controlled target that isn't the target. Now the CBU has done its job, and the area of the three campfires is boiling and flashing. Secondary explosions are coming from the trees as stocks of ammunition, fuel, and explosives begin to cook off.

"Racer, Sun Dog three four has your impacts now. Looks like you struck pay dirt. I'm about five miles north of your bombs on another target, but that's a good one. Racer two and the remainder of the flight are cleared in hot. Lucky shot, Racer, but sometimes that's what it takes." The rest of the flight delivers on the area and the secondaries continue as we rejoin, climbing out toward the last dim glow of the setting sun. Sun Dog will return in the morning to survey the area and report our results. We'll be credited with a cache of supplies destroyed and an estimated number of enemy killed. It will all go on a giant spreadsheet somewhere in a headquarters briefing.

12. BIEN HOA DAYS AND BANGKOK NIGHTS

> Love and war are the same thing, and stratagems and
> policy are as allowable in the one as in the other.

—**Miguel de Cervantes**, from *Don Quixote de la Mancha*

THE SIEGE OF AN LOC in the South of Vietnam had begun just two days after Linebacker in April of '72. Now, almost a year later, we were still pounding the rubble of the town with excess sorties. With few US personnel left on the ground, we demonstrated our support of the Vietnamese forces with mission counts on suspected concentrations of enemy troops or truck parks under the trees. The common way to do the job was the "An Loc Trip Turn." We would load up at Korat, dump bombs with a FAC somewhere in the area of An Loc, then recover at Bien Hoa air base near Saigon. Usually we could fly another short sortie out of Bien Hoa, then load up one more time and dump more bombs on the way back to Thailand. It was decidedly low threat and built up the combat hours for latecomers to the war. Three sorties a day as the action waned was a great catch-up strategy.

With only a handful of Americans left at Bien Hoa, we had to supply F-4 qualified crewmembers to pull duty as supervisor of flying and mobile control officer. Korat shared the duties with Takhli. Each base provided two aviators for twelve-hour shifts for a week at a time. Korat had day SOF and night mobile. Takhli covered night SOF and day mobile. I got the duty of day SOF. I flew a mission in with Art Fournier in my pit and turned my airplane over to the guys who had spent the previous week there.

It was a different life on the ground in Vietnam. The outbound guys turned over their equipment for the task. I got a Michelin man flak vest, a GI Joe steel pot helmet, an M-16 with four full magazines, and a dark blue pickup truck with a UHF radio and an FM hand-held walkie-talkie. Art got similar combat gear but no wheels. When I thought about the job of sitting in the dark out near the runway in the small mobile control unit, I didn't envy him in the slightest. I already had the image of black-pajama-clad VC creeping through the tall grass to kill the Yankee air pirate in the little box with the radios. I gave Art two of my magazines, thinking he might have more need for them than I would.

There was a small maintenance detachment to refuel and reload the Phantoms, patch any minor discrepancies to get the airplane back home, and handle the basic paperwork. Willie Wells was running the show, deployed from the 35th Tac Fighter Squadron in Korea. I'd met Willie when he'd been with his squadron at Korat, during the buildup for Linebacker II. He greeted me and showed me around the place. There was a small operations office, with two tiny briefing rooms in back. A Plexiglas board on one wall listed the expected sorties for the day in grease pencil; the time of arrival, call sign, status of refuel and munitions loads, and departure time. There was a pair of gray metal six-drawer desks, a single four-drawer file cabinet, and a row of three black telephones. A hand-cranked field phone in an olive-drab canvas case completed the communications suite.

"I handle the maintenance and turnarounds. You're in charge of the flying. On the radios your call sign is Phantom four. Don't come to me for decisions on ops, and don't interfere with me getting the airplanes turned. Come and go as you please. Stay on the radio if you aren't in the building. Day SOF works six to six. Try to be on time for swap with the night guy. You've got a reserved room at the BOQ. It's down the street. Any questions?" Willie was concise and to the point. I liked that.

"Oh, see you at the club about 6:30 for dinner. It's the safest place to eat. You probably don't want to go downtown these days," he finished the in-brief. "And one more thing. Hauling that pea-shooter around can get a bit cumbersome. You can lock it up in the safe here. We'll break it out for you if something comes up." That made sense. I'd always thought it best to let someone else do the hand-to-hand, whites-of-their-eyeballs fighting.

I stowed my flying gear in the office along with the rifle, then grabbed the truck and took Art to the BOQ, where we dumped our clothes in our rooms. The SOF and the mobile officer each shared a room with their opposite schedule counterpart. The rooms were in a two-story cinderblock dormitory building, along the main street and just around the corner from a small officer's club. A long hallway ran the length of each floor, with pairs of doors on opposite sides opening into two-man rooms. Five sets of doors and ten rooms in each wing straddled a central shower and latrine area that was prominently designated as the rocket and bomb shelter.

The routine was easy. The shift started at six in the morning and lasted until six at night. During that time, we would get no more than a dozen flights through the reload and launch process. The weather was good, and barring aircraft emergencies there wasn't much to worry about. My hand-held radio kept me in touch with the base command post, so I could wander the area at my leisure. Off duty in the evening I could hang out at the club, see a movie, or simply get a good night's sleep.

An old friend from my days as a pilot training instructor, Jimmie Rutledge, was pulling alert duty as an A-1 pilot for a couple of weeks. The small detachment of propeller-driven attack aircraft flew some local bomb-dropping sorties but mainly was available for quick response search-and-rescue missions. I took the opportunity to visit with Jim at the alert facility. They had a nice chow hall that served a pretty respectable breakfast and a decent cup of coffee. I got the chance to crawl around the big tail-dragger airplane that looked for all the world like something that slipped through a time warp from World War II. Jim's proudest possession was an eighteen-foot-long yellow scarf that he carried in the cockpit. When he returned from a mission he donned the scarf, pulled back the canopy in the turn to final, and flipped the long tails out over the side to trail in the breeze like the Red Baron. It brought a whole new dimension to "scarf in the wind" flying.

The first couple of evenings I spent at the club. The meals were the standard Southeast Asian interpretation of what Americans liked. That meant lots of carbos and beef, few vegetables, and a bottle of ketchup and Tabasco sauce on every table. The club was smaller

than it had been at the peak of the war, and only the bar
remained open. You ate, drank, talked, and relaxed in
the same dingy, smoke-filled room. The waiters were
surly, the waitresses were not the flower of Vietnamese
womanhood, and the requisite Filipino band seemed to
know only two songs, "I Left My Heart in San Francisco" and "We Gotta Get Out of This Place." They al-
ternated through the evening, hoping to create a
longing for home with the Tony Bennett classic and
treating the second song as a national anthem and
protest chant rolled into one.

By the third night the club had pretty much exhausted its entertainment value, so Rutledge took me
down the street to the Rap Bar. The Rap FACs flew
O-2 Cessnas in support of Army troops in the nearby
Military Region 4. We had worked with a Rap on the
An Loc missions, and they always welcomed fighter
types into their hideaway. The bar was simply two
rooms in a BOQ dormitory identical to the one that I
was staying in. Since this dorm building was closer to
the flight line, it was revetted with eight-foot-high walls
of sandbags around all sides. This helped to reduce the
aircraft noise for the first-floor occupants, and provided
a grim reminder that the area was subject to enemy attack at any time. The connecting wall between the two
rooms had been modified with a double-wide doorway,
probably built several years earlier by crews long since
returned to "the world."

The décor was combat-zone eclectic. There were the
usual tattered *Playboy* centerfolds stapled to the walls,
the head-shop kitsch that might or might not reflect a
familiarity with psychedelic pharmaceuticals, and an
array of combat trophies such as AK-47s, deactivated
Soviet grenades, a VC bamboo coolie hat, and a human

skull mounted on a carved wooden base that was occasionally used for the drinking of toasts to fallen comrades, sexual conquests, and almost anything else that might strike the fancy of the moment. The dim lights in red and yellow gave the place an almost surreal atmosphere. It was perfect. One could only imagine how many Stateside basement party rooms would attempt to recreate the Rap Bar in future years.

We sat around sucking up icy beer until about 10:30, when I begged off to get some sleep for my next twelve-hour shift. I walked down the middle of the largely abandoned street, trying to look more like a combat vet than an apprehensive aviator on a rare visit to a military base in the middle of a collapsing regime. I would like to have been surrounded by a lot more traffic and a lot more streetlights. It was all probably just my imagination.

The quarters were quiet as I entered the hall. The lights were dim and the latrine was abandoned. I showered quickly and padded back to my room. Fournier was already out at the end of the runway doing his night-long job of watching for landing and departing aircraft. I crawled into the bunk and immediately went to sleep.

The alarm went off at five, giving me an hour to hit the latrine, take care of morning business, and get suited up to head down to the operations area. I rolled off the mattress, pulled on some clean socks and my combat boots, then strolled down the dimly lit hall, the very model of the well-dressed fighter pilot in Jockeys and jungle boots. No one was home in the communal area, so I had my choice of toilet stalls. I checked the magazine racks in a couple and found one with a *Sports Illustrated* only six months old. I dropped my shorts around my boots, sat on the john, and began to read about George Brett's pursuit of the batting title for 1972.

The rumble of thunder seemed unusual; the weather forecast had been for clear and sunny. There were several deep rumbles and then a few sharper booms. With a particularly loud blast, the lights flickered and then went out. The latrine was suddenly pitch black. I closed my magazine, felt for the rack on the door, and stowed it. I finished my business and pulled up my shorts. With the toilet stall door opened, I still couldn't see a thing. I estimated the wall of sinks opposite the toilets was about ten feet away, and if I could reach the wall I could feel my way to one of the two doorways and get into the hall, where hopefully the gleam of streetlights or rising sun would provide a bit of illumination. I shuffled forward out of the stall and got about four feet before I kicked softly into a body. A muffled wheeze accompanied the light blow of my boot. "Who's there?" I asked. There was no answer.

I sidestepped slowly and cautiously around where I thought the body lay. I asked again, "What's going on?" Still no reply. I started forward again more carefully. A few sliding steps more, and I found the wall. Figuring caution to be the better choice in the stygian blackness, I turned and put my back to the wall and slid down to sit on the floor. I heard breathing, and it wasn't mine. I tried one more time, "Who's here?" Nothing.

IT SUDDENLY DAWNS ON ME. This isn't a thunderstorm. The thunder is man-made, and there's a far greater chance of being struck by the source of this thunder than nature's lightning. We're under rocket attack. The VC are lobbing 122mm rockets into the base from somewhere nearby. Sitting in the dark, I begin to understand the terror of the infantryman as he waits out an artillery barrage. It's an entirely different game than air combat. You can't jink, you can't dodge, there's no skill involved. If the shell has your name on it, you die.

A light comes down the hall. An American with a candle enters the latrine that is now a shelter, and suddenly I see the source of the breathing sounds and the obstacle I encountered. There are five or six people with me in the latrine. Some are in fetal curls along walls, one is under the sinks, and the one I apparently kicked is lying in the middle of the floor. All are American, all are uninjured, all are terrified, and none will respond to my questions. They aren't combat troops, they're personnel and admin clerks; typists and filers caught up in the situation. I stand up, now that I can see the door and bid them all a good day. There's still no reply.

I hurry down the hall to my room to grab a flight suit. As I move, I glance in several open doorways, rooms abandoned by the cowering folks that have just silently shared my experience. Most have the mattresses off the bunk beds, set vertically along the outer walls of the building as an impromptu shelter. There are blankets on the hard floor; apparently the choice of security versus comfort leads them to a painful existence. I have a hard time comprehending this level of fear.

Dressed, I head toward the flight line, where columns of black smoke are rising. Sirens of emergency vehicles seem to come from all quadrants. Marines in helmets and flak jackets are running everywhere. As I pass the Rap building, I notice that the revetment is collapsed on the southwest corner of the building. The sandbags are ripped and toppled. The cinderblock corner of the building is scarred by shrapnel, but unbreached. I'm betting the beer is probably shaken up in the bar.

When I reach the ops building, the door is open and

the front windows are shattered. Acoustic tiles hang from the ceiling, and the tin egg-crate cover from the fluorescent light fixture hangs by a single wire over the gray desk. The night SOF is under the desk in the footwell, sitting quietly and waiting for the sirens to stop. I announce that there is probably an "all clear," since there hasn't been another impact for at least twenty minutes, so he crawls slowly out. He isn't sure whether to hang around or head for the BOQ. The emergency responders seem to be handling things, so I tell him to take off and he seems relieved that he can get away from the flight line. I remind him that it's past six o'clock, so I'm the guy on duty and I now should have the shared helmet and flak jacket. He reluctantly turns over the equipment and leaves.

Somehow the flak jacket and steel pot don't seem as heavy as they did a few days earlier. I find the duty sergeant and ask him if he's seen Major Wells. He points out the broken window at a billow of greasy black smoke rising from the area of the alert revetments. I grab the FM brick and the keys to the truck and head for the flight line. I'm glad the SOF vehicle has both a siren and a red rotating beacon on the roof. While I head down the ramp I pick up the UHF radio microphone and check in with the command post. Just in case they haven't figured it out by now, I tell them that I'm the supervisor of flying and the airfield is closed. They acknowledge, and it only takes two minutes before the FM buzzes on the seat beside me. It's the aircraft commander of a C-141 that I can see parked in the open on the far side of the runway. He's distinctly agitated.

"This is Colonel Johnson. You can't close the damn airfield. I've got to get my airplane out of here. They were lobbing rockets down the taxiway following my airplane after I landed. I almost got killed!" I've got the picture already. This guy is a "telephone colonel," actually a lieutenant colonel who is probably on his bimonthly visit to the combat zone to get his combat pay and income tax exclusion. He's never before seen a shot fired in anger, and he's suddenly got the cold clammy hands that accompany fear. He's gonna earn his pay today.

"I'm sorry, Colonel, but I'll open the airfield just as soon as I can get the runway checked and make sure the field is safe for operations. You might want to get yourself and your crew in a revetment. I can't do anything about your airplane right now. Phantom four, out."

I'm pulling up to the scene of the smoke. I can see Willy's station wagon, and he's standing nearby talking to a firefighter and security policeman. They've cordoned off the area around a "wonder arch" revetment that isn't an arch any more. A rocket has impacted in the front of the shelter, almost dead center on an AT-37 Dragon-Fly loaded with napalm and CBU. The fully fueled jet cooked off immediately, and the combined blast of jet fuel and ordnance has blown the steel and concrete top of the arch open like a Christmas present in the hands of a four-year-old. The cordon is designed to keep the unwary from stepping on or picking up the hundreds of scattered cluster bomblets that litter the area. Four Vietnamese contract workers with push brooms are sweeping the deadly debris into piles near the remains of the shelter. The bomblets roll and bounce in front of the brooms like so many olive-drab tennis balls. The sweepers seem either fearless or incredibly naive. Either way, I'm glad it's not me with the job.

"Hi Raz," Wells waves a greeting. "Enjoying our little wakeup call?"

"Yes, sir. I wasn't sure what it was at first. This happen often?"

"Maybe once a week or so. They seem to be getting a bit more aggressive as we get smaller here. Have you been out to the runway yet? I hear it took a couple of hits."

"Not yet, I wanted to check in with you and see what this was all about. I'll get out there. I've got a trash-hauler colonel wanting to get out of here right away." Willy shakes his head and makes a rude gesture toward the C-141. I'm already back into my truck and headed down the taxiway. There are several sweepers working up and down the runway, and a cluster of trucks just past the 4,000-foot remaining marker. I wave at the sweeper drivers as I speed past, and then slow down approaching the trucks. There's razor-sharp shrapnel from the rocket casings littering the ground everywhere. The trucks are the rapid runway repair crews from civil engineering. They've already manually swept around several large holes in the pavement and are mixing quick-dry cement to fill the gaps. At least one hole has already been patched, and a half-dozen more are ready for the mix. A young first lieutenant seems to be in charge.

"Good morning, sir," he greets me and salutes. "We'll have this cleaned up in about an hour. The goo takes about twenty minutes to set up hard. What time are the first fighters due in?" He's all business and apparently darned good at it.

The FM buzzes before I can reply. "Dunno, I'll check the schedule in a second. Hang on." I squeeze the talk button on the brick, "Phantom four, go ahead."

"Roger, this is MAC 7538 Heavy, we're ready to taxi. When are you getting this airfield open?" It's the trash-hauler again, and he's getting antsy.

The lieutenant overhears and grins. "You should of

seen them walking those rockets up his tail. I thought
they were going to get him before he got that thing off
the runway and over by those trees." He points at the
big silver and white airplane on the west side of the
runway. I'm betting the telephone colonel wishes he
had some of that cool camouflage paint today.

"MAC, this is Phantom four, the runway is closed,
the airfield is closed, and the taxiways are closed. We'll
get you out as soon as we can. In the meantime, address
your problems to the command post. Phantom four,
out." I can't babysit this guy. "Phantom one, Phantom
four." I need to let Wells know about the cratered runway and find out how much time we've got before the
first fighters show up. We may want to divert flights up
the coast to Cam Ranh Bay or Phan Rang if we don't
have time to get things operating here.

"Four, this is Phantom one, what's going on?"

"Roger one, we've got a half-dozen hits on the runway. The engineers estimate about an hour for all the
patches to set up hard, and about the same time to get the
sweepers done. When are the first sorties due in here?"

"Four, I've already canceled the first two flights.
Right now the 10:30 arrivals are still a go. Think we'll
be open for business by then?" Willy is one step ahead
of me, but then he's probably been through this a couple of times already. I relay that the engineers have the
situation in hand and we should be ready.

"Phantom four, Bien Hoa tower, check the approach!" The radio call blasting from the open door of
the pickup sounds frantic. I look away from the repair
work, wondering why the tower sounds so panic-
stricken about something that I'd do routinely prior to
reopening the runway. I'm about to reply when I look
up to see an O-2 FAC aircraft on final, apparently

oblivious to me, my truck, the sweepers, the construction vehicles, and the forty or so workers on the runway. I sprint for the truck and am headed down the runway head-on to the approaching plane.

I grab the UHF mike and flip the channel selector to 243.0, the emergency Guard channel. "Aircraft on short final at Bien Hoa, *Go around!* O-2 on final at Bien Hoa, go around. The runway is closed." I drop the mike and steer with one hand while rummaging in the black briefcase of the SOF kit, trying to reach the emergency flare pistol. I find it and hang out the window firing the red fireworks into the air and noting that the mobile control officer has also fired the remote flares at his end of the runway. A half-dozen fiery trails mark our efforts to attract his attention.

A distinctly Vietnamese voice responds with some rote English, apparently practiced daily during routine operations, "Rogga, Rap 64, unnastan, crear to rand." He understands nothing. He appears to be oblivious to anything in front of him, and he is either going to run into my truck or, if I get out of the way, he'll plow into the repair workers, killing himself for sure and probably a number of them. I opt to stay in his way, hoping he'll finally figure out that ramming a big Ford truck might be painful.

I'm still shouting into the radio that "Hell no, you aren't cleared to land," when he finally glances out the front window and pulls up. He misses the truck by a few feet and climbs off to reposition for another approach. I pick up the FM and call the command post to find out if they know who this guy is and if they've got a Vietnamese officer to explain the situation to him. They tell me they're working on it. Vietnamization seems to be proceeding as we had anticipated.

By noon the operation is running smoothly. Flights are cycling in, and I meet some crews from Korat and exchange the news over lunch. "No, not much going on here. How are things back at Korat?"

The movie that night is *The Godfather.* For some reason, the surround sound of the Mafia turf wars is distinctly disconcerting. I'm never quite sure if the pops and bangs are part of the soundtrack or coming from some activity outside. I still choose the top bunk that night in the BOQ when the movie is over.

WITH THE PRESSURE OF LINEBACKER gone, there is ample flexibility on time off. A long weekend trip to Bangkok could be a monthly excursion. The preferred destination for most fighter crews is the Siam Intercontinental Hotel. It has a great pool surrounded by a large tropical garden, with an outdoor bar to keep the Singha cold and flowing while we lie around in lounge chairs and watch for the arrival of busloads of Pan Am flight attendants. There are never very many; they are always drastically outnumbered, and the tales recounted back at Korat, Takhli, Ubon, and Udorn are probably grossly exaggerated. Still, hope springs eternal.

Rod Bates has been my backseater for several weeks. He was part of a trio of three Academy graduates who all came from the same F-4 training class, two WSOs and one pilot. They arrived just as Linebacker II was launching, and were dumped into the cauldron with little preparation. They did a good job, survived, and were quickly integrated into the squadron. Rod wants to be a pilot and hopes to get selected for pilot training as soon as he becomes eligible. Doing a good job in the F-4 is going to get him the recommendations he needs. He wants a lot of stick time, and I negotiate a contract with him. I'll give him the whole T-37 pilot training course during the flying time going to and from targets, if he'll devote himself to becoming the best WSO in the squadron. He is a sponge for flying knowledge, and he earns it by taking control of his backseat office in a hurry. Within a few sorties he is on top of everything I want, and pushing the envelope in using the aircraft systems to get a jump on the job. Finding tankers is a challenge, and he is asking to take Judys at distances of up to 140 miles. If he can get a beacon paint on the radar, he wants to run the intercept and demonstrate his skill. Lion and Invert are always happy to turn the job over to the aircraft, and probably watch to see if we screw it up and have to come back and ask for help.

Rod seeks my questionable guidance in other areas as well. He confesses that he can't conceive of sex with a Thai. I suggest that there are many beautiful and well-educated Thai girls with whom he might be able to have a relationship. I overlook, in the discussion, the fact that the most likely source of such a meeting will be a bath and massage parlor, strip club, or house of dubious repute. He says he sincerely doubts his ability to perform with an Oriental maiden. I note that he doesn't seem to have a racist bone in his body, then reconsider the pun and reword the comment. I opine that possibly a trip to Bangkok and some research into his attitude might be in order. We're off two days later to the big city, on the air-conditioned bus that leaves Korat each morning.

We arrive at the Siam early in the afternoon and spend a few hours at the pool. Strategy is important, and I want to maximize his opportunities while minimizing the effort involved. Certainly we can't delve into the succulent treats of the Black Pearl of the Orient without proper nutrition. I suggest a good dinner followed by a few drinks at the fleshpots of Pat Pong Road. The strip joints and honky-tonks of Pat Pong have grown from a short neon strip a few years earlier into an industrial-strength concentration dedicated to sin and depravity. Now the area is several blocks long and boasts two parallel streets, Pat Pong I and II. Soul or country, rock and roll or jazz, there's something for everyone, including all the sex any young man could ask for.

Dinner starts at the Dusit Thani Hotel, a huge Las Vegas–style monument to American excess. Certainly not within the budget of the average GI, and definitely too classy for the recreational style of fighter pilots, the Dusit Thani is the sort of place favored by contractors, Congress-critters, embassy officials, and well-to-do parents visiting their offspring in the combat theater. Expense accounts make the tariff acceptable for most of the clientele. Hotel residents and restaurant customers are predominantly Westerners, and other than the staff there is hardly an epicanthic fold in sight. Best to immerse Rod slowly in Asian culture.

A martini, a huge terrine of fresh mussels, a large chunk of what purportedly is "Kobe" beef, a bottle of Château Beychevelle '66, and a dessert of delicate profiteroles chased with a Hennessy Bras Armé make the meal. Admittedly it is a bit short on Thai cuisine, but it is at least served by a Thai waiter. A tweedy British lady sitting at a nearby table compliments us on our selections. Maybe we crass colonials have some sophistication after all.

Then it's off to Pat Pong. It's got all the atmosphere of Bourbon Street, the Ginza, and the dark alleys of Olongapo in the Philippines. There are bars and smoky

eateries, strip joints and dance halls. The male population looks to be split about fifty-fifty between American
military straight from combat and European businessmen seeking something they can't find at home. The females are all twenty-something, heavily made up and
seeking males with some money. Most are Thai, but
there are some Eurasians, taller and often with an eerie
beauty. There are even a couple of Caucasian girls who
have the hollow-eyed, sallow complexion of the drug
addicted, runaways who came to the war trying to follow their boyfriend or husband and now are caught up
in the street life. Girls walk the street trying to attract a
male eye, while taxi drivers chat up GIs, offering them
a quick trip to a whorehouse, drug dealer, tailor shop,
or bargains in souvenir jewelry. Rod and I walk carefully down the sidewalk, checking open doors to bars
and strip joints looking for the right mix of light and
dark, noise and quiet. A well-dressed young man tugs at
Rod's sleeve and suggests that we check out the
cabaret, just up the stairs to the left. We take a chance.

The dark bar has four small round stages, each with
a set of couches surrounding the platform. Girls wander
between the areas as others grind and gyrate to the beat
of rock music spun by a disc jockey behind a glass window on the left. The girls rotate between the stages and
serving drinks to the customers. When their turn comes
they mount the stage, dance for three songs during
which they strip. At the completion of the third song,
they pick up their clothes, redress, and return to shilling
drinks. Some of the girls have established themselves
with free-spending johns, and the management seems
happy to let them drop out of the rotation.

We choose a nearly vacant circle of couches and sit to
watch for a few songs. One stripper is just finishing her

third number. She is replaced by a cute, slender girl who seems a bit shy. She moves to the music, eyes downcast. Midway through the second song, a manager walks by and notes that she is still dressed in her small skirt and taps softly on the railing behind the couch. She looks up, nods quickly, and picks up the pace. The skirt comes off, and as the third song starts she is left wearing only a thin gold chain with a small Buddha around her neck. As the song ends, she removes the chain and flips it to me. She retrieves her clothing and slips from the stage to a side room to dress. Within minutes she returns and comes to claim her chain. I palm her chain and slip the two-baht chain and gold-cased Buddha from my neck. When I drop the heavy gold in her hand, she giggles and shakes her head. I hand her the smaller one.

Rod and I see nothing here to attract his attention. We leave, apparently at the mandated closing time for the many bars along the strip. Hundreds of young men and working girls are pouring out of the gin mills, and all are seeking taxis. We flag a taxi just as the young Thai dancer emerges with a pair of coworkers. She waves timidly at me, and I beckon her over and ask if she would like a ride. She speaks a bit of surprisingly good English and wonders if we would like to accompany the girls to a restaurant. Rod and I are still sated from our luxurious dinner, but this is an opening to get him immersed in the culture. The five of us pack into the cab with the girls on our laps, and they immediately chatter to the driver. We zoom off several blocks to a dark, tree-lined street. The taxi stops outside a large steel gate and honks twice. A guard swings the gate open, and we enter a courtyard filled with cars and fronting a bustling dance hall, bar, and restaurant. It's a classic Capone-era speakeasy. The after-hours business off Pat Pong is booming.

We're the meal ticket for the evening, so we watch the girls eat as Rod and I sip another Singha. The girls are sizing us up for an acceptable business transaction, and I'm trying to see if Rod likes either of the two newcomers. The conversation is limited, with neither side fluent in the other's language. My dancer with the chain wants to take me home, and I'm willing. We find another taxi, and I leave Rod with the two topless dancers. The evening ends with mission accomplishment in question, although Rod has been maneuvered into a tactical position from which it will be difficult to snatch defeat.

The morning sun shining through a wall-to-wall, ceiling-to-floor window wakes me to a Singha headache of monumental proportions. I'm lying naked on my back on a king-size bed in a one-room walk-up apartment in downtown Bangkok. There are no drapes, and the window opens facing the fifth and sixth floor of the Montien Hotel, a respectable downtown residence for tourists and businessmen. The girl is curled next to me, and in the morning light seems decidedly less beautiful than last night. I'm wondering about the show that we might have provided for the guests of the Montien who might have been gazing from their hotel rooms last night. It's too late to worry. I rise and dress. Kiss the dancer good-bye and leave her a hundred baht. I grab a cab downstairs and head back to the Siam.

A shower followed by an almost-American breakfast in the hotel café mitigates the hangover. I change into a swimsuit and head out to the pool with a Frederick Forsyth spy thriller. There's a shady spot with a couple of empty chaises not far from the pool bar. A Coke and a plate of fresh-cut chilled pineapple makes for a potentially relaxing morning. I'm into my book, busily trying to visualize the mechanics of "the Jackal" converting a crutch to an assassin's weapon to assassinate de Gaulle, when Rod emerges from the east wing of the hotel with a sheepish grin. "Well?" is my greeting and request for a debrief.

"No go." He reports an amazing tale of two girls in a taxi attempting to convince him that sex would be a wonderful way to finish his evening. I'm amazed at his powers of resistance. He describes directing the taxi to the Siam and bidding the girls a pleasant morning.

Would he like to try again this evening? He isn't sure. He sprawls on the next lounge and contemplates the long-term impact of international relations.

That night his resolve has wavered, and he agrees to return to Pat Pong. This time we find ourselves in a long, narrow club with raised banquettes along one wall facing a bar with two circular platforms, for a pair of topless go-go dancers. A busty dancer with a wide smile catches my eye, and I simply point back and forth to indicate an intention to talk with her, then wave at the other dancer and point to Rod. She smiles and nods her head. The second dancer, a remarkably tall statuesque beauty, is decidedly Asian, but not Thai. At the next break they join us. The tall girl is half Indian and speaks English better than Churchill. Rod is smitten.

At closing time we grab a taxi with the girls. The driver knows the routine and delivers us almost immediately to a small hotel in a walled enclave. The doorman takes a hundred baht from each of us and directs us to separate doorways, almost like a miniature American motel. There's no key provided. The door locks behind you, and when you leave, you don't return to the room.

I watch the tall girl lead Rod in. The door closes and latches behind them. I think he'll make a breakthrough in attitudes this evening. I join my chesty friend in a little room with a king-size bed, a compact bathroom-shower, and an incongruous rotary switch at bedside that lets you choose among white, red, green, yellow, and blue fluorescents in the ceiling-mounted light fixtures. It's a whimsical "no-tell motel" touch. The next morning Rod and I take the bus back to Korat. The routine of checking the schedule and hanging around the CTF in the evening resumes. Rod expounds to his friends about his adventures in Bangkok.

ALTHOUGH JUST A CAPTAIN, HE is "the very model of a modern major general." He has it all, everything you need to succeed in a politically correct military. He's black, the son of a Tuskegee airman. A graduate of Tuskegee himself and then, through a no-longer-segregated pilot training to become an F-4 backseat pilot, he completes a combat tour riding through missions in South Vietnam. He has filled the combat square and returns to the US to upgrade to the front seat and become an instructor pilot in training. In short order he is selected for the Fighter Weapons School, where he becomes one of the fighter elite with what is generally regarded as a PhD in tactical aviation. He's tall, muscular, and tailored. Articulate, polite, deferential when necessary yet aggressive when appropriate, he's literally a poster child for affirmative action.

But now he's been caught up in the Palace Cobra assignment mill. Arriving at Korat during the peak of the Linebacker campaign, he wangles a job in the wing weapons shop, working for the deputy commander for operations. He organizes the weapons training for new-guy school. He compiles weapons delivery data to report to higher headquarters. He builds charts of dive-bomb parameters with dive angles, airspeeds, release altitudes, and sight settings. Occasionally he flies, but he seldom leads and isn't often seen down among the weeds with the hunter-killers. He's a Weapons School grad, and surely among the best qualified to fly the MiG escort mission. He sees no MiGs, he gets no kills, but he fills another career square with a second combat tour and a wing headquarters assignment. He's a man on the move and one to watch.

Now that the North Vietnam campaigns are over and not likely to be restored, Dick Tolliver begins to appear more often on the schedule. We're going to Bien Hoa for the day. We'll get sent to a forward air controller operating somewhere in the lower half of South Vietnam. He might have some excitement, like a troops-in-contact situation in which an Army unit needs air support, or he might have a concentration of enemy, or probably he will have a chunk of suspected enemy ground for us to stir up with forty-eight 500-pound bombs. Defenses will range from possible small arms fire to maybe nothing at all. The FAC will worry about some enterprising Viet Cong with an SA-7 shoulder-launched heat-seeking missile, but for us in the F-4, the tiny missile, with its limited range, represents very little threat. We'll have time to get a sandwich at Bien Hoa while our airplanes are fueled and armed, then it will be another bomb puke on the way back home. Two missions and about five hours of combat time for Dick's resume.

I'm flying three with Rod in my pit. The wingmen are a couple of lieutenants right out of training who arrived in the squadron just a week or two before the Christmas campaign. They are short on total time, but they make up for hours in the airplane with the intensity of the experiences they had in December. Their

combat baptism reminds me of my first tour in the
F-105. There was no choice but to throw these guys into
the cauldron, and luckily they survived. Now they have
a calm steadiness and a maturity that belies their youth.

We get topped off on Chestnut track and head south
to rendezvous with an OV-10 FAC in Military Region
4. It is the farthest southern tip of South Vietnam, in an
area I've never been to before. The airborne command
post hints that he's got something good for us. We'll
see when we get there. It's relaxing to fly the wing in a
permissive environment. We cruise across Cambodia in
a spread formation, watching the landscape unroll beneath us and admiring the bright blue sky. Rod plays
with the radar for a while, and then I spend some time
giving pilot training lessons, talking about flying instruments, and making small corrections on the attitude indicator rather than trying to chase the altimeter
and airspeed needles. He soaks it up and is always eager for more.

Tolliver follows the inertial nav system to the coordinates the airborne command post relayed and runs us
through the channel changes to contact the FAC and
complete the rendezvous. A hundred miles out we're
talking to Rustic 15, an American probably flying out of
Ubon back in Thailand. He briefs us that he has an ARVN
unit that has been facing a dug-in battalion, or more, of
North Vietnamese regulars. They are in rice paddy country along the coast, at the farthest tip of Vietnam. The
land is flat, the final alluvial spread of the meandering
Mekong, interlaced with hundreds of canals and ditches,
more water than solid ground. I can't begin to imagine
what it's like to be a foot soldier in an Asian army trying
to do battle in that kind of quagmire, and I don't want to
learn as a potential survivor or evader either.

We ease down from our cruising altitude to twelve thousand feet. The landscape is all wrong. The ocean is on the wrong side. The FAC is telling us about the landmarks and the location of the friendlies. He's describing the particular chunk of stream that houses the complex of enemy soldiers. He's spelling out the restrictions for our run-ins and pulloffs so that we don't overfly the good guys on the ground and let a long or short bomb fall among the friendlies. But when he tells us to come off to the west, every mission I've ever flown had west on the land side and water to the east. My mind can't accept a west coast of Vietnam. Yet here we are.

The FAC is in sight, just below us to the left. We drift into a left hand orbit, spread out off of Dick's right wing looking through him to the ground, to follow the FAC's explanations of where all the players are. It flashes through my mind that this is so much more comfortably paced than our frantic run-ins a few months ago—high speed, dodging SAMs, finding targets in a hail of flak, and trying to unravel all the radio calls, RWR squeals and warnings in a package of fifty or more airplanes. Here, we fly circles around an enemy concentration listening to Rustic explain what he wants us to do. It's pretty clear. Friendlies on the east bank, bad guys on the west. Friendlies back about two hundred meters from the river's edge among the dark trees, bad guys right along the water and dispersed along the canals. We should roll in from the north and stay parallel to the river. Come off toward the coast; the west that doesn't seem like it ought to be west. We each have twelve bombs and plenty of fuel, so we'll drop six at a time, making two passes each, and maybe have some time left to strafe. Eight passes for bombs, and then as much shooting as we can fit in.

Tolliver acknowledges the briefing and calls ready to roll in. He's a bit too eager. "Dagger, this is Rustic 15, stand by while I coordinate with the ground commander." The FAC takes one last check with the Army unit to make sure they are all in place, where they said they would be, and know that they had better keep their heads down.

"Okay, Dagger flight. Rustic will be in with a mark in thirty seconds. Daggers, acknowledge, restricted run-ins north to south and off target west. Friendlies two hundred meters east." Rustic makes sure we all understand, and he isn't going to be rushed by an impatient flight lead. We verify the briefing with a quick one, two, three, and four radio call.

The stubby little airplane pulls up into a wing-over and points toward the target. Two puffs of smoke erupt along the riverbank. "Dagger lead, cleared in hot. Hit my smoke." The classic call of the competent FAC. Tolliver is rolling off into his bomb pass as the rest of us remain high and drift to his left side on the pass, expecting him to come off the target as briefed, to the west. I'm watching the impacts of his bombs, a hundred meters or more to the left of the FAC's mark, and I'm caught off guard as I see his airplane nose up turning hard left away from the coastline. He's not jinking, there's no enemy reaction. He's simply turning the wrong way.

"Dagger lead, Dagger three, reverse right. Friendlies are on that side." I jump in and redirect him before the FAC can. I see the airplane slowly come back to the right. The rest of the flight follows him around now to the proper side of the river. Dagger two is ready to drop, and the FAC clears him to once again drop on the smoke from his marks. Two covers the white plumes from the FAC's rockets with six Mk-82s.

We circle and circle, making pass after pass with

Rustic adjusting from one airplane's bomb impacts to the next, or occasionally redefining a target area with another marking rocket. With the bombs gone, we come around for strafing passes and get a rare chance to exercise the 20mm Vulcan. There isn't much to be seen but a lot of muddy rice paddies stirred up and maybe some trees blown down, but the FAC seems happy with the outcome. As we leave for Bien Hoa he gives us a quick report of results, required but not very informative. We get credit for dropping "100 percent within 100 meters." It's not even close to the truth, but no one knows what 100 meters really is, and it sounds much better than saying all ordnance obeyed the law of gravity and hit the ground.

We contact Bien Hoa approach, and Dick follows the controller's radar vectors to the traffic pattern at the big base on the north side of Saigon. We're guided to the initial approach for runway 27, left hand traffic pattern. As we enter the pattern, Tolliver flips a wing down to the left, signaling he wants the number two man in the formation to come over to the left wing where three and four are flying. It's "echelon left" with all four airplanes in a row, the standard for a right-hand break or pitchout to downwind. It's the wrong direction for the current traffic pattern. I move the element back and down, give a small hand wave to the astonished lieutenant on the right wing, and move my wingman with me over to echelon right. As we fly over the approach end of the runway, I watch Tolliver roll into a hard left break for the traffic pattern without even a look before leaping. We take four seconds' spacing between airplanes and follow him around to landing.

Once the aircraft are parked and we're all aboard the

crew van to the operations building, Tolliver looks at me and scowls. He doesn't say much, and the rest of the guys are left to chatter about the FAC, the target, the weather, and what's for lunch at the club while we get fueled for the return flight.

At the debriefing, we don't spend time on the flight, the refueling, the tactics, or the target. Dick looks at me and accuses, "Why did you do that on initial? You're trying to make me look bad, just because I'm black." It's sudden and makes no sense. I didn't expect thanks, but also didn't think any of us were guilty of aeronautical sin.

"Dick, we tried to make you look good. Breaking into the echelon and scattering airplanes all over the base would make you look bad. You made a minor mistake, and we covered for you. If you don't think a good flight is supposed to do that, you're wrong. And frankly, it makes no difference to me if you're black, white, or polka dot." I've got a feeling now that the return to Korat is going to be a bit quiet.

Not quite a week later, I'm passing through the intel area of the command post. Barry Johnson steps out of the control room for a break and sees me. He calls me back, "Hey, Raz, were you on that Phu Ken mission with Tolliver last week?"

It doesn't ring any bells. "I don't think so. Never heard of the place. It sounds like a name I would remember. I had a Bien Hoa turn with Dick. What about it?"

"That's it. The Bien Hoa turn. Tolliver was leading. Down in MR 4, south of Saigon. We got a message in this morning from Seventh Air Force about it. Seems like the ground commander was impressed. Apparently there was a pretty extensive tunnel network through the area, and after you guys left the ARVN sat there and watched the Cong haul off dead, wounded, and even body parts for the next three days. They want to recommend Tolliver for a DFC."

"Are you sure?" Amazing. A no-threat flight in a no-challenge area with a nothing-in-sight target moving a bunch of mud and bamboo around leads to a gong recommendation for someone who just sort of muddled through it. It's really the way most medals are won. Real bravery is seldom seen or reported, and real heroes downplay their actions. Medals most often come through coincidence. Being in the right place and the right time, and then not getting killed. Tolliver is going to add to his list of credentials. The very essence of the modern major general. Still a captain, but someday . . .

"Yeah. They said you guys probably killed all the VC in the Phu Ken region." Johnson shakes his head walking away. He's probably thinking the same thing I am. Even the blind pig finds an acorn once in a while. Drop bombs on detailed targets in heavily defended areas to destroy critical military infrastructure and nothing seems to happen. Plop a bunch of high explosives in a marshland, and suddenly you've dealt the enemy a telling blow. What a strange war.

13. WOLFS AND LAREDOS AND TIGERS, OH MY!

The nation that will insist on drawing a broad line of demarcation
between the fighting man and the thinking man is liable to find
its fighting done by fools and its thinking done by cowards.

—Sir William Butler

IT WAS A RETURN TO those days of war as a routine.
There were way too many airplanes for way too few
targets. Somehow the reluctant warriors who had so far
found more critical need for their skills elsewhere now
quickly filled the squadrons. Their timing was excel-
lent. We got Phantom drivers with six, seven, and in
one instance nine years of experience in the airplane,
who had never been to Southeast Asia. They came from
training squadrons and flight test facilities and Pentagon staff jobs. There would be few promotions for
those who hadn't been to the show, and now it looked
like the last chance to log combat time. How they had
dodged the Cobra for so many years no one would ever
know, but suddenly they were eager.

The answer to finding targets was a regeneration of
the fast–forward air controller programs. Every Thai-

land base with F-4s had flown fast-FAC missions during the period between Rolling Thunder and Linebacker. It was a good concept. Forward air controllers specialized in chunks of landscape. They learned the nooks and crannies of the jungle and the road networks. They could visit their area and tell in a heartbeat that a new "tree" wasn't really a tree but really camouflage over a parked truck or a munitions storage area. They could find the temporary bridges and see the influx of heavy traffic by the changes in the tracks or the shifting of the mud around a riverbank. But traditional FAC airplanes were small and slow and exceedingly vulnerable. That's where the fast-FAC came in.

Sure, you couldn't see the details as well from 450 knots as you could at 80 miles per hour, but you could survive. You could specialize in an area, and you could learn the skills necessary to control flights of other fast movers, to talk their eyes onto the target and direct their weapons deliveries to best effect. You couldn't loiter for hours, but with lots of tankers available, you could cycle to a gas station overhead and be back in your area in twenty minutes. Run a four-hour mission with three tanker hits and you could get pretty familiar with a stretch of landscape. You could make the fast fighters much more effective than having them do their own armed reconnaissance missions.

There had been some great fast-FAC operations dating back to 1966, with the F-100 Misty program. In 1970, '71, and early '72, the Wolfs from Ubon, Laredos at Udorn, and Tiger FACs from Korat had written large in the history of fighter aviation. They flew low, studied hard, knew the areas, and got results. You could do some serious war fighting with a sharp group of fast-FACs.

Or you could build a fraternity of pretty boys with

tiger-striped scarves and secret handshakes who trafficked in the mythology of specialization. Days into the new year, Korat had the Tiger FAC program going again. It was an "invitation only" organization, populated by a group that had either been or was destined to be staff officers, generals' aides, or headquarters executives. They had a couple of warriors, mostly among the backseaters, but the bulk of the group were looking for something that would get them maximum combat hours and an impressive line in a performance report that would be read in a promotion board by someone who wasn't sure which end of the jet the hot air came out of.

The missions were mostly flown in Cambodia. You could get killed in Cambodia, but not quite as easily as in North Vietnam. There were no SAMs, and you were a long way away from any MiGs. There weren't any radar-guided big guns, but there were more than enough 37mm and 57mm flak sites. There were plenty of 23mm twin-barreled cannons ready to stitch your intakes shut. And there were lots of bad guys with rifles more than eager to shoot into the air at big, noisy, smoky jets.

I was on the wing of Tiger two, with Kirby in my backseat. There was no shortage of things to dislike about Tiger FAC missions. Every Tiger had a personal call sign. The flight used that name rather than a rotating, tactical call sign. It wasn't a bad convention when dealing with a slow-mover FAC who routinely flew single-ship, but with a pair of Phantoms, you now had to remember that the second aircraft in the flight wasn't "two" but "bravo," which was confusing because traditionally the letter designations were reserved for front- and backseaters in the same airplane. So the lead aircraft, Joe Green, was Tiger two even if he was leading, and I was Tiger two bravo. If we were shot down, I'd become Tiger two bravo alpha and Kirby would be bravo bravo. But I wouldn't get shot down, so there was no need to worry about that.

The FAC carried a pair of LAU-32 rocket pods with seven white phosphorus-marking rockets in each, and a pair of 370-gallon outboard tanks. He was clean and fast and maneuverable. The FAC wingman carried twelve Mk-82 500-pound bombs and the same tanks. We were fat and dirty and heavy. It was a recipe for continually being out of gas, outside the turn, on the verge of a stall, and out of control. But at least you ran out of gas faster than the FAC, so you could demand that he knock it off and take you to the tanker. The goal of every fast-FAC wingman was to get rid of the bombs as early as possible in the mission, then simply fly as a protection and extra set of eyes for the FAC. Getting stuck with iron into the second or third target period was never good. The FAC, however, wanted you to keep the bombs as long as possible. If he could get sets of fighters from one of the controlling agencies, he would always use those first and save the wingman to be used only on a fleeting target, or if no other assets were available.

The FAC tanker was always in a high orbit, waiting patiently at 28,000 feet to feed the FAC and his wingman. The FAC loved it, but when the wingman still had the bombs, it was almost impossible to get hooked up without being in afterburner on at least one engine. The wingman hated it. Somehow the pretty boys in the tiger-striped scarves must have slept through the lessons on wingman consideration. They never seemed to notice.

We were operating in Cambodia, along the network of Mekong tributaries that fanned out and eventually dumped into the sea beyond Phnom Penh. It was mostly jungle, with little villages of grass-topped huts. Dirt tracks crisscrossed the area, and except for the huge temple complex of Angkor Wat there was little of significance in the region. The Khmer Rouge insurgents fought against their own people, and the North Vietnamese transited the area to resupply their forces in South Vietnam. If you got lucky you could find a convoy or a storage area that would generate some serious secondary explosions. If it was a typical day, you simply flew patterns over the dark green trees looking for something unusual or some antsy gunner to show himself with a string of yellow tracers that arced behind your aircraft and disclosed the location of the hapless shooter.

It was early in the day, and a low-hanging cloud layer wasn't dissipating. Joe Green had a gun site plotted on his maps that had shot at his wingman yesterday. It was a ZU-23mm, a twin-barreled gun that could put out an incredible amount of fire. It didn't have any radar guidance, and for fast movers it wasn't a very serious threat unless you flew low over it or were attacking something close. The charts said a 23mm could be effective up to 8,000 or 10,000 feet, but most of us knew that you seldom saw effective fire much beyond 2,500. You might consider it a bit like a rattlesnake. It was certainly deadly, but you could quite easily walk around it without harm.

WITH HALF THE AREA UNDER low clouds and the other half not disclosing any lucrative targets, Joe decides it's a good idea for me to kill the snake. I'm tired of trying to nurse a bomb-laden airplane into unnatural maneuvers to keep up with Joe's target-hunting gyrations.

Kirby is not sure this is a good idea at all. We head for the coordinates and find the rough position of the gun alongside a dirt road through the jungle. He may be lurking, just like that snake, under an overhanging cloud layer at about 800 feet. We fly by once and don't get any reaction. Joe decides to fire a marking rocket under the edge of the clouds and see what happens. I wait, flying a high orbit parallel to Green's track as he rolls into a shallow dive and fires the willie-pete rocket into the jungle. As if on cue, the response to the pop of the white smoke on the ground is a string of angry yellow hornets erupting from just under the edge of the cloud bank. The gun is occupied. The snake is home.

"Okay, Kirby, we'll be dive toss, low angle. I'm going to drop pairs until we get a good position on this guy. I'll call the roll-in and you tell me when you're locked up." I've already got the switches set up and am listening to Kirby's litany of reasons why we shouldn't be doing this. They all make sense, but a kill's a kill and my fangs are out.

"Tiger two bravo's in." I point the nose at the puff of white smoke rising above the trees. Green gives me the required clearance to drop, and Kirby calls the radar lockup. The gunner now does his part and starts fighting for his life. We're under the cloud bank, and I'm trying to get the pipper to link up with the source of the string of yellow tracers that are coming by the canopy. Kirby's voice is now several octaves higher than usual. Bombs come off and I break hard left, then quickly back to wings level and pop through the cloud layer back to on top and out of sight of the gunner.

I circle back around to the north of the gun and try to see under the cloud deck for the bomb impacts. We've hit long. "Okay, Kirby, here we go again. Same drill." I try to circle a little bit farther to the west to take a slightly different approach, but the cloud layer hampers the approach, and the only way to the gun is from the clear side and then underneath the layer. We're locked up again, the gun is firing again, the tracers whizzing by the canopy again have got Kirby screaming again. This is getting personal.

The second pair are just short of the gun. We've got him bracketed, but he's still shooting. Gutsy little guy. Bet he can't hear anything anymore. "One more time, Kirby. Just one more time and we've got him."

"Let's go. I wanna get this over with, Raz." Yeah, the kid's all right. He doesn't really enjoy it, but he hangs on for the ride pretty good. I roll in and put the pipper between the two clouds of gray smoke from the first two passes. The yellow tracer string resumes. The bombs come off. We break right off the target and keep a hard level turn up beneath the clouds to watch the impacts end the tracer stream. Scratch one gun battery.

BOB MCKELVEY HAS BECOME THE squadron commander of the 34th. I met him at Luke during the F-4 checkout. He's one of the small group of previously fighter-qualified pilots taking the short course in the Phantom. We both arrived at Korat during the middle of the Line-backer campaign, but McKelvey didn't get assigned to either of the F-4 squadrons. Despite having less than thirty hours' experience in the airplane, he got an assignment to the wing staff as chief of the standardization and evaluation branch. These are the people who in a peacetime operation administer check rides for pilots to ensure their qualification and ability to perform the mission. Typically they are highly experienced people with an in-depth understanding of the aircraft, the weapons, the missions, and the tactics. But at this stage in the war, nothing is very typical.

Standardization is important. Establishing routine procedures that everyone uses makes it easier to get the job done. Whether it is an agenda for a flight briefing or a sequence for taxiing, having a standard procedure is important. When it comes to contingencies in flight or, even more critically, for emergencies, it can mean life or death. With almost eight years of combat operations from Korat, the major standards have been well established.

The second part of the job, evaluation, becomes far less important in combat than in peacetime. The real evaluation of your combat capability is generally handled by the enemy. If you do things right, you live and the enemy suffers. If you don't have your act in order, you die and the enemy celebrates. During the early days, no one considered the idea of combat area flight checks as being necessary. As time passed, however, the bureaucracy grew and evaluation was added to the list of squares to fill and paperwork to complete. Now you need an annual instrument check, so you fly a combat mission dropping bombs, dodging the guns and finding a tanker in the murky haze, then return to fly a series of practice, simulated instrument approaches with a flight examiner so that you can be qualified to do tomorrow and the next day what you did yesterday and a week ago.

Operational qualification at Korat is mostly about paperwork and less about combat effectiveness. In peacetime operations, you have to demonstrate detailed knowledge of weapons and tactics. You might have to conduct a briefing on how to deliver a nuclear weapon on a target in heavily defended Eastern Europe. Or you might have to plan a low-level conventional attack along a detailed mountainous route to meet a precise time on target, and then deliver a series of practice bombs on a controlled gunnery range within established criteria. In combat, you have to take a flight examiner along on a mission and survive.

Stan-eval is the perfect slot for Bob McKelvey. He can supervise a bunch of people who know what they are doing, even if he isn't yet very competent in the airplane himself. He can run the office and attend wing staff meetings, so he won't have to go to war every day. When he does fly, he can give a check ride and use that as a justification for taking the simpler, less-threatening missions. It's a perfect way to fill a combat tour without running a major risk. It will look good on the performance report. He does a good job. The paperwork is done right. The documentation is up to speed when the inspection team rolls through in January, and it only seems reasonable that when George Dornberger leaves, Bob should get the opportunity to command a fighter squadron. The timing is perfect. Linebacker has ended. We aren't bombing the places with MiGs and SAMs and lots of guns defending the targets. As squadron commander, he can pick and choose the missions he flies, and the menu of choices doesn't carry a lot of danger. People who have been squadron commanders, chiefs of standardization, inspectors, and executives to senior commanders are the ones who make general. Occasionally guys with those qualifications are also warriors, but just as often they aren't.

I'm in my usual position for evenings when I don't go downtown, leaning on the end of the CTF bar exchanging tall tales with one or another of the squadron good guys. It's a quiet night without even a poker game. McKelvey comes in, looking around the bar as if seeking someone in particular. He's not a regular visitor to the bar, preferring to spend time at the officer's club for dinner and then in his room reading, writing letters, and catching up on important paperwork. He looks a bit more tense than usual.

"Hi, Raz. How ya doing this evening?" Always good to have a bit of sociable conversation with the troops. Makes you seem accessible and one of the boys.

"Fine, sir. What brings you into this den of iniquity?"

"We got a hot one coming up tomorrow, and I was looking for some of the guys that will probably be on it." That's not good news, and the CTF is not a real good place to bring it up, if it really is some sort of special mission. There hasn't been anything really heavy happening for almost three months now. Nothing in the news or in this morning's intel briefing has indicated any probability of resuming bombing of North Vietnam. The big story has been the C-141 Freedom Bird flights picking up the POWs out of Hanoi. We've been getting plenty of pictures in *Stars and Stripes,* as well as in the command post, of the ceremonies of the prisoners' release and their welcomes as they arrive at the Philippines.

"Intel reports a lot of noise indicating that the North Vietnamese have moved an SA-3 into Khe Sanh in the South. There are already confirmed reports about a couple of SA-2 batteries, and now the SA-3 will make it damn near impossible to operate the C-130s to support the Marines. Looks like we're going to go in tomorrow and clean them out."

Now that puts a new perspective on things. While the missions have gotten almost meaningless in Cambodia, the facts are that the North Vietnamese regulars are continuing to flow into the South. Their goal remains to support the Vietcong, overthrow the semi-democratic regime in the South, and reunify the country under a Communist revolutionary government.

I've seen enough SA-2s over the years to have great respect for the weapon, but I also have learned exactly how my equipment works to warn me of the missile's operations. I know what my RWR is telling me, and I know what my ECM pods can do, and I know how to attack an SA-2 site and survive. The missile is slow off the pad and, if seen, can be outmaneuvered.

The SA-3 Goa is smaller, faster, and with shorter range. Some analysts compare it to the Army's Hawk, which is very, very good. The SA-3 uses different radars, the Flat Face and Low Blow, which are supposed to be detected by our radar-warning receiver, but since we haven't previously encountered one, we can't really be sure. One never wants to trust his life to the advertising copy of the manufacturer. Smaller and faster means harder to see and less reaction time to maneuver to avoid it. This could be a bitch.

Soviet doctrine on deployment of the missile is to use it in combination with the SA-2 in overlapping coverage. Where the larger missile has gaps, the smaller one fills. Where the small missile can't reach, the bigger one can. Cover the whole mess with the usual array of optical and radar-guided guns to create a true nest of vipers.

"So, Boss, you think this is gonna go?" Got to say something, even if it doesn't mean much. Fill the conversational void.

"Yeah, Raz. We've got a preliminary frag already. We're gonna send in a couple of hunter-killer teams and then some bomb flights to follow up after you guys root 'em out."

I hate the sound of that, "you guys."

He continues, "It's gonna be a tough one. You'll want to be in on it, naturally. We'll have some losses, of course. But, there'll be Silver Stars for everyone." I'm wondering about the old maxim of leadership by example. I don't hear anything about the squadron commander at the point of the spear. The idea that a mission is flown for decoration is absurd and offensive. Frankly, I have absolutely no desire to be in on it. I've come to believe that you are given a certain allocation of heartbeats for your life, and if you use them up too fast, it's over. There's gonna be a lot of heartbeats expended on this mission.

"Well, Boss, I've already got mine. Maybe you want to go. It might be the last chance to get yours." The conversation is over. I've struck a chord, and McKelvey leaves.

A few hours later the schedule comes out. The squadron commander will be the supervisor of flying, monitoring operations from the control tower. I'm leading the F-4 element in the second hunter-killer team.

An hour before briefing time, the mission is unexplainably canceled. Maybe weather, maybe revised intel, maybe something else has intervened. We never hear more about the SA-3.

CHARLIE PRICE IS TIGER FIVE. He's been around for almost a full year. Charlie has been on my wing, and I've been on his. He knows what he's doing. At least he knows what he's doing in the air. On the ground is a different story. He's brought his wife to war. She's living in Bangkok with a cluster of other wives who, despite regulations to the contrary, have come to share the experiences and provide spousal support. Most weekends she hops the bus and comes to Korat city for a couple of days. She visits the club for meals, lounges by the pool with other wives during the day, and gossips incessantly about the indecent behavior of the other fighter pilots who drink too much, have foul mouths, and probably cavort with local women. Charlie is one of the guys for ten days in a row, then the devoted husband for a three- or four-day visitation. It's a schizophrenic life that has to impose pressure on him.

Charlie is working the area just east of the Angkor Wat complex, heavy jungle infested with campsites for Khmer Rouge and, probably, rest areas for North Vietnamese transporting arms and supplies to units infiltrating South Vietnam. He's got the standard Tiger two-ship flight and is dragging a floundering wingman through low altitude maneuvers trying to see what is going on under the canopy of heavy green. Today there is a cloud deck covering most of the working area; mid-level stratus forecasts a slow-moving warm front, which will bring heavy rain tomorrow or the next day. The countryside is relatively flat, so it's easy to duck down through the clouds and then search for targets. There's enough space beneath to work flights dropping bombs in the low-threat environment.

Back and forth he crisscrosses the jungle and meandering streams, concentrating on what is different today from yesterday. He's looking for the telltales of new activity. Tracks in the dirt road meaning heavy trucks, discolored leaves on trees indicating branches cut and now dying used as camouflage, clusters of trees that weren't there the last time he overflew the area. It's tough for slow-FACs, but fast movers have to really be prepared, and flying the airplane must be second nature. There's little time to look, react, calculate altitudes, think about airspeeds. You feel the bird, you sense the speed, you trust your instincts. Feedback from the stick in your hand tells you what the airplane is doing. The G loads tell you what your turn capability is, the angle-of-attack tone tells you what potential you have left.

It's late and nearly time to get home. The wingman has saved four bombs, just in case they find something but don't have time or fuel left to get another flight in on the target. It's the third session of the day. They've refueled from a nearby tanker three times already, and logged more than four and a half hours' maneuvering at low altitude and usually with three or four G on the airplane. Charlie is tired. It's time to expend the last bombs and go home to Korat. Maybe Momma will come up to visit this weekend and they can hang around a bit. Yeah, that will be good.

There, just a bit beyond that cluster of hootches. It looks like something under the trees. Price bends the airplane around in a hard turn, looking to see if there are trucks or crates or armed men. It's time to find a target. "Tiger five's got something for you, bravo. Looks like some trucks under the trees. Let's get ready to drop your stuff and head for home." He comes harder left and eases the airplane up to get ready for his marking pass. Got to get a bit higher and try to keep it on the steep side. Definitely want to give the wingman a good spot to hit. It's embarrassing to put a mark down and then have to talk him onto a target a hundred meters away. Much better to hit the target with the rocket and then simply have the wingman hit the smoke.

"Tiger five is in to mark." He rolls over, inverted momentarily and floating upward as he looks through the top of the canopy, straining to keep the trees in sight that cover the hidden trucks. He's into the clouds, and then on top of the thin layer. He continues the pull downward, trusting that the transition back through will come as quickly on the downward flight as it did on the upward. Nose down now, he pops out of the cloud layer and searches for his references again. Where's the target? Ahh, over there, just a little bit. Got it in sight now. Looking good. Altitude? Oh, shit! Pickle. Rocket fires. Charlie pulls.

The airplane shudders and protests as he pulls to recover. The AOA tone beeps, then goes steady and then chatters as he pulls into a high-speed stall. The nose is coming up, but slowly, and the altimeter is unwinding too fast. The trees loom. He pushes the throttles forward, trying to keep some energy to get some more G and then more capability to make the pullout. Jungle fills the windscreen. The nose is up now, but the airplane is still going down. Tiger five smashes into the tops of the trees pancake style, then bounces back into the air. The engines unwind, and both immediately flame out as leaves and branches choke the intakes. Instinctively Charlie slams both throttle to the firewall, demanding afterburner and hopefully triggering a restart.

The airplane is shuddering and sinking without thrust. The control stick is stiff and seemingly ineffective. Then the bang of a compressor stall as one engine lights off. Slowly it spools up and maybe will give a bit of thrust. The warning light panel is sparkling like a Christmas tree with nearly a dozen red, yellow, and green lights vying for attention. Generators, hydraulic systems, fuel gauges, overheat lights, engine fires, all saying "pick me, pick me" to fix first. Just fly the airplane now. Just see if the engine will push it fast enough to stay airborne.

The engine winds up slowly; 70, now 80 percent. It stops accelerating at 85 percent. Charlie hits the master jettison button and blows everything off the airplane. Tanks, rocket pods, pylons, bomb-suspension gear, everything must go. Rummage sale at the Wat tonight for slightly used F-4 parts. Will a two-engine airplane fly on one with only 85 percent power? No one knows. It's never been done before. He needs three hands, one to hold the throttles forward, one to milk the stick trying to squeeze a few feet of altitude out of the bird, and one to stay ready on the ejection handle. There's no electricity, so no intercom, and Price can't know if his backseater is all right and whether or not he is about to eject them both. He tries to see a head in the rearview mirrors but can't get a free hand to do any kind of signaling.

That's all he's going to get. Either the second engine is windmilling or the tachometer is frozen. It isn't going to start. The one engine running at partial power is keeping them airborne, but the airplane is definitely flying sideways. It shudders continually and wants to roll off to the right. It's a battle to keep it flying and head for the border. Can he make it to Ubon, or at least across the border to Thailand for a safer pickup after ejection?

Tiger five's wingman catches up, or, more accurately, slows down to join his stricken leader. The airplane is barely staying airborne, but it's impossible to estimate for how much longer. The damage is incredible. The bay panels on both engines are gone, from the trailing edge of the wing all the way back to the nozzles. The flap on one side is totally ripped off, while the other flap is simply torn. The speed brake panel on one side is hanging, slightly skewed. A landing gear door is missing, and the strut and wheel assembly are partially exposed. Fluids are leaking from a half-dozen rips and tears in the underside of the fuselage. The wingman calls Charlie on the radio, but there is no answer. He moves forward on the wing and waves at Price. Charlie responds with a quick okay sign. The airplane is flying.

They stagger through the sky toward Ubon. The wingman handles radio calls and coordinates with Ubon tower for an emergency recovery. Fortunately, the mishap has taken place conveniently close to the border, and they won't have to nurse the crippled airplane very far. Good weather helps, as they can see the base and get lined up on the runway for a simple straight-in approach.

The flaps are so badly damaged that there will be no attempt to lower them. There's no way of knowing what additional damage might occur. With little margin of power, Charlie is going to have to make a tough decision about the landing gear. It might come down normally, it might not come down, or it might only come down partially. Once it is down, will he have enough power to have any options left? The drag of the gear might overcome the ability of the single trashed engine to maintain flight. He certainly won't have power to go around if the landing looks bad. He doesn't know if, once down, he will be able to raise the gear again. Wait too long to try the landing gear, and he risks sinking into the ground. Lower it too early and he may not have power to get to the runway. Too low and with a sink rate, ejection might not be an option. The tail hook works. It comes down when he lowers the handle, and his wingman signals with an okay sign.

Short final now, about four miles from the runway, descending through about eight hundred feet. He reaches for the gear handle, and with his breath held pulls it out and then slaps it down, activating the emergency gear extension. The airplane shudders and sinks momentarily as bent and torn gear doors open, and with one last bump the landing gear drops into place. A glance to his right at the other airplane gets a reaffirming hand signal. He's cleared to land and he's got three down and locked. Over the overrun, easing off the throttle, onto the runway, hook engaged. Tiger five is yanked to a stop by the arresting gear. He's on the ground.

Fire engines and rescue people swarm around as a helicopter hovers overhead. Charlie pulls the throttles to cutoff and opens the canopy. In seconds he and his backseater are unstrapped and on the ground, being helped away from the smoking airplane. It will never fly again, and no one is even sure how it was flying seconds ago.

THE YEAR IS NEARLY OVER. It's June, and I've got my assignment to Europe to continue flying the F-4 in Spain. The Linebacker campaigns had only some of the intensity of that earlier tour in the F-105, but Linebacker II at Christmas was an experience that is going to become part of history. Since the cessation of North Vietnam bombing, the daily grind has been more like flying to a gunnery range in training than real combat. The snake can jump up and bite on any given day, but it is much more likely to be weather or maintenance or your own stupidity that kills you than a determined enemy.

Seven of us are scheduled to complete a year of combat flying on the first of July. We could easily fly our last sorties during the last few days of June, but by delaying a few days the scheduler will get each of us an extra month's combat pay and income tax exclusion. It's something that airlifters have been doing for eight years of the war, scheduling trips into the area over the last and first days of a month. Usually it's far from the minds of fast-mover flyers. It makes no difference to me, but the plan is made without my input. We'll all fly missions on the first of the month. We'll all have a barbecue on the lawn outside the CTF. We'll all have a party in the banquet room of the officer's club in party suits. We'll all get a squadron plaque, a handshake, and our release to return to the real world where things have changed.

Seven is an odd number, and it doesn't recognize the concept of two-seat airplanes. We need one more person for an end-of-tour flight. I'll take the hospital commander, squadron flight surgeon, and savior of Roscoe in my backseat for my final combat mission. Doc Zimmerman has been trained to operate the radar, align the inertial navigation system, change radio channels, and generally do all the things a brand-new WSO does. He takes pride in his designation as "combat doc" and nags incessantly to get on the combat schedule rather than trying to log time on maintenance flights or, even worse, by riding on a trash-hauler. I wouldn't consider going to Hanoi with him, and he probably wouldn't be too eager for the experience either. But for a simple bomb-dumper into Cambodia or South Vietnam, the doc is more than adequate. I've got no problem with the idea. I like the doc and consider him a friend. He'll be going home next week as well.

The mission is uneventful. Takeoff, tanker, FAC rendezvous, bomb the trees, and come home. It's so much different than the terror-filled final flight of my F-105 tour. We've had no losses for weeks. We've had no sig-

nificant missions for months. We come back to Korat
and get to do a flyby. The wing even has a regulation
for end-of-tour buzz jobs. Can't be done with ordnance
remaining. Missiles on board are okay. Must be done
over the runway, not the main base. Weather minimums
are specified. One pass only. Must remain subsonic;
don't need any broken windows. Pull-ups are authorized, rolls are not. Formations are fine, but single-ship
is approved also. Rolls are authorized for passes on
MiG-kill missions, but there haven't been any of those
for six months. The bureaucracy has even spread to the
regulation of celebration. Everything must be properly
managed. It's symptomatic of the entire war.

The doc flies the airplane back to Korat as I remove
my helmet and quietly peel the olive-drab camouflage
tape away, restoring it to peacetime white. I'm no longer
at war and won't be hiding in the elephant grass after a
terror-filled ejection. Today, as I replace my helmet, I
shake the stick to take control from Zimmerman and
waggle the wings to move my wingman into close formation. We're just a two-ship, so we stay together. I call the
tower and let down to approach the field. We're cleared
for the pass, and we come down farther to 100 feet. I hold
the airspeed at 400 knots until we reach the overrun. We
throttle up, light the burners, and run the length of the airfield reaching just a bit over 600 knots by the end of the
runway. I wave at my wingman and leave him behind as I
pull five Gs and come up into the vertical. Doc is grunting under the load in the backseat, but I feel fine today.
Symbolically I'm leaving Korat behind. The airspeed is
more than enough to take us to the moon, but I come out
of burner at 10,000 feet and roll the airplane over on its
back to pull back down and circle for landing.

The parking area celebrations are more perfunctory

than truly sincere. The level of relief at the end of combat is directly related to the level of fear and apprehension with which you've been dealing. There has been little true fear for the past six months, and the people who meet us are simply filling a schedule to make sure that all of the end-of-tour aircrews get met by someone with a bottle of two-buck champagne and a handshake. I don't mind at all.

The party at the CTF starts in the early afternoon. As flights finish and the celebrants arrive, the stereo gets turned up and the lawn captures the overflow from the bar. The drink of choice for the end-of-tour crews is bubbly. We finish off the meager stocks of André champagne and call the officer's club for their supply. Then we hit on the NCO club for any sparkling wine they might have. Before long we've exhausted it all, including a few bottles of very questionable "cold duck" from the base exchange shop. We harass the sleeping C-130 crews that fly the night airborne command post missions by tossing empty bottles on the corrugated tin roof of their hootch. The bottles roll and rattle down the slope in a symbolic ritual commemorating Rolling Thunder. The guys emerge bleary-eyed into the afternoon sun to gripe and curse at us. We respond with a wire-cutter and snip the external power cords from the air conditioners to their rooms, leaving them hot and sweaty as a penalty for the impertinence of daring to challenge our celebration.

The party ends late, and only after we've sung songs, raised toasts, wrestled on the lawn, then cast an orange smoke grenade into the CTF and pinned the door hasp, locking two dozen revelers in the tiny bar. Two of the larger lieutenants, former football players, rescue the occupants by plunging through the aged plywood wall beside the door. A good time is had by all, and the morning-after headaches are well earned. The singing isn't good but it's loud, and most of the participants recall all the words. The next night, the ceremonial dinner at the club is more refined and suitable for attendance by the wives—those women who weren't authorized to be there, but were anyway.

Two days later I'm headed back to the States. There's no slack given aircrews in the processing. The harassment starts immediately when boarding the C-130 at Korat. Everyone who is headed for home must spread their suitcases on the tarmac before boarding the airplane. Briefcases and hang-up bags lie flat. Suitcases, like my bulging zippered B-4 bag, must be opened and laid out. A large German shepherd and a slack-jawed air police two-striper step over, onto, and through the array of personal effects. The dog sniffs and the cop prods. Eventually we are cleared. This is customs inspection, and they are looking for drugs. The easy availability of heroin, hashish, and other recreational pharmaceuticals makes it necessary.

We land at Bangkok, where we transfer to a contract airline, a DC-8 painted in the livery of an airline that no one has ever heard of before. We have to go through customs before boarding. Bags open, inspected, disheveled again. July in Thailand on the white cement of the airport ramp leaves everyone appropriately sweaty and miserable prior to boarding and strapping in for the flight to the Philippines, where we will be asked to debark, find our bags on the ramp, and have them inspected once again. Can't have illicit drugs somehow migrating into the suitcases during flight.

Refueling at Honolulu, we've finally set foot in the United States. More customs inspections. But, I ask, wasn't the airman at Korat a certified customs inspector?

Or maybe the one in Bangkok or at Clark? It makes no difference, apparently. My beleaguered B-4 bag takes this opportunity to express its own protest by refusing to re-zip. One of the customs inspectors, obviously familiar with the life cycle of an Air Force issue zipper, offers me a piece of clothesline to secure my bag closed.

San Francisco repeats the process one last time upon arrival at Travis AFB. It is a commercial contract flight, and it could land at San Francisco airport because most of the passengers are proceeding onward to other places in the nation, but that wouldn't be the military way. Hog-tied suitcase, oil-stained hang-up bag, and scuffed leather briefcase in tow, I grab a taxi for the long drive to the other airport. There is a bus, but I'm tired of being crammed into cattle cars, huddling while I await the next round of abuse.

I've heard the reports. I've seen the news photos. Dog-tired, sweaty, and suffering the depth of jet lag that only comes from a trip crossing fourteen time zones and the international dateline, I pay the cabbie and turn my bags over to the smiling skycap at the curb. American Airlines to San Antonio. He nods and tags the scruffy baggage. He grins at the clothesline. I look around for the war protesters, the name-callers, the spitters. There's no one beyond the normal airport people going about their business. Maybe some of them are against the war, but none approach me with taunts of baby-killing or any semblance of disrespect. Maybe it's the scowl and the bags under my eyes, maybe it's the "try me" glare, or maybe the protesting isn't as rampant as the media would have us believe. Nobody cares. No one bothers me. I get my ticket and head toward the gate to wait for a departure in a couple of hours. A call from a nearby phone booth to San Antonio. No answer. I leave a message on the answering machine that I'll be home almost exactly on the schedule I sent in a letter a few days earlier. All the connections have been close to on time. I'll get into San Antonio about eight o'clock in the evening. I nap in a chair near the departure gate.

The sun is just setting as the flight touches down in San Antonio. I've caught glimpses of the white buildings and parallel runways at Randolph AFB, and have seen the lights on the Hemisfair tower downtown as we maneuver to land. Passengers file out of the airplane and are greeted by family and friends. I look around but no one is here. I retrieve my tired belongings and get a taxi to take me home.

The cab pulls up before the small brick rancher in Universal City. The porch light is on, and the living room light glows softly through the window. I drag my bags to the door and ring the doorbell. No answer. My dog, Count, barks from the backyard at the sound of the chimes. I ring again, then rummage through my briefcase to retrieve a house key not used in a year. There's no one home. I open the backdoor and Count bounds in, jumping to lick my face and greet me. No notes, no explanations. She still lives here, but she didn't lie that night so long ago when I told her about the assignment. As Santana might sing, "My house is dark and my pots are cold." Welcome home.

14. WIN, LOSE, OR DRAW?

War is an ugly thing, but it is not the ugliest of things;
the decayed and degraded state of moral and patriotic
feeling which thinks that nothing is worth war is much
worse. A man who has nothing for which he is willing to
fight, nothing he cares about more than his own personal
safety, is a miserable creature who has no chance of being
free, unless made and kept so by better men than himself.

—John Stuart Mill (1806–1873)

WASHINGTON, DC, IS A CITY of beautiful buildings and
soaring monuments. The capital dominates with its ma-
jestic dome and broad stairways. The Supreme Court
similarly rises among the stately trees, with strength in
its columns and classic façade. The memorials to the
greats of our nation are white, broad, and tall, befitting
the stature of the military and political leaders that they
honor. But the Wall is black and buried, a depression in
the ground symbolizing the depression of the nation
that did not win the war or respect the men who fought
it. You can see the Washington Monument from miles
away, and you won't need a map to find Lincoln or Jef-
ferson or the World War II memorial, but you could
walk within a hundred yards of the Wall and never see

it. We seem to want to hide it, maybe hoping that an obligation has been fulfilled but no one wants to admit
that the obligation existed in the first place.

The names are listed in a paper directory, dog-eared
and dirty from thousands of hands searching through it
for a friend or family member who was lost. It's
chained to a plywood pedestal like a small-town phone-
book at a gas station pay phone, almost as an afterthought by the government that maybe some visitor
might want to know where on the wall among the
58,000 names their special person is memorialized. But
they do want to know. They come from across the country to see and to feel and to remember. Some say they
come for closure or to heal, but that is only a few. More
come for respect and to belatedly honor the fallen. And
some come out of guilt that they didn't go or didn't do
the right thing at the time.

The sidewalk along the brooding black marble wall
slopes gradually, there are no steps along the way. It's
almost a metaphor for the gradualism that led us to failure. It marks the descent into the immorality of sending
men to die for a cause that the nation wants to ignore.
But when you reach the deepest point, the walk rises
again and gradually, over time, returns to the level of
the street and the city. All things pass, and maybe this
represents a return to normalcy and patriotism and
honor, belief in your country's might and the principles
that the other soaring white monuments of Washington
commemorate. Maybe.

Children visiting the Wall from the inner cities of
America laugh and tussle on the grass, showing little of
the solemnity that we might wish for this spot. They
don't know, these many years later, exactly what this is

all about. They don't make a great distinction between Verdun and Vietnam. But that guy over there, the one in the dark suit with the sunglasses, he knows the difference. The gray-haired fellow coming down the walk with his grandson holding his hand, he knows many of these names. The heavy-set fellow in the West Point sweatshirt, sitting on the park bench with the cane by his side, he was there. The one in the tattered field jacket, with the beard and dirty matted long hair? Probably not. Odds are he's ten years too young and simply another poseur and wannabe. There are many of them these days. You can buy the jacket in any town, and the medals can be found on eBay. But that's the stereotype: the homeless, drug- or alcohol-addicted hulk destroyed by the war. The reality is that the great majority of that war's survivors are quiet old men, living out their lives and remembering.

The POWs were released just weeks after the Christmas bombing, but as the years pass we continue to question. Were there more? Were some held back? We want a full accounting, but is that even possible? Most of the POWs tell you that the names they know are all accounted for, yet there are names that didn't show up, and remains aren't returned, and final disposition is unsure. We may never know.

We lost a huge part of America during the long drawn-out years of the war. We learned that you don't have an obligation to your country, and that nothing is worth fighting for beyond your own slice of the pie. It was reasonable, maybe even more respectable to resist a war, denying that there was a national interest or a reason for involvement if it meant that you wouldn't be inconvenienced. As the embassy fell in 1975, we watched the last of the Vietnamese being evacuated or left behind, after they depended upon us for the future of their nation. Many gloated that America had been brought low, and would never be respected or influential again. Yet nearly thirty years later, we see a Vietnam that's more capitalist than before the Communist victory. There is a real Hilton hotel in Hanoi, and the Web site touts an "American breakfast" included in the room rate. The free market is creating a booming economy in which entrepreneurs are succeeding, and the dependency upon Marxist largesse to support the individual is abandoned. Americans are returning to Vietnam as tourists, and Vietnamese students are migrating to American colleges and universities to learn how best to succeed in the free market world.

For many years after the collapse of Saigon, the rallying cry of the modern American was "no more Vietnams." That was supposedly the proper position for the politically correct pacifist, who may have thought nothing was worth the sacrifice of war or the disruption of life in service to their country. The draft was gone, and military service became increasingly viewed as a refuge from real life for those who could not succeed in business. Yet the service academies continued to attract eager, conscientious, talented young men, and now women. The enlisted corps continued to provide opportunity for growth, leadership, and responsibility for men and women who saw service above self as a worthwhile life. And there are still wars. Despite the reluctance of the majority of Americans to get involved or fight for anything, there are still wars.

And we are prepared. The damage done by the years of Vietnam was not totally without benefit. We learned lessons. We responded when we could have tucked our tail between our legs and slunk into the back rooms of society. We built a fighting force and trained a leadership cadre that could meet future challenges if only we could avoid the political pitfalls that nearly destroyed us in Southeast Asia. Not everyone likes it, but it undeniably works.

War is the ultimate game. It's played for high stakes and, damage to your self-esteem notwithstanding, you've got to keep score. Did we win? Everyone says no. But if we lost 58,000, and by most estimates the enemy lost between 2 and 3 million people, wasn't their victory pyrrhic? "What price victory?" is a cliché, but the cost of winning in SEA was high for whichever side will, in the balance of history, be declared the winner.

No one can reasonably claim that we won. But does that mean we lost? There were lessons from those years and they have had an impact. The political lessons haven't all been learned, but the military lessons certainly have. During 1966, when I flew the F-105 in Rolling Thunder, we lost an airplane every 65 missions over North Vietnam. For every five pilots that started the tour, three would be shot down before completing it. In 1991, during Desert Storm, the average loss rate for fixed wing aircraft was one every 3,500 missions. During Iraqi Freedom, more than 16,000 fixed wing combat sorties were flown, and only one aircraft was shot down. Clearly we learned something from our experiences. If the political and military errors of the Vietnam War led to the changes that resulted in the low loss rates of the two Iraq wars, then we won something.

Quite clearly the major lesson of the air war was that gradualism in the application of force may be politically expedient, but militarily it is folly. Never has the theory of Douhet been more clearly proven than in the eleven days of Linebacker II. The idea that a strategic bombing campaign can be decisive without a ground operation to accompany and seize territory has been debated since the Italian aviation pioneer suggested it. Unleashing the full force of available airpower on North Vietnam effectively destroyed all significant military targets in the Red River Delta and, as reported by the POWs on the scene, it virtually demoralized the North Vietnamese. With the reasonable political goals of ending US involvement, gaining release of the prisoners, and providing an incentive to the recalcitrant negotiators to sign an agreement, the campaign was a clear success, but five years too late.

The flawed personnel policies of the Air Force took a bit longer to correct. The principle that all pilots are interchangeable when the need arises has been effectively abandoned. The related concept that all tactical pilots can be effective in all missions has also been tossed out. Today's Air Force employs a multiple track pilot training system that channels officers into high performance or heavy aircraft early in the process. There is little crossover between career fighter pilots and career airlifters or bomber types. Specialization in mission is not quite as rigid, but training focuses on the primary missions of aircraft designed for specific purposes. For nearly twenty years now, we've had experts in air-to-air combat and experts in ground attack.

The equipment to support such specialization has proven itself in US conflicts as well as in the hands of our closest allies. The air superiority fighter, the F-15 Eagle, has achieved an unequaled record in combat against other airplanes. It isn't simply the airplane, however, that makes it work. The integration of a more agile airplane with improved weapons is the obvious part of the package. A less visible component is the synergy gained from working closely with controllers in the "son of Disco," the AWACS that keeps the big picture of the battle available. Add a program of serious continual training with dissimilar aircraft types under instrumented conditions that allow recreation of every detail of every training mission back on the ground, and you have an effective war-fighting capability.

The ground attack mission is equally specialized. The North Vietnam air war taught us a lot about the modern air defense system. Fighting through an integrated system of modern surface-to-air missiles, radar-controlled high rate-of-fire guns, and ground-directed interceptors to a target takes more than just a good airplane. We learned about radar warning, electronic jamming, and communications security. We developed weapons to attack and suppress enemy defenses. We've even developed aircraft that are extremely difficult to detect by radar, infrared, or visual search. Neutralization of the enemy defenses is one of the first steps toward a guarantee of success.

New generations of weapons have come from the lessons of the war. Seldom is it necessary to go nose-to-nose with the target. Now we employ standoff weapons that can be released at some distance from the target, well clear of the defenses. Many generations after the initial laser-guided and TV-guided weapons of Vietnam, we now have more precise weapons with more flexibility. Laser systems have given way to satellite-positioned weapons that can be programmed in flight to find their precise target coordinates, day or night, in good weather or foul. Fewer airplanes, less exposure, higher probability of target kill, and less collateral damage are the benefits.

Training has improved. From the specialized preparation for tactical aviators in undergraduate pilot training to the improved simulations in initial qualification courses, the pilot arriving in his first operational unit is better equipped than ever before for a difficult job. Large-scale integrated force exercises on realistic training ranges keep the skills sharp. The old philosophy that training is dangerous has been properly trashed. Training is essential to survival in battle, and now we do it as realistically as possible and with the benefit of the highest of technologies.

Politically, we've learned as well. We learned that it is possible to fight, with just cause, without unleashing the nuclear genie. More important, we've learned that once the decision to fight is made, a war should be pursued vigorously, with all reasonable force, to a quick conclusion. Clear objectives, firm resolve, and competent military leadership can lead to more positive results. Clemenceau said that war was too important to be left to the generals, but the French outcome in World Wars I and II challenge that assertion. Quite clearly we have learned, and properly so, that war is too important to not be left to the generals. Once the political decision to fight is made, the war *must* be left to the generals. The evidence of Desert Storm and Iraqi Freedom is too great to deny.

We will always have two classes in our military. There are warriors, those who can face the challenges of battle, overcome their fears, and fulfill their mission. These are the ones who don't seek personal glory, but simply find themselves drawn to the ultimate challenge of war. And there are careerists. These are the ones who know that the military is a structured bureaucracy that offers incredible opportunity for those who will learn the detailed rules of the culture and abide by them. Occasionally the two classes come together, but in most instances they clash, sometimes violently, sometimes subtly. The warriors need no more than the satisfaction of the war. The careerists go to war to credential themselves for future advancement.

When the country is at peace, the warriors train and the careerists seek offices with potential. The warriors are deployed to forward bases, honing their skills and fulfilling the need to deter potential enemies. The careerists are in staff offices, attaching themselves to senior officers, careerists themselves, and writing the policies and regulations that will define them.

When conflict erupts, the careerists are often placed in command, where their dependence upon structure leaves them unable to deal with the fog of war and incapable of breaking out of the corporate group-think mindset. If the conflict is short they can survive, and their career continues. If the conflict is protracted, as was the war in Southeast Asia, they institutionalize themselves, circle the proverbial wagons, and begin to write the justifications for their failures.

The Vietnam War left the US with both classes. We had fine, capable staff officers aplenty, now with combat qualifications in greater or lesser degree, to populate our headquarters buildings and government offices. They attended the embassy soirees in their dress uniforms and appropriate assortment of medals, knowing which spoon to use and whether to shake hands with glove on or removed. They looked good in the background for photos of presidents and senators and congress-critters.

We also had a group of warriors, blooded in battle and knowing what it would take to build the force to fight the future wars. They knew the lessons of history and felt little need to relive them. In the ensuing years after Vietnam, leaders like Chuck Horner, Charlie Gabriel, Joe Ralston, Ron Fogleman, Mike Ryan, and others shaped the thinking and rebuilt the force. They knew the differences between the two classes, and while they couldn't wholesale change the culture, they could get the right people in the right jobs to make sure the same mistakes wouldn't happen again. The results of the most recent conflicts have validated their efforts.

Did I win or lose in the war? Life is filled with choices and occasionally no choice at all. Few are as fortunate as I have been in knowing exactly what I wished to do in my life and then finding myself with the skills and talents necessary to fulfill my dream. I had the choice to become a fighter pilot, but then no choice in my war. I learned a violent trade in an unforgiving environment during Rolling Thunder. It was a choice to return to the war, and then a huge disappointment to see what we had become. You can't go home again. Not all will agree with my views nor even understand my motivations. They might not be willing to make the sacrifices or confront their fears. That is fine. They live their lives and I have lived mine. I've had few regrets. I won my wars.

Anybody who doesn't have fear is an idiot.
It's just that you must make the fear work for you.
Hell when somebody shot at me, it made me madder than hell,
and all I wanted to do was shoot back.

—BRIGADIER GENERAL ROBIN OLDS, USAF

APPENDIX 1
Linebacker Losses

Operation Linebacker was conducted from May 10 through October 23, 1972. During that period, the following aircraft were lost in missions over North Vietnam:[1]

Date	Aircraft	Crew
10 May	F-4D 65-0784	Maj. Robert Lodge
		Capt. Roger Locher
	F-4E 67-0386	Capt. Jeff Harris
		Capt. Dennis Wilkinson
	F-4J 155797	Cdr. Harry Blackburn
		Lt. Stephen Rudloff
	F-4J 155800	Lt. Randy Cunningham
		Lt.(jg) Willie Driscoll
11 May	F-105G 62-4424	Maj. William Talley
		Maj. James Padgett
	F-4D 66-0230	Lt. Col. Joseph Kittinger
		1/Lt. William Reich
12 May	F-4E 66-0299	Capt. Samuel Adair
		1/Lt. Dennis Cressey
	F-4D 66-8799	Capt. Lonnie Bogard
		1/Lt. William Ostermeyer

1. Losses reflect only aircraft lost over N. Vietnam or as a result of Linebacker missions. This does not include losses in Laos or S. Vietnam. Chris Hobson, *Vietnam Air Losses: USAF, Navy, and Marine Corps Fixed-Wing Aircraft Losses in SEA, 1961–1973* (Hinckley, England: Midland Publishing, 2001).

Date	Aircraft	Crew
17 May	A-7E 158015	Cdr. T. R. Wilkinson
	F-105G 63-8347	(crew unknown)
18 May	F-4D 66-7612	1/Lt. Wesley Ratzel
		1/Lt. Jonathan Bednarek
19 May	A-7B 154541	Lt. Aubrey Nichols
20 May	F-4D 65-0600	1/Lt. John Markle
		Capt. James Williams
21 May	F-4E 67-0358	Lt. Col. R. E. Ross
		1/Lt. W. N. Key
	F-4B 153032	Lt. Cdr. H. Sampson
		Lt.(jg) R. G. Draggett
22 May	F-4D (unknown)	(unknown)
23 May	A-7B 154405	Cdr. Charles Barnett
	F-4D (unknown)	Capt. William Byrns
		Capt. William Bean
24 May	F-8J 150311	Lt. Carroll Beeler
	A-7E 156877	Lt. Cdr. H. A. Eikel
25 May	A-4F 155045	Cdr. Henry Strong
26 May	F-4D 66-7621	Capt. A. Arnold
		Capt. T. Kinkaid
27 May	A-4F 155048	Lt. Thomas Latendresse
	A-4F 154197	(unknown)
29 May	A-6A 155650	Lt. Cdr. Phillip Schuyler
		Capt. Lou Ferracane
1 June	F-4E (unknown)	Capt. G. Hawks
		Capt. David Dingee
6 June	F-4D 66-0232	Maj. James Fowler
		Capt. John Seuell
7 June	RA-5C 156616	Lt. Cdr. C. H. Smith
		Lt. L. G. Kunz
8 June	F-4E 67-0303	Capt. John Murphy
		1/Lt. L. D. Johnson
11 June	A-6A 154145	Capt. Roger Wilson
		Capt. William Angus
13 June	F-4E 67-0365	1/Lt. Gregg Hanson
		1/Lt. Richard Fulton
	A-7A 153206	Lt. Cdr. Francis Davis
16 June	RF-8G 145613	Lt. P. Ringwood
	A-7A 153197	Lt. John Cabral

Date	Aircraft	Crew
17 June	A-7E 157531	Cdr. Darrel Owens
	A-7A 153230	Lt. Larry Kilpatrick
18 June	F-4J 157273	Lt. Cdr. Roy Cash
		Lt. R. J. Laib
20 June	F-8J 150923	Cdr. James Davis
21 June	F-4E 69-0282	Capt. George Rose
		1/Lt. Peter Callaghan
24 June	F-4E 66-0315	Capt. David Grant
		Capt. William Beekman
	F-4D 66-7636	1/Lt. James McCarty
		1/Lt. Charles Jackson
25 June	A-7E 157437	Capt. C. M. Hovston
27 June	F-4E 67-0243	Capt. John Cerak
		Capt. David Dingee
	F-4E 68-0314	Lt. Col. Farell Sullivan
		Capt. Richard Francis
	F-4E 69-7271	Capt. Lynn Aikman
		Capt. Thomas Hanton
	F-4E 69-7296	Maj. R. C. Miller
		1/Lt. Richard McDow
1 July	F-4E 67-0277	Maj. Paul Robinson
		Capt. Kevin Cheney
3 July	F-4E 69-0289	Capt. Stephen Cuthbert
		Capt. Marion Marshall
5 July	F-4E 67-0339	Maj. William Elander
		1/Lt. Donald Logan
	F-4E 67-0296	Capt. William Spencer
		1/Lt. Brian Seek
	F-4D 66-7680	Capt. Michael Vanwagenen
		Maj. E. K. Johnson
6 July	F-4D 65-0800	Maj. Harland Davis
		1/Lt. Frederick Koss
7 July	A-6A 155690	1/Lt. Alan Kroboth
		Capt. Leonard Robertson
8 July	F-4E 69-7563	Lt. Col. R. E. Ross
		Capt. S. M. Imaye
9 July	A-4F 154972	Cdr. Frank Green
10 July	F-4J 155803	Lt. Robert Randall
		Lt. Frederick Masterson

Date	Aircraft	Crew
	F-4D 66-7707	Lt. Col Brad Sharp
		1/Lt. Michael Pomphrey
11 July	A-4F 155046	Lt. Cdr. Henry Lesesne
12 July	F-4E 69-0302	1/Lt. James Huard
		Capt. Samuel O'Donnell
17 July	F-4D 66-8772	1/Lt. G. K. Tushek
		Capt. Wayne Brown
	A-7C 156792	Cdr. William Yonke
	A-7C 156771	Lt. D. K. Anderson
	A-7B 154521	Lt. Leon Haas
19 July	F-4D 66-0253	Capt. H. D. Wier
		1/Lt. K. G. Edwards
20 July	F-4D 66-0265	Capt. Joe Lee Burns
		1/Lt. M. Nelson
22 July	RF-8G 146873	Lt. Cdr. Gordon Paige
23 July	A-7B 154531	Lt.(jg) Gary Shank
	A-7B 154532	Lt. Cdr. Clarence Tolbert
24 July	F-4E 66-0369	Capt. S. A. Hodnett
		1/Lt. D. Fallert
29 July	F-4E 66-0367	Capt. James Kula
		Capt. Melvin Matsui
	F-105G 62-4443	Maj. Tom Coady
		Maj. H. F. Murphy
30 July	F-4D 66-7576	Lt. Col. William Breckner
		1/Lt. Larry Price
	F-4D 66-7770	Capt. D. A. Crane
		1/Lt. D. W. Petkunas
	F-4D 66-7597	Capt. G. B. Brooks
		Capt. J. M. McAdams
31 July	A-7A 153193	(unknown)
2 August	F-4J 155817	1/Lt. R. O. Lamers
		1/Lt. Sam Cordova
6 August	A-7B 154508	Lt.(jg) Michael Penn
	A-7A 153147	Lt. J. R. Lloyd
9 August	F-4D 65-0599	Capt. J. L. Beavers
		1/Lt. W. A. Haskell
10 August	F-4D 66-0281	Capt. Patrick Matthews
		1/Lt. Herbert Stark
12 August	F-8J 150336	Lt. David Thompson

Date	Aircraft	Crew
13 August	RF-4C 68-0604	Capt. William Gauntt
		1/Lt. Francis Townsend
16 August	F-4J 157262	Cdr. John Pitzen
		Lt. Orland Pender
17 August	A-7A 153207	Lt. Cdr. Dale Raebel
19 August	RF-4C 69-0355	Capt. Roger Behnfeldt
		Maj. Tamotsu Shingaki
	A-6A 157018	Lt. Roderick Lester
		Lt. Harry Mossman
22 August	F-4E 68-0477	Maj. Lee Tigner
		1/Lt. William Crockett
25 August	F-4D 66-7482	Lt. Col. Carl Bailey
		Capt. Jeff Feinstein
	F-4B 153020	Lt. Cdr. Michael Doyle
		Lt. John Ensch
26 August	F-4J 155811	1/Lt. Sam Cordova
		1/Lt. D. I. Borders
27 August	F-4B 151013	Lt. Theodore Triebel
		Lt.(jg) David Everett
3 September	F-4E 68-0335	Capt. William Wood
		Maj. Robert Greenwood
	A-4E 152000	1/Lt. D. R. Eisenbrey
5 September	RF-8G 146861	Cdr. R. Harrison
	F-8J 150299	Lt. J. Schultz
6 September	A-6A 155626	Lt. Cdr. Donald Lindland
		Lt. Roger Leserth
	A-4F 155021	Lt. W. F. Pear
7 September	A-7B 154393	Lt. Cdr. Donald Gerstel
8 September	F-4J 157302	Cdr. R. P. Bordone
		Lt. J. H. Findley
9 September	F-4E 69-7565	Capt. William Dalecky
		Capt. Terry Murphy
10 September	A-7C 156798	Lt.(jg) Stephen Musselman
	F-4E 69-7251	(unknown)
11 September	F-4E 69-0288	Capt. Brian Ratlaff
		Capt. Jerome Heeren
	F-4J 155526	Maj. Lee Lasseter
		Capt. John Cummings
	F-4J 154784	Capt. Andrew Dudley

Date	Aircraft	Crew
		1/Lt. James Brady
12 September	F-4E 69-7266	Capt. Randolph Zuberbuhler
		Capt. Frederick McMurray
	A-7A 153213	Lt. G. H. Averett
13 September	F-4J 153854	(unknown)
16 September	F-4D 66-8785	Capt. W. A. Kangas
		Capt. Frederick Cunliffe
	A-6A 157028	Cdr. Verne Donnelly
		Lt. Cdr Kenneth Buell
17 September	F-105G 63-8360	Capt. Thomas Zorn
		1/Lt. Michael Turose
	A-7C 156781	(unknown)
	F-4D 65-0593	Capt. E. B. Dyer
		Capt. D. E. Henneman
19 September	A-7E 158653	Lt. W. A. Robb
	F-4D 65-0467	(unknown)
20 September	A-7B 154363	(unknown)
21 September	F-4D 66-8769	Maj. Roger Carroll
		1/Lt Dwight Cook
22 September	RF-4C 69-0351	Capt. J. G. Watts
		1/Lt. J. H. Pomeroy
	F-4E 67-0385	Capt. G. A. Lentz
		1/Lt. Nick Holoviak
24 September	A-7B 154436	Lt. Daniel Borah
26 September	A-4E 151009	Capt. James Walsh
28 September	F-111A 67-0087	Maj. William Coltman
		1/Lt. Robert Brett
29 September	F-105G 63-8302	Lt. Col. James O'Neill
		Capt. William Bosiljevac
5 October	F-4D 66-8738	Capt. Kenneth Lewis
		Capt. John Alpers
	F-4E (unknown)	Capt. James Latham
		1/Lt. Richard Bates
6 October	F-4E 69-7573	Capt. J. P. White
		Capt. A. G. Egge
	F-4E 69-7548	Lt. Col. Robert Anderson
		1/Lt. George Latella
10 October	F-4E 67-0254	Capt. Peter Cleary
		Capt. Leonard Leonor

Date	Aircraft	Crew
11 October	A-6A 155700	1/Lt. John Peacock
		1/Lt. William Price
12 October	F-4E 69-0276	Capt. Myron Young
		1/Lt. Cecil Brunson
16 October	F-111A 67-0066	Capt. James Hockridge
		1/Lt. Allen Graham
17 October	F-4D 66-6708	(unknown)
23 October	F-4D 65-0632	(unknown)

APPENDIX 2
Linebacker II Losses

Operation Linebacker II was conducted December 18–29, 1972. During that period, the following aircraft were lost in missions over North Vietnam:[1]

Date	Aircraft	Crew
December 18/19 night	B-52G 58-0201	Lt. Col. Donald Rissi
		1/Lt. Robert Thomas
		Maj. Richard Johnson
		Capt. Robert Certain
		Capt. Richard Simpson
		Sgt. Walter Ferguson
	B-52G 58-0246	Maj. Cliff Ashley
		Capt. Gary Vickers
		Maj. Archie Myers
		1/Lt. Forrest Stegelin
		Capt. Jim Tramel
		M. Sgt. Ken Connor
		Lt. Col. Hendsley Conner
	F-111A 67-0099	Lt. Col. Ronald Ward
		Maj. James McElvain
	B-52D 56-0608	Capt. Hal Wilson
		Maj. Alexander Fernando

1. Losses reflect only aircraft lost over N. Vietnam or as a result of Linebacker missions. This does not include losses in Laos or S. Vietnam. Chris Hobson, Vietnam Air Losses: USAF, Navy, and Marine Corps Fixed-Wing Aircraft Losses in SEA, 1961–1973 (Hinckley, England: Midland Publishing, 2001).

Date	Aircraft	Crew
		Capt. Henry Barrows
		Capt. Charles Brown
		Capt. Richard Cooper
		T. Sgt. Charlie Poole
December 19	A-7C 156783	Lt. Carl Wieland
December 20/21 night	B-52G 57-6496	Capt. Terry Geloneck
		1/Lt. William Arcuri
		Capt. Craig Paul
		Capt. Warren Spencer
		1/Lt. Michael Martini
		S. Sgt. Roy Madden
	B-52G 57-6481	Capt. John Ellinger
		(5 crew, names unknown)
	B-52D 56-0622	Maj. John Stuart
		Maj. Randolph Perry
		Capt. Irwin Lerner
		Capt. Thomas Klomann
		1/Lt. Paul Grainger
		M. Sgt. Arthur McLaughlin
	A-6A 155594	Cdr. Gordon Nakagawa
		Lt. Kenneth Higdon
	B-52D 56-0669	Capt. Vincent Russo
		Maj. Frank Gould
		Capt. James Farmer
		Lt. Deverl Johnson
		(2 crew, names unknown)
	B-52G 58-0198	Lt. Col. James Nagahiro
		Capt. Donovan Walters
		Maj. Edward Johnson
		Capt. Lynn Beens
		Capt. Robert Lynn
		A1C Charles Bebus
		Lt. Col. Keith Heggen
	B-52G 58-0169	Capt. Randall Craddock
		Capt. George Lockhart
		Maj. Bobby Kirby
		Capt. Ronald Perry
		2/Lt. Charles Darr
		S. Sgt. James Lollar

Date	Aircraft	Crew
December 21/22 night	A-6A 152946	Lt. Cdr. Robert Graustein
		Lt. Cdr. Barton Wade
	B-52D 66-0061	Capt. Peter Giroux
		Capt. Thomas Bennett
		Lt. Col. Gerald Alley
		Capt. Peter Camerota
		1/Lt. Joseph Copack
		M. Sgt. Louis LeBlanc
	B-52D 55-0050	Lt. Col. John Yuill
		Capt. Ian Drummond
		Lt. Col. Louis Bernasconi
		Lt. Col. William Conlee
		1/Lt. William Mayall
		S. Sgt. Gary Morgan
December 22/23 night	F-111A 67-0068	Capt. Robert Sponeybarger
		1/Lt. William Wilson
December 23	F-4J 153885	Lt. Col. John Cochran
		Maj. H. S. Carr
	EB-66	Maj. Henry Repeta
		Maj. George Sasser
		Capt. William Baldwin
December 24	A-7D 71-0312	Capt. Charles Riess
	A-7E 157503	Lt. Phillip Clark
December 26/27 night	B-52D 56-0674	Capt. Robert Morris
		1/Lt. Robert Hudson
		Capt. Michael LaBeau
		Capt. Nutter Wimbrow
		1/Lt. Duane Vavroch
		T. Sgt. James Cook
	B-52D 56-0584	Capt. James Turner
		Lt. Robert Hymel
		Lt. Col. Donald Joyner
		Maj. Lawrence Marshall
		Capt. Roy Tabler
		T. Sgt. Spencer Grippin
December 27	F-4E 67-0292	Maj. Carl Jeffcoat
		1/Lt. Jack Trimble
December 27/28 night	A-6A 155666	Capt. Ralph Chipman
		1/Lt. Ronald Forrester

Date	Aircraft	Crew
	B-52D 56-0599	Capt. John Mize
		Capt. Terrence Gruters
		Capt. Dennis Anderson
		Capt. William North
		Lt. William Robinson
		T. Sgt. Peter Whalen
	B-52D 56-0605	Capt. Frank Lewis
		Capt. Samuel Cusimano
		Maj. James Condon
		Maj. Allen Johnson
		1/Lt. Bennie Fryer
		M. Sgt. James Gough
	F-4E 67-0234	Capt. John Anderson
		1/Lt. Brian Ward
December 28	RA-5C 156633	Lt. Cdr. Alfred Agnew
		Lt. Michael Haifley

GLOSSARY

AAA: antiaircraft artillery. Air defense guns ranging from 23mm up to 130mm, with air-bursting projectiles. Fired singly or in batteries, either visually or radar directed.

AB: afterburner

acro: acrobatic flying

AFB: Air Force base

AOA: angle of attack

ARM: antiradiation missile. Airplane-carried missile that homes on enemy radar.

ARVN: Army of the Republic of Vietnam. Acronym for the South Vietnamese Army.

ATC: Air Training Command

AWACS: airborne warning and control system. A large airplane equipped with radar to manage and control air operations.

BARCAP: barrier combat air patrol

BDA: bomb damage assessment. A report of the results of an attack, it could be through reconnaissance photos or an observer estimation.

bear: an electronic warfare officer flying in the backseat of a Wild Weasel aircraft. Origin of the term varies. Some think it refers to the "dancing bears" of old circuses—a gruff furry creature that does tricks. Others say it came from an ejection experiment conducted for the B-58 aircraft in which a live bear was strapped into an ejection seat and blasted out of an airplane. When recovered, the bear was very upset.

bingo: radio call indicating a fuel state at which all remaining fuel will be needed to return to home base and a planned landing.

BITs: built-in-tests

BLC: boundary layer control

BUFF: slang acronym for B-52 bomber: "big ugly fat fucker."

BX: base exchange. Military version of a department store.

B-sweep: a radar type with square scope and vertical cursor that scans left and right.

camo: camouflage

CAP: combat air patrol

Cat IV: the Category IV requirement, sixty days and about thirty hours of flying time.

CBU: cluster bomb unit. A wide range of weapons that either dispense bomblets from a fixed unit or drop from the aircraft, then open to deploy small baseball-size bomblets. Early versions such as CBU-2 required low, level delivery. Later models such as CBU-24/27/52/58 consisted of a bomb-like shell that was delivered from a diving pass and was activated by a timer fuse at a preset altitude above the ground.

comm: communication

CTF: crew training facility

DFC: Distinguished Flying Cross, decoration for air combat equivalent to the Bronze Star.

Disco: an EC-121 airborne command and control aircraft carrying a large radar. Capabilities included monitoring of flight paths of airborne aircraft, overseeing border violations, and vectoring aircraft toward other aircraft. A forerunner of AWACS.

DME: distance measuring equipment. An instrument readout that provided distance in nautical miles from a TACAN station or to a Doppler destination.

DMZ: demilitarized zone

DNIF: duty not including flying. A medical term describing conditions in which illness such as the common cold temporarily grounds an aviator.

DO: deputy commander for operations. Senior staff officer responsible for flying operations.

ECM: electronic countermeasures

emergency fuel: a fuel state in which all remaining fuel may not be sufficient to safely land the aircraft, even if traffic priority is given.

EOT: end of tour. Last flight of a combat tour.

FAC: forward air controller. A pilot flying a small spotter plane, qualified to direct air strikes by fighters. Used in areas in close proximity to ground troops, as well as for detailed reconnaissance of specific geographic sectors.

Fan Song: a ground-based radar assembly that provides azimuth, elevation, range, and command guidance for the SA-2 surface-to-air missile.

Firecan: a small ground-based radar used primarily for aiming and ranging antiaircraft artillery.

frag: abbreviation for fragmentary order. Units received only part of the daily strike plan, only a portion or fragment of the total operations order. The daily tasking for a wing was called the "frag."

Freedom Deal: operation code name for the post-Linebacker bombing campaign in Cambodia.

G: the force of gravity

GCA: ground-controlled approach. A precision radar landing maneuver.

GCI: ground control intercept. Acronym used to describe air defense interceptor radar control systems.

GIB: guy in back. Slang term to indicate the rear cockpit crewmember of an F-4. Originally a rated pilot, by the period covered here, the position was manned by navigators.

Guard: a dedicated radio frequency for emergency communications. UHF Guard channel is 243.0 mHz. Also the auxiliary radio receiver used by tactical aircraft.

HSI: horizontal situation indicator. A composite flight instrument that displays aircraft heading, bearing, and distance to selected navigational aids or waypoints.

INS: inertial navigation system. A self-contained navigation system and attitude reference used by the F-4 to orient the airplane attitude indicator, provide input to the dive-toss weapons computer, and display latitude/longitude information. It detects motion and translates that into speed, time, and distance calculations. Can display ground speed, distance, and heading to any destination.

IP: instructor pilot

Jolly Green Giant: rescue helicopter. HH-3C heavy-lift, long-range helicopter equipped with winch to lower rescue personnel or to raise survivor aircrew from the jungle.

Judy: brevity code word indicating that the pilot has sufficient radar or visual information to complete an intercept without further assistance from ground radar controlling agencies.

karst: prominent limestone formation, often reaching several hundred feet high, that thrusts upward from the jungle

klong: an open canal or manmade lake used for irrigation and often for waste disposal. Also, call sign of in-theater C-130 airlift missions. Used to denote almost any C-130 in the region.

knot: unit of speed measurement equal to one nautical mile per hour. A nautical mile is longer than a statute mile used in miles per hour. One hundred knots equals 115 miles per hour.

LGB: laser-guided bomb

LORAN: long-range air navigation, a system of ground-based stations that provide triangulation data to accurately position an aircraft.

MER: multiple ejector rack. A suspension rack carried on the centerline station that had six bomb stations, allowing for multiple weapons to be carried from a single aircraft position. Depending upon weapon dimensions and weight, the rack was used to carry from two to six munitions. Release was sequenced to avoid weapon interference, and a time interval for release was preflight-selectable.

MiG: any of a range of Soviet-built interceptors from the Mikoyan design facility. Highly maneuverable lightweight fighters armed with cannon and various air-to-air missiles depending upon type. MiG-17, 19, and 21 were flown by the NVNAF.

MiGCAP: MiG combat air patrol

minimum fuel: a fuel state in which all remaining fuel may be required to achieve a safe landing in normal sequence with other aircraft. An advisory that delays may result in problems.

Mk-8x: a series of low-profile, low-drag, general purpose bombs ranging from Mk-81 at 250 pounds through 82 (500 pound), 83 (1,000 pound) and 84 (2,000 pound).

mobile control: The mobile control or runway supervisory unit (RSU) was a small auxiliary control tower, located at the approach end of the active runway. The mobile officer was an aircrew member whose duty was to observe landing and departing aircraft for proper configuration and warn of potentially hazardous situations. A "gear-checker."

MPC: Military Personnel Center

napalm: also called incendigel. A flammable chemical compound dropped and then ignited by magnesium flare fuses. Described officially as "anti-PAM" munitions, i.e. anti-personnel and materiel.

nav: a navigator

NCO: non-commissioned officer

ORI: operational readiness inspection

PJ: acronym for para-rescue specialist. A crewmember on a Jolly Green Giant trained to aid aircrew members being rescued. PJs were trained to swim, parachute, rappel, etc., to reach the ground to aid the downed crewman.

POL: petroleum, oil, and lubricants. The fuel required to run the machinery of war, along with all of the equipment to store, transport, and process it.

recce: reconnaissance

RHAW: radar homing and warning. Generic name for a radar-warning receiver. Also called APR 36/37 or RWR.

ROE: rules of engagement. The rule book on what, where, when, and how targets can be attacked. The intensely political nature of the war made the ROE a frustrating set of restrictions that often seemed to favor the enemy and endanger the aircrews rather than the other way around.

RWR: radar-warning receiver. At this period, usually APR 36/37. A detection and display system to provide information about radar that may be scanning or locking on to an aircraft. Also called RHAW for radar homing and warning. Earlier version was APR 25/26, and later version immediately after Linebacker was ALR-46, an advanced digital system.

SAC: Strategic Air Command

SAM: generically, any surface-to-air missile. Most typically during this period the Soviet-built SA-2, Guideline, a radar-guided large missile. Also, in some areas of Southeast Asia, the SA-7, Strela, an infrared guided man-portable antiaircraft missile.

Sandy: call sign of rescue support aircraft, usually A-1 propeller driven aircraft noted for their long flight endurance and wide range of munitions carried. Derived from the mission of search *and* rescue.

SEA: Southeast Asia

Shotgun: radio call indicating the firing of an anti-radiation missile.

Shrike: AGM-45 anti-radiation missile. Approximately the size of the air-to-air radar-guided Sparrow, the Shrike is the primary ARM employed by all Wild Weasel aircraft throughout the war.

SOF: The supervisor of flying was an additional duty for a senior pilot. Either working from the control tower or from a radio-equipped vehicle, the SOF was responsible for monitoring airfield conditions, weather, and maintenance. He coordinated assistance for airborne aircraft in emergencies.

stab-aug: stability augmentation. An aircraft system employing sensors to minimize oscillations around all three axes of flight: yaw, roll, and pitch. Supersonic aircraft are inherently unstable, requiring some automated systems to aid the pilot in maintaining control. Stab-aug depends upon both electrical and hydraulic systems to function. Autopilot tasks are an advanced component of the stab-aug system.

Standard: AGM-78 anti-radiation missile. Large missile, programmable by the Weasel crew to provide initial guidance toward an emitting radar on the ground.

TACAN: tactical air navigation system. The primary means of fighter jet navigation, it depends upon ground-based stations that emit radio signals offering a bearing to the station and a distance from the station. Locations can be described relative to a TACAN station by giving a radial and DME.

TDU: threat display unit. The component of the APR-36/37 that displayed the frequency band of detected threat radars as well as status of a SAM launch sequence.

TFS: tactical fighter squadron

Thud: a nickname for the F-105 Thunderchief. Originally considered pejorative, it is now regarded as a term of endearment for an aircraft that performed exceptionally well in a difficult task.

UHF: ultrahigh frequency. The radio band used by USAF aircraft ranging from 225.00 to 399.9 mHz.

UPT: undergraduate pilot training. Flight school for new USAF pilots where they receive initial training and earn their wings.

VI: visual inspection

Wild Weasel: name of a specially equipped and dedicated aircraft used to detect and attack SAM sites. Often simply "Weasel." Initially F-100F, then F-105F, F-105G, and F-4C. The final dedicated Weasel used until Desert Storm was the F-4G. Also used to refer to the pilot of the aircraft.

willie-pete: white phosphorus

Winchester: Radio call indicating that all ammunition has been expended.

WRCS: weapons release computer system

WSO: weapons system operator or officer. See GIB.